D0593116

PSYCHOLOGICAL PRACTICE IN A CHANGING HEALTH CARE SYSTEM

Robert L. Glueckauf, PhD, is Associate Professor and Clinical Training Director of the Doctoral Program in Clinical Rehabilitation Psychology at Indiana University-Purdue University Indianapolis, where he has been since 1988. He obtained his doctorate in clinical psychology at Florida State University in 1981. Dr. Glueckauf is a past president of the American Psychological Association's Division of Rehabilitation Psychology. He serves as Associate Editor for *Rehabilitation Psychology.* He has authored over 40 empirical and theoretical articles, books, and chapters in the field of health care and rehabilitation. His current scholarly activities include outcome studies of psychosocial interventions for at-risk teens with disabilities and their families, and process research on professional–client interactions in medical settings.

Robert G. Frank, PhD, ABPP, is Dean of the University of Florida's College of Health Professions (HP) and Vice President of Rehabilitation and Behavioral Health Systems. He received his doctorate in clinical psychology from the University of New Mexico. Dr. Frank has a diplomate in clinical psychology and is a Fellow of the American Psychological Association. His research has focused on psychological responses to catastrophic illness or injury. In 1991 he was selected as a Robert Wood Johnson Health Policy Fellow. He also served as Chairman of Missouri's ShowMe Health Reform Initiative, which was instrumental in writing comprehensive health reform legislation considered during the 1994 legislative session. Dr. Frank has also worked on a number of federal health reform bills introduced during the 102nd and 103rd Congresses. He has published more than 40 papers in peer-reviewed journals.

Gary R. Bond, PhD, is Professor of Psychology and Director of the Doctoral Program in Clinical Rehabilitation Psychology at Indiana University-Purdue University Indianapolis, where he has been since 1983. He received his doctorate in psychology from the University of Chicago in 1975. He has received 5 national awards for his research on the effectiveness of psychiatric rehabilitation programs. His publications include 50 articles in peer-reviewed journals and 20 book chapters. He has consulted and presented widely to mental health and rehabilitation organizations throughout the United States.

John H. McGrew, PhD, is Assistant Professor of Psychology and core faculty member in the Doctoral Program in Clinical Rehabilitation Psychology at Indiana University-Purdue University Indianapolis, where he has been since 1989. He received his doctorate in clinical psychology from Indiana University-Bloomington in 1991. Dr. McGrew serves as the principal investigator of a grant investigating the long-term community outcomes of discharged patients following the closure of a large state hospital, and the co-principal investigator of a grant developing and evaluating the use of provider profiles for determining capitation cost-groupings for community mental health centers in Indiana.

Janet O'Keeffe, DrPH, RN, received a Bachelor of Science in Nursing from the State University of New York, and a Master's and Doctoral degree in Public Health from the UCLA School of Public Health. She has extensive experience as an R.N. in a wide range of health care settings: acute care, rehabilitation, and long-term care. She was awarded a Congressional Fellowship from the Women's Research and Education Institute and worked in the U.S. House of Representatives. She has worked on a wide range of health, aging, and disability issues for the American Psychological Association, first as Assistant Director of Public Interest Policy and then as Acting Director of APA's Public Policy Office. She is currently a senior policy advisor in the Public Policy Institute of the American Association of Retired Persons. Her research and analysis focuses on long-term care services for persons with physical and mental impairments, the integration of health and long-term care, and the Medicaid program.

PSYCHOLOGICAL PRACTICE IN A CHANGING HEALTH CARE SYSTEM

ISSUES AND NEW DIRECTIONS

Robert L. Glueckauf
Robert G. Frank
Gary R. Bond
John H. McGrew

Editors

Janet O'Keeffe
Editorial Consultant

SPRINGER PUBLISHING COMPANY

Copyright © 1996 by Springer Publishing Company, Inc.

All rights reserved

No part of this publication may be reproduced, stored in a retrieval system, or transmitted in any form or by any means, electronic, mechanical, photocopying, recording, or otherwise, without the prior permission of Springer Publishing Company, Inc.

Springer Publishing Company, Inc.
536 Broadway
New York, NY 10012-3955

Cover design by Tom Yabut and Margaret Dunin
Production Editor: Pamela Ritzer

96 97 98 99 00 / 5 4 3 2 1

BF
75
P744
1996

Library of Congress Cataloging-in-Publication Data

Psychological practice in a changing health care system: Issues and new directions /
    Robert L. Glueckauf . . . [et al.], editors.
        p.   cm.
    Includes bibliographical references and index.
    ISBN 0-8261-9280-7
    1. Psychology—Practice—United States. 2. Clinical psychology—Practice—United States 3. Psychotherapy—Practice—United States 4. Managed mental health care—United States 5. Psychologists—Training of—United States. 6. Clinical psychologists—Training of—United States.   I. Glueckauf, Robert L.
    BF75.P47   1996
    362.2—dc20   96–26099
                                                                                        CIP

Printed in the United States of America

UNIVERSITY
OF
PENNSYLVANIA
LIBRARIES

Contents

v

Contributors

Bruce Caplan, PhD
Department of Rehabilitation
  Medicine
Thomas Jefferson University
  Hospital
Philadelphia, PA

Bruce A. Crosson, PhD
Department of Clinical and Health
Psychology
University of Florida
Gainesville, FL

Marie A. DiCowden, PhD
The Biscayne Institutes of Health
  and Living, Inc.
Miami, FL

Debra Lina Dunivin, PhD
Office of U.S. Senator
  Daniel K. Inouye
Washington, DC

Joseph D. Eubanks, PhD
Texas Neuroscience
  Institute
San Antonio, TX

Rebecca C. Foote, PhD
Deaprtment of Clinical and Health
  Psychology
University of Florida
Gainesville, FL

Ronald Fox, PhD
Piedmont Care
Chapel Hill, NC

Alan L. Goldberg, PsyD
Private Practice
Tucson, AZ

Lee Hersch, PhD
Augusta Psychological
  Associates
Staunton, VA

Philip J. Hofschire, MD
Great Plains Physician Group
Omaha, NE

**U.S. Congressman,
  Andrew Jacobs, Jr.**
U.S. House of Representatives
Washington, DC

Brick Johnstone, PhD
Department of Physical Medicine
and Rehabilitation
University of Missouri School of
Medicine
Columbia, MO

Robert M. Kaplan, PhD
Department of Family and
Preventive Medicine
University of California
San Diego, CA

Donald Kewman, PhD
Department of Physical Medicine
and Rehabilitation
University of Michigan
Ann Arbor, MI

A. John McSweeny, PhD
Department of Psychiatry
Medical College of Ohio
Toledo, OH

Barbara G. Melamed, PhD
Ferkauf Graduate School
Yeshiva University
New York, NY

Paul D. Nelson, PhD
American Psychological
Association
Washington, DC

Janet O'Keeffe, DrPH, RN
American Association of Retired
Persons
Public Policy Institute
Washington, DC
Formerly with the American
Psychological Association
Washington, DC

Alexandra L. Quittner, PhD
Department of Psychology
Indiana University
Bloomington, IN

Robert J. Resnick, PhD
Department of Psychiatry
Medical College of Virginia
Richmond, VA

Foreword

The Honorable Andrew Jacobs, Jr.
Representative, U.S. Congress

Alexander Hamilton said it: "Here, Sir, the people rule.

Let no one doubt that with regard to the salient public policy issues, whether well-informed or ill-informed at any given time, the people of the United States do rule. When President Bill Clinton made his initial address to Congress in January 1993 about his health care proposal legislation, the polls showed that the public was strongly favorable. In subsequent months, according to public opinion surveys, the people's support diminished. A great public debate ensued. Or perhaps the debate was not so great. It was driven by enormously expensive television and newspaper advertising, which has always meant something very different from equal time allowed for the various sides. In most instances, the best-financed interests are those who, quite naturally, favor the status quo. By midsummer 1994, the public was opposed to the "Clinton plan," although a majority surveyed still seemed to favor so-called universal coverage.

It was in that uncertain context that the Congress embarked on the final stage of its efforts to reach an agreement on some sort of health care financing reform legislation. The failure to pass any such legislation by the end of 1994 was a result of many factors, including the lack of public support for any one of the several health care reform packages proposed in Congress, confusion over the basic issues, fears about a "government take-over," and the impression (reinforced by a media campaign) that there was no health care crisis

Traditionally, mental health has been included in national health care legislation, including both the Medicaid and Medicare programs. It was to some extent included in legislation recommended by the U.S. House Ways and Means Committee and by the Senate Finance Committee in the 103rd Congress. The public evidently supported the notion that its well-being would be served by the inclusion of such services. One senses, however, that the general public does not focus on the need for investment in mental health, nor on how attention to psychological functioning in general medical care might prove beneficial as well as cost-effective.

This volume contains a series of chapters discussing critical issues in the U.S. health care system, especially those relating to access to, and delivery of, psychological health services. It is important to note that this conference focused on psychological services as a component of the health care system, not simply on mental health services. As is true of much of the informed health care reform debate, the arguments in this book are complex and not easily reduced to television sound bites. The underlying issues touch the lives of all the American public: the rich and the poor, big and small employers, physicians, nurses, psychologists, and other health care providers. Many profound nonlegislative changes are already occurring in the United States regarding how individuals acquire access to health care, who provides those services, who makes the decisions about access, what new technologies are used, how health care is delivered, and how much we pay for those services. The health care system will continue to evolve, with or without new law. As suggested by this book's findings, some of the directions of change do not help solve our current problems, but instead create new problems or exacerbate old ones. Unfortunately, as is true with other major societal changes, the public is often only vaguely aware of ongoing modifications in health care, except as these changes impinge on their individual lives.

I hope that psychologists, who are the primary target audience for this book, will begin to translate the important ideas and findings summarized in the following pages into forms that are readily understandable and relevant to legislators and to the general public, to inform public policy better. As suggested by this book's findings, some of the directions of change do not help solve our current problems, but instead create new problems or exacerbate old ones. Unfortunately, as is true with other major societal changes, the public is often only vaguely aware of ongoing modifications in health care, except as these changes impinge on their individual lives.

I hope that psychologists, who are the primary target audience for this book, will begin to translate the important ideas and findings summarized in the following pages into forms that are readily understandable and relevant to legislators and to the general public, to inform public policy better.

Part I

INTRODUCTION

Health Care Reform and Professional Psychology: Overview of Key Issues and Background of Book

John H. McGrew, Robert L. Glueckauf, Gary R. Bond, and Robert G. Frank

As this book goes to press, there are now available literally hundreds of articles and books on health care reform and changes in the health care system. What is different about this book?

The focus of this book is on the practice of psychology as a health care profession in health care settings (e.g., hospitals, rehabilitation centers, medical centers, and nursing homes). Health care psychologists provide a broad array of services to children and adults with acute and chronic medical conditions, such as neurological and functional assessments, health promotion and intervention strategies, independent living and vocational consultations, and psychiatric rehabilitation. It is the fastest-growing sector of professional psychology.

This book is not another collection of dry, abstract opinions of a few scholars or editors. Rather, in large part, it represents the collaborative efforts and viewpoints of the broader community of health care psychologists, representing a wide range of interests and expertise in health care psychology. These efforts culminated in an intensive, 2-day national conference on health care reform sponsored, in part, by the American Psychological Association (APA) and its health-oriented divisions, and attended by many prominent leaders in psychology. This book, then, is a direct outgrowth of that conference. A specific discussion of the conference is included later in this introduction.

The book not only identifies issues and problems facing psychology within a changing health care system, but also indicates possible future directions and solutions to these problems. An explicit goal of the book is to alert concerned professionals to the issues facing psychology and to outline possible directions and strategies to help psychology shape its future. Before introducing the book in detail, however, it will be useful to outline the health care context that formed the basis for this volume.

BACKGROUND: THE GENERAL HEALTH CARE CONTEXT

The U.S. health care system is undergoing rapid change and growth. In 1929, expenditures on health care totaled $3.6 billion, or 3.5% of gross national product (GNP). In 1950, that amount had risen to $12.7 billion, or 4.4% of GNP (Rice, 1990). By 1984, expenditures on health care had exploded to $387 billion, or 10.6% of GNP, and by 1994, expenditures were expected to exceed $1 trillion, an estimated 13% of GNP (Graig, 1993).

Growth was even faster in public health care programs. Between 1970 and 1990, Medicare spending increased at an average rate of 14.3% (Jencks & Schreiber, 1991). Moreover, overall health care spending is expected to continue to grow as a percentage of the GNP. Expenditures are predicted to be $1.5 trillion, or $5,550 per capita, by the year 2000 (15% of GNP) (Division of National Cost Estimates, 1990) and to reach as high as 26% of GNP by 2020 (Sonnefeld, Waldo, Lemieux, & McKusick, 1991).

No other country currently spends as much on health care. In 1990, the United States spent $2,566 per person on health care, whereas Canada spent $1,770; Germany, $1,456; Japan, $1,171; and the United Kingdom, $972, in constant 1990 dollars (Scheiber, Poullier, & Greenwald, 1992). Moreover, in contrast to the rapidly rising costs of health care in the United States, costs for most of these countries has stayed steady during the past decade (Graig, 1993).

Despite the high cost of health care in the United States, and in contrast to other Western democracies, access to services is not available to every American (Graig, 1993). Estimates of the number of Americans without either public or private insurance on any given day range from 31 to 37 million, the number without coverage at some time during the year is estimated to be 48 million (Friedman, 1991). African Americans, the unemployed, children under 18 years of age, and the poor are more likely to be uninsured (Short, 1990). However, employment is no guarantee of coverage. More than one half of those who are uninsured (56.4%) are working adults (Graig, 1993).

In effect, then, there has been a rationing of health care benefits to those who can afford it, to those who work for employers willing to pay for the benefit, or to those either poor enough or disabled enough to qualify for public-provided health care coverage. However, even for those who can obtain insurance, benefits have eroded. Coverage is more likely to include larger deductibles, permanent exclusions for preexisting conditions, higher copayments, and more restrictive limits on single incident or lifetime benefits.

Although the United States has the most expensive health care system in the world, our citizens are no healthier than those in Western democracies that spend far less. For example, among the 24 nations included in the Organization for Economic Cooperation and Development, U.S. life expectancy at birth for males and females ranked 17th and 16th, respectively (Scheiber, Poullier, & Greenwald, 1991). Also, among industrialized countries, the United States ranks near the bottom in both infant and perinatal mortality rates (Anderson, 1989). In addition, although Americans are living longer, they are experiencing worsening health (i.e., increased morbidity), especially for middle-aged and older people (Verbrugge, 1990). People report more restricted activity days and an increased percentage report limited major and secondary activities because of illness. The prevalence of chronic conditions (e.g., diabetes, heart disease, hypertension, and cancer) has also increased since 1957 (Verbrugge, 1990). Moreover, even though U.S. mortality rates have fallen, there is scant evidence linking this change to improved medical care (e.g., Milio, 1983). Lowered mortality rates are most likely attributable to better nutrition and hygiene (McKeown, 1975). Cross-country comparisons also indicate little correlation between available health resources and health outcomes (Aday, Begley, Lairson, & Slater, 1993), thus making the point that an expensive health care system is not necessarily a better one.

These trends in costs, outcomes, access, and quality have led many Americans to question our health care system seriously. In 1988, only 10% of Americans surveyed agreed with the statement that the U.S. health care system works pretty well and that only minor changes are needed versus 56% of Canadians surveyed (Blendon & Taylor, 1989). By 1990, roughly two thirds of Americans favored a government-funded national health plan, and 84% thought that the federal government should take a major role in reforming the health care system (Navarro, 1994). Moreover, surveys by the National Association of Manufacturers revealed that corporate managers viewed escalating health care costs as a greater threat to business competitiveness than the federal debt (Graig, 1993).

Politicians also began to take notice. The unexpected victory of Democrat Harris Wolford over the preelection favorite Richard Thornburgh for a vacant Pennsylvania seat was widely attributed to Wolford's campaign for comprehensive and universal health care coverage. According to a July 1992 Gallup poll taken before the presidential election, voters considered health care reform the second most important election issue, after jobs (Navarro, 1994). Governor Bill Clinton's successful campaign for the presidency highlighted the health care reform issue; once elected, President Clinton made health care reform the focus of his domestic legislative agenda during the second year of his presidency.

Outpacing the government, insurers and health care providers also enacted their own solutions to the spiraling costs of health care. The use of alternative delivery systems increased rapidly during the past decades. From 1976 to 1991, the number of health maintenance organizations (HMO) increased from 174 plans serving 6 million members to 553 plans serving 34 million members, or about 13% of the U.S. population (National Center for Health Statistics, 1992). In addition, by 1991, enrollment in preferred provider organizations (PPO) and nontraditional HMOs (which allow enrollees to consult non-HMO providers for a penalty) reached 28.5 million (Aday, Begley, Lairson, & Slater, 1993). Physician practice also has changed. Whereas 10.6% of physicians worked in group practice in 1965, 30% did in 1990. The size of the groups also has increased from a mean of 6.6 physicans to 9.6 physicians. Moreover, more than 70% of physician groups now contract or do business with HMOs on a referral basis, and 56% contract with PPOs (American Medical Association, 1990). Increasingly, hospitals also are forming alliances. Only 30% of hospitals were affiliated with another hospital in 1979; however, by 1987, this number had reached 45%, and it is projected to reach 80% by the year 2000 (Luke, Begun, & Pointer, 1989).

HEALTH CARE CONTEXT FOR PSYCHOLOGY

What was psychology's position during the rapidly evolving health care scenario of the early 1990s? Professional psychology's reactions to the early reform initiatives of the Clinton administration were similar to those of most allied health disciplines: rally the troops, establish a grassroots network, and lobby influential members of Congress. There were two primary themes that pervaded the early presentations of APA's Practice Directorate, the group primarily responsible for organizing APA's health care reform campaign: (a) health care coverage should include unlimited outpatient psychotherapy benefits, and (b) regulatory controls should be imposed on managed care (Glueckauf, 1993; Glueckauf, Frank, Bond, & McGrew, 1994).

Unfortunately, these early advocacy efforts were not only "out of sync" with most congressional health subcommittee proposals but also misrepresented the views of a large body of practicing psychologists. From its inception, the APA's Practice Directorate's health care reform campaign had been skewed toward the interests of psychologists in independent private practice whose orientation was psychoanalytic or psychodynamic, and whose primary identity was "mental health." This constituency had the most to lose in a reforming health care system that emphasized utilization review and cost controls. The decision-making and economic constraints imposed by managed care systems, particularly the requirements of preauthorization, intensive use review, and reduced fees, were anathema to psychoanalytically oriented, solo practitioners (Glueckauf, 1995; Levant, 1994; Saeman, 1994a).

It was not until August 1993, that leaders from the mainstream of rehabilitation and health psychology began to voice their concerns about the direction of APA's advocacy efforts. They objected to the APA's Practice Directorate's portrayal of psychologists as "mental health providers" on two grounds. First, the label, mental health provider, perpetuated the myth that physical and mental health are independent, nonoverlapping processes. Research over the past decade, however, has shown the opposite to be the case. Cognitive, emotional, and biological factors function as codeterminants of health and illness across a variety of contexts and medical conditions (Cohen & Rodriguez, 1995; Melamed, this volume).

Second, the term *mental health practitioner* inaccurately described the activities and roles of psychologists working in a variety of health care settings. Psychologists working in neurorehabilitation settings, for example, may spend most of their time teaching compensatory techniques for memory dysfunction, social problem solving, and impulse control. These services bear little resemblance to traditional mental health services, such as individual and group insight-oriented psychotherapy.

Apart from definitional concerns, rehabilitation and health psychology leaders had little enthusiasm for the APA's Practice Directorate's "frontal attacks" against managed care. They had already concluded from years of experience in working with managed care systems that little would be gained in fighting against this economic tidal wave. Instead, they were eager to pursue solutions for operating effectively within the prevailing system.

Mainstream health care psychology leaders, furthermore, had a different agenda for promoting professional psychology than the APA's Practice Directorate leadership. They were convinced that legislative advocacy efforts should focus on the cost-savings of problem-focused psychological intervention (rather than unlimited outpatient psychotherapy), particularly those treatments that had a strong scientific basis and focused on health and lifestyle management (e.g., smoking cessation and assertive community treatment), as well as psychology's contribution to quality assurance and program evaluation (Cummings, Pallak, Dorken, & Henke, 1992; Cummings & VandenBos, 1981). In addition, they thought that several long-term strategies should be enacted by APA, such as evaluating the "market needs" for psychologists in a reforming health care system, developing standard practice guidelines, and assuring access to psychological services for at-risk children and adults with chronic medical conditions.

In an effort to bring forward this agenda, the editors of the current text crafted a grant proposal for a National Conference on Health Care Reform and Psychological Practice in Rehabilitation and Health Care Settings (Glueckauf, Frank, Bond, & McGrew, 1993). Several parties both within and outside APA provided grant funding for the conference, including the APA Board of Directors; APA Council of Representatives; APA Divisions 12-5 (Pediatric Psychology), 22 (Rehabilitation Psychology), 38 (Health Psychology), 40 (Clinical Neuropsychology), and 42 (Psychologists in Independent Practice); the National Academy of Neuropsychology; and the Department of Psychology at Indiana University-Purdue University at Indianapolis (IUPUI).

The Indianapolis Conference

On May 6 to 8, 1994, the National Conference on Health Care Reform and Psychological Practice in Rehabilitation and Health Care Settings was held on the campus of IUPUI. The conference brought together 55 representatives from psychology's major health care specialties, key APA officers and staff members, and U.S. congressional representatives Ted Strickland and Andy Jacobs, Jr. The common linking factor among this diverse group of participants was a strong commitment to ensuring the advancement of psychological practice in health care settings during the era of health reform.

The primary objectives of the working conference were (a) to formulate a comprehensive statement on the role of psychological practice in health care settings in a changing a health care system, (b) to provide the ground-work for developing an information base on the benefits of psychological practice in rehabilitation and health care settings, and (c) to develop strategies for lobbying Congress and individual states to include psychological services for persons with health problems in a comprehensive health care benefits package (Glueckauf et al., 1994).

The conference focused on four key themes: (a) the adequacy of psychology's work force, that is, the size and characteristics of the psychological work force needed to provide services in a reformed health system, (b) the level of access to psychology services in health care settings, (c) demands for quality assurance and health outcomes standards, and (d) the educational preparation of psychologists for work in rehabilitation and health care settings.

Several important recommendations and action steps emerged from the Indianapolis conference. As a first step in disseminating conference information, the organizing committee drafted an "Executive Summary" that was published in its entirety in Division 22's *Rehabilitation Psychology News* (Glueckauf et al., 1994) and in abbreviated form in a variety of other sources, such as *The National Psychologist* (Saeman, 1994b). Several other initiatives followed, including Bob Frank's invited address on the Outcomes of the Indianapolis conference at the 1994 APA convention in Los Angeles (Frank, 1994); the publication of a special section on psychology in health care in *Professional Psychology: Research and Practice* (Johnstone et al., 1995); the creation of an interdivisional consortium of health care psychologists to foster changes in quality assurance and outcome evaluation practices, in public education about psychological services in health care settings, and in education and training models for research and practice in health and rehabilitation (see Johnson, 1995), and the publication of the current text.

The Book.

Originally, we had planned a proceedings volume from the conference to ensure rapid information dissemination for lobbying purposes. However, before we could even begin this effort, the health care reform climate had changed dramatically. By the fall, 1994, Clinton's health care reform bill was "on its last legs." Moreover, sweeping Republican victories in the U.S. congressional elections in November 1994 sounded the end of 40 years of Democratic domination of both the U.S. Senate and the House of Representatives, and silenced populist voices for national health care reform. The elections were widely touted as an indictment of Clinton's health care reform plan, specifically, and of any increase of federal government's role in managing the health care system. Republicans further interpreted the elections to indicate public confidence in the reforming ability of competition and the free market. Thus, the architects of large-scale health care reform were replaced by conservative voices counseling slow-paced, incremental reform, primarily in federal insurance regulations (e.g., increased insurance portability and limiting exclusions on preexisting conditions).

However, the pressures within the health care system have not changed. The trends and changes in health care cost, systems, and delivery begun in the past three decades will undoubtedly continue (Rice, 1990). There will be continued conversion to managed care, states will continue to experiment with local reform, and some reform will be enacted at the federal level. Indeed, as of this writing, there are again serious discussions in Congress about making substantial changes in health care, but limited to federally funded health care programs (i.e., Medicaid and Medicare).

The current text not only summarizes and integrates the major findings of the May, 1994, Indianapolis conference, but also addresses the changes in the health care climate since the conference took place. The book is divided into six parts. Part I serves as an introduction to the book and to the health care system. Parts II to V concern the four key themes of the conference, and are based on and follow a format similar to that used at the conference. These sections are divided into three subsections: a brief introduction to and overview of each section by the section editor, a comprehensive review chapter describing the issues and possible action steps related to each area, and a consensus chapter outlining the major findings and recommendations. Part VI provides an overview summary and conclusions for the book.

The intended audience for the book is broad. We hope the book will be of use to policy makers, health care administrators, health care educators, and health care practitioners. Certainly, the book will be of interest to psychologists and allied professionals (e.g., social workers, physiatrists, psychiatrists, psychiatric and rehabilitation nurses, mental health and rehabilitation counselors, and psychology graduate students).

Several individuals deserve special acknowledgment in helping to complete this book. Pat DeLeon, Tom Boll, and Lee Sechrest deserve special thanks for their guidance in developing the conference content, format, and procedures. Janet O'Keeffe has provided invaluable editorial assistance, in addition to authoring two chapters. Finally, special thanks go to the Springer Publishing Company staff members, particularly Dr. Ursula Springer, and Managing Editor, Bill Tucker, for their editorial support throughout this process.

REFERENCES

Aday, L. A., Begley, C. E., Lairson, D. R., & Slater, C. H. (1993). *Evaluating the medical care system: Effectiveness, efficiency, and equity.* Ann Arbor, MI: Health Administration Press.

American Medical Association. (1990). *Medical group practice in the United States.* Chicago: American Medical Association.

Anderson, O. W. (1989). *The health services continuum in democratic states: An inquiry into solvable problems.* Ann Arbor: Health Administration Press.

Blendon, R., & Taylor, H. (1989). Views on health care: Public opinion in three nations. *Health Affairs, 8,* 149–157.

Cohen, S., & Rodriguez, M. (1995). Pathways linking psychological and physical disorders. *Health Psychology, 14,* 374–380.

Cummings, N. A., Pallak, M. S., Dorken, H., & Henke, C. J. (1992). *The impact of psychological services on medical utilization and costs* (HCFA Contract No. 11-C-98344/9 report). Baltimore: Health Care Financing Administration.

Cummings, N. A., & VandenBos, G. R. (1981). The twenty year Kaiser-Permanente experience with psychotherapy and medical utilization: Implications for national health policy and national insurance. *Health Policy Quarterly, 1,* 59–87.

Division of National Health Care Costs, Office of the Actuary, Health Care Financing Authority. (1990). National Expenditures, 1986–2000. In P. R. Lee & C. L. Estes (Eds.), *The nation's health* (3rd ed., pp. 207–221). Boston: Jones and Bartlett.

Frank, R. G. (1994, August). *Health care reform and psychological practice in rehabilitation and health care settings: An update from the Indianapolis conference.* Invited address at the 102nd annual convention of the American Psychological Association, Los Angeles.

Friedman, E. (1991). The uninsured: From dilemma to crisis. *Journal of the American Medical Association, 265,* 2491–2495.

Glueckauf, R. L. (1993, winter). Health care reform and psychological practice in rehabilitation and health care settings. *Rehabilitation Psychology News, 21(2),* 1–3.

Glueckauf, R. L. (1995, August). *Boundaries among health care psychology specialties: A call for experimentation and unification.* Invited address at the 103rd annual convention of the American Psychological Association, New York City.

Glueckauf, R. L., Frank, R. G., Bond, G. R., & McGrew, J. (1993, November). *Health care reform and psychological practice in rehabilitation and health care settings: A national conference.* Conference grant funded by the Board of Directors and Council of Representatives of the American Psychological Association, Washington, DC.

Glueckauf, R. L., Frank, R. G., Bond, G. R., & McGrew, J. (1994, summer). National conference on health care reform and psychological practice in rehabilitation and health care settings. *Rehabilitation Psychology News, 21(3),* 1–5.

Graig, L. A. (1993). *Health of nations: An international perspective on U.S. health care reform* (2nd ed.). Washington, DC: Congressional Quarterly.

Jencks, S., & Scheiber, G. J. (1991). Containing U.S. health care costs: What bullet to bite. *Health Care Financing Review,* 1991 Supplement, 9–12. (Suppl.).

Johnson, S. B. (1994, December). *Psychologists in medical settings consortium.* Memorandum from Suzanne Bennett Johnson, President, Division of Health Psychology, Department of Psychiatry, University of Florida Health Sciences, P. O. Box 100234, Gainesville, FL 32610.

Johnstone, B., Frank, R. G., Belar, C., Berk, S., Bieliauskas, L. A., Bigler, E. D., Caplan, B., Elliott, T. R., Glueckauf, R. L., Kaplan, R. M., Kreutzer, J. S., Mateer, C. A., Patterson, D., Puente, A. E., Richards, J. S., Rosenthal, M., Sherer, M., Shewchuk, R., Keigal, L. J., & Sweet, J. J. (1995). Psychology is health care: Future directions. *Professional Psychology: Research and Practice, 26,* 341–365.

Levant, R. F. (1994, August). A strategy for managed care. *Practitioner (APA Practice Directorate), 7(2),* 1, 19, 22.

Luke, R. D., Begun, J. W., & Pointer, D. D. (1989). Quasi-firms: Strategic interorganizational forms in the health care industry. *Academy of Management Review, 14,* 9–19.

McKeown, T. (1975). *The role of medicine: Dream, mirage, or nemesis?* London: Nuffield Provincial Hospitals Trust.

Melamed, B. G. (1996). Introduction. In R. L. Glueckauf, R. G. Frank, G. R. Bond, & J. H. McGrew (Eds.), *Psychological practice in a changing health care system: Issues and new directions.* New York: Springer.

Milio, N. (1983). *Primary care and the public's health.* Lexington, MA: Lexington Books.

National Center for Health Statistics. (1992). *Health, United States, 1991* (DHHS Publication No. PHS 92-1232). Washington, DC: U.S. Government Printing Office.

Navarro, V. (1994). *The politics of health policy: The U.S. reforms, 1980–1994.* Cambridge, MA: Blackwell.

Rice, D. P. (1990). The medical care system: Past trends and future projections. In P. R. Lee & C. L. Estes (Eds.), *The nation's health* (3rd ed., pp. 72–93). Boston: Jones and Bartlett.

Scheiber, G., Poullier, J., & Greenwald, L. (1991). Health care systems in twenty-four countries. *Health Affairs, 10(3),* 22–38.

Scheiber, G., Poullier, J., & Greenwald, L. (1992). U.S. health expenditure performance: An international comparison and update. *Health Care Financing Review, 13(4),* 1–87.

Saeman, H. (Ed.). (1994, July/August). Psychology as health profession is major thrust, not mere addition: An interview with Robert G. Frank, Ph.D. *The National Psychologist*, 4.

Saeman, H. (Ed.). (1994, July/August). Psychology is health profession—not only mental health—group insists. *The National Psychologist*, 3.

Short, P. (1990). *Estimates of the uninsured population, calendar year 1987.* (DHHS Publication No. PHS 90-3469). Washington, DC: U.S. Government Printing Office, Agency for Health Care Policy and Research.

Sonnefeld, S. T., Waldo, D. R., Lemieux, J. A., & McKusick, D. R. (1991). Projections of national health expenditures through the year 2000. *Health Care Financing Review, 13(1),* 1–29.

Verbrugge, L. M. (1990). Longer life but worsening health? In P. R. Lee & C. L. Estes (Eds.), *The nation's health* (3rd ed., pp. 14–34). Boston: Jones and Bartlett.

Chapter 2

The American Health Care System

Janet O'Keeffe

This chapter provides a brief overview of the financing and organization of the American health care system, a discussion of its major problems, and a review of the reforms that are needed to fix them. To analyze accurately the many issues that will be presented in this book, it is essential to have an understanding of the current health care system, particularly its financing, and the problems that are driving reform efforts. Without knowledge of our current health system and its problems, it will not be possible to chart a course for psychological practice in a changing health care environment.

HOW THE U.S. FINANCES HEALTH CARE

The two major problems with our health care system are the interrelated issues of lack of access and out-of-control costs. Clearly, if health care were more affordable, financial barriers to access would not be a major concern. Unlike virtually all Western industrialized democracies, the American health system is financed through a combination of uncoordinated private and public programs that, despite their high cost, fail to provide coverage for all Americans.

Private Programs and Policies

In the late 1930s, to assure a secure source of revenue following the Great Depression, hospitals organized to establish the first nonprofit health insurance company—Blue Cross (Iglehart, 1992b). At the time of its introduction, Blue Cross hospital insurance was community rated. Under community rating, everyone who applies for coverage is accepted, and everyone pays the same premium regardless of health status, or risk of illness or injury. In this way, adherence to the central principle of health insurance—that the healthy subsidize the sick—is assured. Blue Shield was subsequently established to cover payment for physician services.

Over the next several decades, the number of people with private insurance increased, in large part because of the preferential tax treatment of employee health benefits, which provided an incentive for employers to offer health benefits to their workers. This incentive was increased during World War II when employer-provided health benefits were exempted from the wartime freeze on wages (Friedman, 1986). As more employers began to offer insurance as a fringe benefit, an increasing number of commercial (i.e., for-profit) insurers entered the market, and competition for low-risk groups began. As a result, the practice of experience rating was introduced, which sets premiums according to past or anticipated health claims experience.

Employers contributed to this practice by bargaining for lower rates with insurance companies on the basis of their own claims history and the characteristics of their work force. As a result, employers with a predominately young work force in low-risk occupations were able to negotiate much lower premiums than those with older workers in high-risk occupations. Experience rating gradually replaced community rating among commercial insurers, and the health insurance market became increasingly segmented, with each employer group, in effect, forming their own insurance pool. This development reduced the ability to spread risk over a large population, which is essential to keep premiums affordable for everyone—not just the young or healthy. Clearly, with ever-increasing health care costs, it is not possible for the premium contributions of a small group (e.g., a business with 15 to 20 employees) to cover the cost of even a single catastrophic illness or injury.

From the 1950s through the 1990s, tremendous increases in health care costs have affected the availability of health insurance in two major ways. First, as health care has become increasingly expensive, insurance premiums have likewise escalated, thereby excluding many Americans who cannot afford to buy insurance. It is not uncommon to find insurance policies costing $5,000 per year for individual coverage and $10,000 per year for family coverage. Given that 50% of American households earn less than $31,000 per year, insurance is simply unaffordable for many (U.S. Department of Commerce, 1993). Second, in an effort to maintain their profits, health insurers have instituted more intensive medical under-writing. The competition for low-risk groups has led not only to numerous preexisting condition exclusions and an increase in the number of individu-als deemed ''medically uninsurable'' but also to the exclusion of those who are judged likely to develop such conditions no matter how minimal the risk. As a result, entire occupations, industries, and geographic areas are routinely excluded from coverage by many health insurers on the grounds that individuals in these areas and groups are at high risk for needing health care (Kincaid, 1995).

As rising health care costs have pushed premiums higher, an increasing number of large firms have chosen to self-insure, thereby saving them-selves the cost of insurance company commissions, overhead, and profits, and allowing them to obtain the financial benefits of investing large reserves. The Employee Retirement Income Security Act (ERISA), which governs employer health benefit plans, also exempts employer health plans from state insurance regulations and taxes, and from many consumer protections, thereby providing another financial incentive to self-insure. Because employers who self-insure simply pay their employees' health care bills out of their before-tax profits, they have become increasingly concerned about controlling costs and assuring maximum benefits for dollars spent.

By 1990, approximately one half of all Americans with employer-provided insurance were covered by plans that were to some extent self-insured (Sullivan & Rice, 1991). Consequently, the market that remains for private insurance consists primarily of small companies and organiza-tions, and the self-employed. As the market has shrunk, the competition to screen out bad risks has intensified, with many insurers going to extremes to avoid rather than manage risk (O'Keeffe, 1992). These trends combined with massive cost increases caused the number of uninsured to grow by 30% between 1980 and 1991. In 1991 alone, 3.3 million people lost coverage (Levit, Olin, & Letsch, 1992). In this same period, public programs covered an increasing portion of the population, but this increase did not offset the decline in the proportion with coverage through private insurance.

Recently released census data indicate that in 1993 the proportion of the population under 65 years of age without insurance was 18.1%—41 million people (Bureau of National Affairs, 1995a). However, because this figure is derived from cross-sectional data, it underestimates the scope of the problem. If we look at longitudinal data, an even higher percentage of the population is without insurance for significant periods. A Census Bureau study found that 30% of the under-65-year-old population—61 million Americans—lacked insurance for at least a month during a 28-month period between 1987 and 1989 (Rubin, 1993).

Limitations of Private Insurance

Although the 41 million Americans without insurance are often cited as the major reason for reforming our health system, there are millions more who are underinsured. This is related to several factors: (a) lack of coverage for preexisting conditions; (b) exclusion from coverage of certain categories of health care and related services, including preventive and diagnostic services, prescription drugs, extended rehabilitation, durable medical equipment, and long-term care; (c) exclusions for ''experimental'' drugs, treatments, and procedures, the determination of which frequently differs among insurers; (d) annual and lifetime caps and high copayments for certain conditions or treatments, usually for mental health and substance abuse services; (e) no limits on out-of-pocket payments for covered services; (f) no limits on expenses that exceed ''usual, customary and reasonable'' charges for covered benefits; and (g) a host of other exclusions based on restricted definitions of ''medical necessity,'' or arbitrary limitations on services, such as physical therapy. Estimates of the number of people under 65 years old who are underinsured range from 38 million (those who have insurance but have no limits on out-of-pocket expenditures) to 55 million, if those who are at risk of being impoverished should they experience a major costly illness are added (DeLew, Greenberg, & Kinchen, 1992; U.S. Congress Office of Technology Assessment, 1988). In one study of uncompensated hospital care, 47% of the 1,689 patients who could not pay all their hospital expenses *had* health insurance (Saywell, Zollinger, Chu, MacBeth, & Sechrist, 1989).

Limitations in insurance coverage are often not apparent until a person becomes seriously ill. Consequently, most Americans report high levels of satisfaction with their current health insurance coverage. It is only when they experience a serious illness or accident that requires a wide range of ongoing medical, rehabilitative, and support services, that they discover how few of these services are covered. They also find out that hospital and physician charges the insurer determines are above ''usual, customary, and reasonable'' charges are neither paid by the insurer nor applied to the out-of-pocket limits. Thus, for persons who incur major costs, out-of-pocket expenses are often far higher than stated limits.

Additionally, many insurance plans nominally include a particular benefit, but the services covered are so limited that they are often insufficient. As an example, a plan may provide a durable medical equipment benefit of $300, but an electric wheelchair needed by a person with quadriplegia can cost $10,000 or more. In another example, a plan may cover only 60 days of inpatient rehabilitation, but persons with a neurological disability (e.g., stroke or spinal cord injury) may require intensive rehabilitation for 8 weeks or longer, and intermittent outpatient rehabilitation services for another 6 to 12 months. In the case of a child with cerebral palsy, rehabilitation may be required throughout the child's lifetime. Even limited benefits may not be reimbursed if an insurer determines that rehabilitation services are being provided to ''maintain'' and not to ''improve'' function. Persons with serious mental illness generally exhaust their inpatient lifetime mental health benefit within a year. Health insurance also rarely, if ever, covers long-term care, services, and supports for persons who are disabled as a result of a congenital condition, a chronic disease, or an injury. The rationale often given for not covering these services is that they are not ''acute,'' not ''medically necessary,'' or not ''health related.''

One of the most troubling aspects of our system of private health insurance is that it cannot be counted on in the event of sickness or accident. Because policies issued to individuals and small groups are often nonrenewable, many individuals are at risk of having their coverage terminated when they, or someone in their family or small group, becomes ill. Once a member of the group has a serious illness, finding insurance to cover the group becomes much more difficult and expensive, and coverage usually cannot be obtained without preexisting condition exclusions. In testimony offered to the U.S. Bipartisan Commission on Comprehensive Health Care Reform, a couple with a group policy for their family business was forced to drop coverage for their employees when their premiums rose from $198 per person to $766 per person *per month* after their child was born with a birth defect. The couple was forced to drop health care coverage the following year when the monthly premium was further increased to $1,375 per month (U.S. Bipartisan Commission on Comprehensive Health Care, 1990).

Employees in large groups also experience problems with coverage of benefits because so many are covered by self-insured plans and are not protected by the limited state regulations that govern commercial insurers, including those that mandate coverage of specific benefits, such as mental health treatment. If persons in a self-insured plan have been denied *covered* benefits and suffered negative effects as a result, ERISA does not permit them to sue for damages. At best, they can sue to have the insurer pay for the covered benefit. ERISA also permits employers to change the provisions of their benefit plans, an issue that is increasingly affecting retired workers, particularly those under 65 years of age who are not eligible for Medicare, many of whom retired because of poor health.

Since 1993, the Federal Accounting Standards Board has required companies to include the cost of retiree health benefits as liabilities on their balance sheets. As a result, many employers are cutting back or entirely eliminating retiree health benefits. A recent Supreme Court case upheld employers' rights to do so, ruling that "employers . . . are generally free under the Employee Retirement Income Security Act (ERISA), for any reason at any time, to adopt, modify, or terminate welfare plans," as long as the original contract contains provisions to do so (Bureau of National Affairs, 1995b).

Recent congressional hearings highlighted the problems faced by retired persons with serious health conditions who are unable to purchase private insurance because they are considered "medically uninsurable" and who will not be eligible for Medicare for many years. Even for those retirees who may not be excluded for health reasons, the cost of health insurance is often prohibitive, amounting sometimes to one half or more of their annual pension. Some retirees who are able have reentered the labor force solely to obtain health insurance (Retiree Health Benefits, 1993; Willis, 1991). In sum, the security afforded by a comprehensive health insurance policy is increasingly tenuous, and the benefits provided are often inadequate to meet the health care needs of those covered, particularly those with disabling chronic conditions.

Public Programs and Policies

In the United States today, persons under 65 years of age without private health insurance can receive health care through several public programs, such as government-financed community health centers and public health service hospitals. They also have access to emergency medical care in life-threatening situations in both private and public hospitals through specific statutory requirements placed on these entities. Historically, many hospitals were founded by religious or charitable groups whose major purpose was to provide free care for the poor and destitute. However, the particular statutory obligation of hospitals to provide charity care had its origins with the passage of the Hospital Survey and Construction Act in 1948, more widely known as the Hill Burton Act. The act provided federal funds to build hospitals, and, in return, required hospitals to provide a defined amount of free and below-cost care each year for 20 years to uninsured and low-income persons.

A right to emergency care is also ensured through a variety of state and federal statutes, including hospital licensing laws and tax-exempt status standards. Under the tax code, nonprofit hospitals are required to provide some charity care to their communities in exchange for their exemption from federal and state taxes. More recently, in response to egregious cases of hospitals denying care in emergency situations, an antidumping law was enacted in 1986 that prohibits hospitals from refusing to treat persons with life-threatening conditions, those with medically unstable conditions, and pregnant women in active labor.

Publicly financed programs and statutory obligations evolved in part because of a recognition that government and health providers have a responsibility to provide health care for certain categories of vulnerable persons, and to all individuals in life-threatening situations, sometimes referred to as "the rule of rescue." They have also evolved because of concerns about the detrimental impact of specific communicable diseases (e.g., tuberculosis and sexually transmitted disease) on society as a whole, as well as pragmatic economic interests. For example, in the late 1790s when recruitment of merchant seamen became difficult because port hospitals did not want to provide care to seamen from other towns, the government began garnishing seamen's wages to fund a system of merchant marine hospitals, which later evolved into the U.S. Public Health Service (Shefler, 1993).

The government has always assumed responsibility for the health care of members of the armed forces and veterans with service-connected health conditions and disabilities—groups it could not afford to leave to the uncertain coverage of the private market. The federal government also provides health care for Native Americans through the Indian Health Service. This program was enacted in 1955 based on federal treaty obligations (Taylor, 1992). The Indian Health Service, and the Department of Defense and Veterans Administration health programs are systems of "socialized medicine," with all health facilities owned and operated by the government, and health personnel, including doctors, salaried by the government. The responsibility to provide health care to the armed forces was incrementally expanded to the dependents of military servicemen and women; first through the Emergency Maternal and Infant Care Act of 1943, which ensured that spouses and children of low-ranking servicemen would be able to obtain health care, and then in 1956, when Congress permanently extended federal health care benefits to spouses and dependents through the Civilian Health and Medical Program of the Uniformed Services (CHAMPUS) (Friedman, 1986).

Thus, a variety of publicly financed health programs were established incrementally over several decades, as federal and state governments gradually assumed responsibility for ensuring access to health care for some groups. These public programs paved the way for the enactment of Medicare and Medicaid in 1965.

Medicare

Medicare is a government-financed and -administered "single-payer" national health insurance program that was originally intended to cover only persons older than age 65. Because health insurance is primarily obtained through employment, at the time of Medicare's enactment, 44% of the elderly had no hospital insurance (Iglehart, 1992b). In 1973, Medicare was expanded to cover permanently disabled persons (and their dependents) receiving Social Security Disability Insurance (SSDI) benefits for at least 2 years and persons with end-stage renal disease. In 1990, Medicare covered 13% of the U.S. population (Levit et al., 1992).

Although Medicare is often viewed as a source of comprehensive health care for persons older than age 65; in fact, the program covers only a limited amount of services. Hospital services are covered through the Medicare Hospital Trust Fund—Part A. Because enrollment in Part A is mandatory and requires no premiums, it establishes an entitlement to most hospital services, hospice care, and a limited postacute nursing home and home health benefit. Coverage for physician and other outpatient services is available to all Medicare eligible individuals regardless of income through Medicare's Supplementary Medical Insurance—Part B. The $553 annual Part B premium is heavily subsidized from general revenues. Approximately 89% of Medicare's revenue is obtained from payroll and income taxes levied on persons younger than age 65 (Iglehart, 1992a). For Medicare eligible persons whose incomes are just above the federal poverty level and who have less than $4,000 in assets, Medicaid is required to pay the Part B premium, the deductible, and any copayments incurred. However, only one third of the poor elderly are eligible for this Medicaid coverage, and it does not include payment for services that Medicare does not cover, such as prescription drugs (Commonwealth Fund Commission on Elderly People Living Alone, 1987). Additionally, of the 4.2 million eligible, 1.8 million are not receiving this assistance because they do not know it is available (Families USA Report, 1993).

Persons with Medicare coverage are not assured access to comprehensive health care because its limited package of benefits pays primarily for acute care. Most notably, Medicare does not pay for prescription drugs, many preventive and early diagnostic services, and long-term care. Additionally, the program requires considerable cost-sharing. Hospital coverage is subject to a $716 annual deductible, and there is substantial cost-sharing for hospital stays more than 60 days, no cap on out-of-pocket liability, and no coverage for persons needing more than 150 days of hospital care.

Deficiencies in coverage for expensive items, such as prescription drugs and extensive cost-sharing impoverish one third of the near poor elderly each year. Fear of such impoverishment or the inability to pay for needed services leads 72% of persons older than age 65 to purchase supplementary coverage through private "Medi-Gap" policies, which generally pay all of Medicare's cost-sharing requirements. However, most of these policies do *not* pay for any benefits that Medicare does not cover, specifically prescription drugs and long-term care. The few policies that cover prescription drugs are medically underwritten, thereby excluding many persons who want to purchase such coverage. Forty-two percent of the poor elderly pay as much as 10% of their income to purchase Medi-Gap policies (Commonwealth Fund Commission, 1987). Finally, Medicare does not provide payment for any health services received outside of the United States. Thus, Americans older than age 65 who live or travel abroad are not covered.

Medicaid

Medicaid is a combined federal and state funded, means-tested health care program for targeted categories of the poor, such as mothers with children who are enrolled in the Aid to Families With Dependent Children Program (AFDC), and recipients of the Supplemental Security Income Program (SSI), which provides cash benefits to persons with disabilities younger than age 65 and the elderly poor. Strict categorical eligibility and unrealistically low-income requirements greatly reduce the number of poor persons eligible for Medicaid. Medicaid income eligibility for a family of three averages $5,100 nationwide, an amount equal to 44% of the federal poverty level. In the state of Alabama, a family of three is not eligible for Medicaid if their income exceeds $1,788 annually (less than $150 per month), which is 16% of poverty (Kaiser Commission on the Future of Medicaid, 1992).

Thirty-six states have a "medically needy" standard that allows persons whose income and assets exceed eligibility guidelines, to "spend down" to the state determined poverty level to become eligible for Medicaid (i.e., they can deduct their health care expenses from their income to meet state income eligibility requirements). In states without this standard, persons who are not categorically eligible through AFDC or SSI are not eligible for Medicaid even if their medical expenses *exceed* their income. The failure of the program to cover the poor is evident in the fact that 25% of poor children and 40% of poor adults are not covered by Medicaid, and have no other source of health insurance (Kaiser Commission on the Future of Medicaid, 1992).

Although limited in its coverage of the poor, Medicaid provides a more comprehensive array of benefits than Medicare. These benefits include preventive, diagnostic, acute, rehabilitative, and long-term care services. However, unrealistically low reimbursement rates restrict access to health care by discouraging program participation by health care providers. Additionally, because some services, such as long-term care, are generally covered only when delivered in institutions, families with long-term care needs are generally required to institutionalize their disabled parents or children to receive assistance. Because they are reluctant to do so, most families assume the personal and financial costs of long-term care until they are either impoverished or no longer physically or emotionally able to provide the level of care required.

Finally, although federal Medicaid mandates require states to offer certain services and prohibit them from arbitrarily limiting services based on diagnosis, states are permitted to place limits on the duration and amount of services provided. For example, when a lawsuit was brought against the state of Tennessee for reducing Medicaid coverage of hospital days from 20 to 14 per year, the Supreme Court ruled that it was permissible for states to place a limit on the number of hospital days that Medicaid would cover. In its ruling, the Court stated that Medicaid's purpose is to assure the delivery of necessary medically care, "not adequate health care" (Supreme Court, 1985). The "necessity" for hospital care for periods longer than 14 days was apparently not considered by the Court.

In sum, although Medicare and Medicaid provide an entitlement to some health care for eligible individuals, the health care guaranteed through these public programs is oriented primarily to acute medical needs and, in addition, under Medicaid, the provision of long-term care to the impoverished severely disabled population of all ages. The guarantee of emergency care, the financing of primarily acute care, and the failure to assure universal access to preventive and primary care have led to higher overall costs for the health system. People are unable to obtain preventive, early diagnostic, and primary care, but are admitted to the most expensive institutions when their health status has deteriorated sufficiently to require emergency treatment.

The recognition of a moral obligation to save life, but not to provide a comprehensive array of health services, has resulted in a health care system where uninsured women go without prenatal care costing about $800, but hospitals will provide neonatal intensive care—often costing over $100,000—to save the life of an uninsured infant born prematurely. Similarly, Medicare will pay for hospital care for a person who has had a stroke but not for the medication to treat the hypertension that caused the stroke. A recent study found that Medicaid and uninsured patients are hospitalized at much higher rates for preventable complications of diabetes and asthma than are patients with private insurance (Weissman, Gatsonis, & Epstein, 1992).

Clearly, as the cost of technologically advanced interventions continues to climb, it is irrational to require treatment at the acute end of the health care continuum for health conditions that, if not totally preventable, could be treated at a far lower cost in a system designed to provide comprehensive primary health care to all its citizens. However, the continuing escalation of costs in both Medicare and Medicaid have made federal and state governments wary of expanding coverage under these programs because of fears that significant costs would be incurred before cost-savings would be realized.

HOW MUCH DO AMERICANS PAY FOR INSECURE AND INADEQUATE COVERAGE?

In 1992, only 30.7% of our nation's trillion-dollar health bill was paid through private health insurance premiums and self-insured plans (Burner, Waldo, & McKusick, 1992). The low proportion paid by private insurance is due to the fact that it primarily covers younger, employed people who have lower health expenses on average, and also because the industry works assiduously to exclude both those who need health care and those they deem to be at high risk for needing health care. In the same year, federal, state, and local governments (i.e., the American taxpayer) paid 45.9% of the nation's annual health care bill through a variety of health programs: Medicare; Medicaid; the Department of Defense; CHAMPUS; the Veterans Administration; federal and state employee and retiree programs; and other discrete health programs, such as Community Mental Health Centers.

If we consider the federal tax subsidy for employer-provided insurance—estimated at more than $66 billion for fiscal year 1996 (Bureau of National Affairs, 1995a)—public financing of health care through taxes contributes well over 50% of total payments for our health care bill, a share that will increase as the "baby boom" cohort ages and becomes eligible for Medicare. Thus, the public sector is currently the largest single financier of health care in this country. Clearly, the characterization of our current health system's financing as predominately private is inaccurate. Yet while the health care system flourishes on public funding, many aspects of the system respond only minimally to public needs.

The United States spends a trillion dollars annually on health care. Eighty-one percent is paid by individuals in the form of direct out-of-pocket payments, health insurance premiums, and general and earmarked taxes. Employers pay a significant portion of health care costs (19%) but recoup these expenses by charging higher prices to the public for goods and services, and through lowered compensation to employees and lower returns to investors (Burner et al., 1992; Reinhardt, 1993). Because most of the payments for health care are indirect and hidden—through pretax employer and employee contributions and general and earmarked taxes, most Americans do not realize the amount they are paying to finance a system that does not guarantee secure comprehensive health coverage throughout their lifetime. It is clear that the American public pays enough money into our current system to guarantee universal coverage to a high quality of health care. What is needed is a system to distribute it more equitably and efficiently.

FEATURES OF A SYSTEM THAT GUARANTEES A SECURE RIGHT TO COMPREHENSIVE HEALTH CARE

To guarantee a meaningful and secure right to health care for all its citizens, a health care system must have the following features: (a) mandatory universal coverage; (b) equitable financing; (c) a mandated comprehensive benefits package; (d) an efficient delivery system that provides coordinated, comprehensive health care in accessible settings; and (e) appropriate and adequate mechanisms to contain overall health care spending. Each of these features is discussed in turn.

1. *Mandatory universal coverage.* A meaningful and secure right to health care can only be assured through the establishment of a system of health insurance that provides continuous coverage for everyone regardless of age, health status, disability, employment, income, or any other factor. Because it is highly unlikely that the United States will enact a public, single-payer system of national insurance for the entire population, a system of universal coverage will most likely have to be achieved through a combination of private and public coverage, as is currently the case. However, universal coverage through a multipayer system will require not only that private insurers accept all applicants, but that every American enroll in a health plan. Mandating that insurers must accept all applicants while permitting the purchase of insurance to be

voluntary would lead to adverse selection and would perpetuate the current situation where people without insurance do not pay premiums but incur costs that are then shifted to those Americans who are already contributing. Leaving anyone out of the system also undermines the central premise of insurance that makes it work: The healthy subsidize the sick and because everyone is at risk for needing health care, everyone must contribute.

2. *Equitable financing.* An equitable financing mechanism is needed so that persons with low incomes do not have to pay a disproportionate share of their income for health insurance. Given that 15% of the U.S. population lives in poverty and 50% of households have less than $31,000 annual income (U.S. Department of Commerce, 1993), health insurance is unaffordable for many individuals and families. Therefore, the financing mechanism will need to be progressive, with those who are better off financially paying more than those who are less well off. This would be a marked change from the current system of financing, which is extremely regressive, providing the greatest subsidy for health insurance to high-income groups through the tax exclusion for employer-provided insurance.

Currently, those with the highest incomes pay the lowest percentage for their health insurance. In 1987, the Economic Policy Institute reported that families with incomes between $16,000 and $21,000 spent 15% of their income on health insurance premiums, out-of-pocket health costs, and taxes to support government health programs, whereas families with incomes between $72,000 and $93,000 spent only 11% of their income (News in Brief, 1993). Similar regressivity is present in the financing of the Medicare program, which subsidizes both high- and low-income elderly with the taxes of low-income workers, many of whom have no insurance for themselves and their families.

The simplest form of financing from an administrative perspective is a payroll tax. This approach is used by both public single-payer and private multipayer systems in other countries. Additional financing mechanisms would be required for individuals without earned income, such as early retirees who are not yet eligible for Medicare, and other individuals younger than 65 years who do not work but who have income from other sources. A recent study by the Economic and Social Research Institute found that the elimination of employer-provided insurance and the imposition of a 7.75% payroll tax could save up to $3.1 trillion in health spending over the next 10 years (Rich, 1993). However, there is powerful opposition to a payroll tax from businesses, particularly small businesses with low-wage employees, and businesses that currently do not provide insurance. For those who do provide insurance, a payroll tax in the range of 6% to 8% on annual earnings of $31,000 (U.S. median earnings) would cost far less than the average cost of a health insurance premium, which for small and medium-size businesses can range as high as $4,000 to $6,000 per person and $10,000 or more for family coverage.

Because it is unlikely that the United States will enact a payroll tax to finance health care, financing will most likely continue to be provided through the payment of premiums. The basic tenet of social insurance is that the healthy subsidize the sick and that those with large out-of-pocket costs resulting from illness or injury should not also be burdened by higher premiums. Therefore, premiums will need to be community-rated so that everyone pays the same irrespective of their health condition or risk of illness. Community rating also has the potential to reduce the overall cost of health care by providing incentives to all purchasers to work together to control aggregate costs (U.S. General Accounting Office, 1993).

However, financing universal coverage through community-rated premiums rather than a payroll tax will necessitate some form of subsidy for low-income persons who otherwise could not afford to pay the community rated premium. Subsidies could be provided through an employer mandate to provide coverage and through the tax system. Financing through premiums paid to a private system of multiple, competing, for-profit insurers will also necessitate some form of risk adjustment or reinsurance because such a system will not spread risk, as well as a system with a single insurer, or a few dominant insurers, and, as a result, there will be a greater chance for each plan to incur catastrophic costs. Clearly, financing universal coverage through a multipayer system will be much more administratively complex and costly than financing through a single-payer system, such as Medicare.

3. *Mandated comprehensive benefits.* A health system should provide the full range of services needed to prevent and treat illness, and to maintain physical and mental health and functioning. To do so, the current system's acute care bias needs to be altered to eliminate the incentives that have led to the neglect of coverage for preventive, primary, and rehabilitative services. To ensure that these services are covered, a comprehensive health benefits package would have to be mandated. Decisions regarding which services to include in a mandated standard benefits package should be based

on a consideration of their effectiveness and their cost-effectiveness.

4. *An efficient delivery system.* To assure the continuing affordability of health insurance, health care must be delivered efficiently. As a first step, the excess capacity in our current system should be reduced to a minimum. A reduction in the numerous inefficiencies and duplications in the system would also be important steps toward guaranteeing the efficient provision of coordinated health care in a range of settings.

5. *Cost-containment.* A health care system must contain appropriate and effective mechanisms for cost-containment. The rate of increase in health care costs over the past two decades is clearly unsustainable and must be reduced to keep health insurance both affordable and comprehensive. The debate over the best way to contain costs is likely to be divisive and contentious. However, without adequate cost-containment mechanisms, the cost of insurance will continue to climb, taking scarce resources away from other areas of our economy. Additionally, if the health care industry and health care providers are successful in blocking cost-containment mechanisms that affect their charges for products and services, it is virtually inevitable that both benefit coverage and financial protections for consumers will be reduced.

6. *Additional steps.* Although the five features of a health care system discussed previously are necessary to assure secure access to comprehensive health care for all Americans, they are not sufficient. There are many other factors that affect the availability and cost of health services. For example, it is generally recognized that the shortage of primary care physicians and the oversupply of specialist and subspecialists in the United States is a major factor contributing to excessive health care costs, while failing to produce measurable improvement in health status indicators (Grumbach & Fry, 1993; Schroeder & Sandy, 1993). Therefore, a coherent health policy must also address this imbalance and provide incentives to increase the number of primary care physicians relative to specialists (Grumbach & Fry, 1993; Schroeder & Sandy, 1993).

A first step might be to amend the current taxpayer subsidy to train physicians through the Medicare program so that taxpayer funding of graduate education is provided only to correct regional and national shortages (e.g., the lack of primary care physicians) or to increase underrepresented minorities in specific professions (e.g., the number of Native American mental health providers).

Additionally, health care delivery systems will need to have mechanisms to control the inappropriate use of specialists for conditions that could be handled by less costly primary care health providers.

Another factor contributing to health care cost inflation is the uncontrolled proliferation of both proven and unproven technology. Paradoxically, the overabundance of technology simultaneously increases cost and decreases access. As one analyst noted, it is ironic that many women in the United States cannot afford to have a mammogram because there are too many underused mammography machines driving up the average cost of the procedure (Starr, 1992). A rational and coherent national health policy would either regulate the dissemination of technology to more appropriately meet the needs of the population or design a system that provides incentives to purchase only that technology that will be appropriately used to full capacity.

In the area of health research, although the public provides $10 billion each year to fund research at the National Institutes of Health (NIH), little of this research is focused on the prevention of illness and the amelioration of the functional impairments that often result from technological advances in treatment and an attitude that we must save and extend life regardless of the personal or societal cost. It is essential that research priorities be altered to give equal attention to the prevention of accidents and illnesses, the maintenance of health and functioning, and the rehabilitation of persons with functional impairments.

Other barriers to health care will also need to be addressed, including the geographic inaccessibility of health services to many Americans living in rural areas. This will not require that the full range of specialized services be located in every geographic area. Rather, it will require that persons in underserved areas be provided primary care in accessible locations, and the means to access specialty services that are not in their immediate geographic area. Finally, we need to invest a greater proportion of our resources in the public health infrastructure, particularly in the area of infectious disease prevention and control. The emergence of multiple drug-resistant tuberculosis, which can cost $400,000 per patient to treat, underscores the importance of public health services in controlling our nation's health care expenditures.

PSYCHOLOGISTS AND THE HEALTH CARE SYSTEM

At the beginning of this chapter, it was noted that psychologists need to understand our current system and its problems to assess the many forces affecting the provision of psychological services in our changing health care environment. It is imperative that strategies designed to address the practice needs of psychologists in health care settings not be at odds with strategies to reform the system overall. Strategies to assure access to and reimbursement for psychological services must consider the need for systemwide reforms. In particular, it is essential that psychologists both understand the need to contain costs and show a willingness to work with public and private third-party payers to do so, while assuring that cost-containment measures and proposed reforms do not undermine the delivery of high-quality, cost-effective psychological services.

Because cost is the major factor driving reform efforts at the federal, state, and local levels, it will likely be difficult to obtain reimbursement for psychological services not currently covered, particularly those submitted without a Diagnostic and Statistical Manual (DSM) code, unless efficacy and cost-effectiveness are clearly demonstrated. Thus, more research is needed to document the ability of psychological services provided in health settings to improve both physical and mental health outcomes, and to do so at a reasonable cost (O'Keeffe, Quittner, & Melamed, this volume).

Education and Training

As previously discussed, cost-containment measures and the reduction of excess capacity in the health care system are essential if health care is to remain affordable. Given this and the fact that bachelor's- and master's-level health and mental health practitioners (e.g., nurses and social workers) are educated to provide some counseling services in health and mental health settings at generally lower cost than doctoral-trained providers, reimbursement for psychological services may move toward the lowest acceptable provider charge. Therefore, it would be prudent for education and training programs to assess current and future needs for practitioners, and to use this information to guide both admissions policy in current programs and, more important, to determine if new programs are needed.

Clearly, more data are needed on the number of psychologists practicing in all mental health and health care settings; the type, intensity, and duration of services they are providing; areas of unmet need (e.g., publicly funded mental health facilities); and variations in the cost and source of payment for services. The same data are also needed for those providers who could compete with doctoral-trained psychologists. In extremely pragmatic terms, it is inadvisable to increase the number of psychologists providing psychological services, if employment opportunities and reimbursement policies preclude their making a living in the field.

In closing, the U.S. health care system is likely to undergo considerable change over the next 20 years. Given the nation's history of health care policy making, barring a significant increase in the number uninsured, incremental change will probably be the norm, necessitating continual adaptation by providers of services. Clearly, current rates of increase in total health care expenditures are unsustainable. Because it is highly unlikely that the private sector will successfully address the two major interrelated problems with our system—access and affordability—we can expect increasing involvement by both state and federal government to both control costs and improve access.

Because most of the U.S. population cannot afford to pay for health care services directly, third-party reimbursement—public or private—is the predominant source of payment. Insurance companies and employers who purchase insurance or who self-insure are increasingly demanding accountability and cost-concessions from providers. Although individual psychologists may believe that their services are essential and their charges are reasonable, they need to understand cost concerns from a broader perspective.

For example, the APA provides health insurance for approximately 400 employees, their spouses, and dependents. APA, like other employers, is experience rated by the insurance industry, and thus has little choice of insurance companies and even less control over the cost of premiums for comprehensive coverage. In 1995, the total cost for APA's preferred provider health insurance plan was $4,000 for individual coverage, $7,500 for a couple or an employee and children, and $11,500 for family coverage. APA pays approximately 80% of this cost, the exact subsidy dependent on income and level of coverage. Given this tremendous cost, it is not surprising that employers are concerned about health care costs. In some cases, employers are deterred from hiring new workers because of the high cost of health insurance coverage in today's experience-rated market. Many small businesses do not provide any coverage for the same reason.

If psychologists are to adapt to a changing health care system and to advance their professional agenda within the context of systemwide reforms successfully, they must continually pursue information about the health care system, its problems, and the reforms that are needed to address the access and cost problems. They also need to become active participants in health policy making at the local, state, and federal levels, whether as expert advisers or as constituents supporting legislative and regulatory changes. Unless they continue to be both informed and involved, psychologists will in effect relinquish control over their professional practice in the U.S. health care system.

NOTE

1. A recent proposal to finance universal coverage for the state of California estimated that a payroll tax of 7.75% (6.75% paid by the employer and 1% paid by the employee) would be sufficient to fund the proposed system (California Department of Insurance, 1992).

REFERENCES

Anderson, J., & Binstein, M. (1992, May 31). Insurance company bean counters. *The Washington Post*.

Bureau of National Affairs. (1995a). Employer-provided health benefits continue to be leading tax expenditure. *BNA's Health Care Policy Report, 3*, 295.

Bureau of National Affairs. (1995b). Supreme Court eases employer's ability to amend plan to cut off health benefits. *BNA's Health Care Policy Report, 3*, 421.

Burner, S. T., Waldo, D. R., & McKusick, D. R. (1992). National health expenditures projections through 2030. *Health Care Financing Review, 14*, 1–29.

California Department of Insurance. (1992, August). *Issues in financing a universal health care system. A health care reform working paper*. California: Author.

Commonwealth Fund Commission on Elderly People Living Alone. (1987, November 20). *Medicare's poor: Filling the gaps in medical coverage for low-income elderly Americans*. Baltimore, MD: Author.

DeLew, N., Greenberg, G., & Kinchen, K. (1992). A layman's guide to the U.S. health care system. *Health Care Financing Review, 14*, 151–169.

Families USA Report. (1993, March 27). *The Washington Post*, p. A6.

Friedman, E. (1986, May 5). Fifty years of U.S. health care policy. *Hospitals, 60*, 95–96, 98, 100, 102, 104.

Grumbach, K., & Fry, J. (1993). Managing primary care in the United States and in the United Kingdom. *New England Journal of Medicine, 328*, 940–945.

Hahn, B., & Lefkowitz, D. (1992). Annual expenses and sources of payment for health care services. (AHCPR Publication No. 93-0007). *National Medical Expenditure Survey research findings* (Vol. 14). Rockville, MD: Public Health Service.

Iglehart, J. K. (1992a). The American health care system—Medicare. *The New England Journal of Medicine, 327*, 1467–1472.

Iglehart, J. K. (1992b). The American health care system—Private insurance. *The New England Journal of Medicine, 326*, 1715–1720.

Kaiser Commission on the Future of Medicaid. (1992). *Medicaid at the cross-roads*. Menlo Park, CA: Henry J. Kaiser Family Foundation.

Kincaid, M. L. (1995). *Health insurance underwriting guidelines used in Texas: A report of the Office of Public Insurance Counsel*. Austin, TX: Office of Public Insurance Counsel.

Levit, K. R., Olin, G. L., & Letsch, S. W. (1992). Americans' health insurance coverage, 1980–1991. *Health Care Financing Review, 14*, 31–57.

News in brief. (1993, May 17). *Health Care Reform Week, 22*, 4.

O'Keeffe, J. (1992). Health care financing: How much reform is needed? *Issues in Science and Technology, 8*, 42–49.

Reinhardt, U. E. (1993). Reorganizing the financial flows in American health care. *Health Affairs, 12* (Suppl.), 172–193.

Retiree health benefits: The impact on workers and businesses: Hearing before the Subcommittee on Labor of the Committee on Labor and Human Resources, U.S. Senate, 103d Cong., 1st Sess. (1993).

Rich, S. (1993, May 20). Payroll tax-based health plan backed. *The Washington Post*, p. A20.

Rubin, A. J. (1993, September 25). Leap of faith. *Congressional Quarterly*, 7–10.

Saywell, Jr., R. M., Zollinger, T. W., Chu, O. K., MacBeth, C. A., & Sechrist, M. E. (1989). Hospital and patient characteristics of uncompensated hospital care: Policy implications. *Journal of Health Politics, Policy and Law, 14*, 287–307.

Schroeder, S. A., & Sandy, L. G. (1993). Specialty distribution of U.S. physicians: The invisible driver of health care costs. *New England Journal of Medicine, 328*, 961–963.

Shefler, L. (1993, March). No easy cure. *Pitt Magazine*, 12–18.

Starr, P. (1992). *The logic of health care reform*. Knoxville, TN: Grand Rounds Press.

Sullivan, C. B., & Rice, T. (1991). The health insurance picture in 1990. *Health Affairs, 10*, 104–115.

Supreme Court rules hospital stay reduction does not discriminate against handicapped. (1985, Spring). *Health Advocate*, 10.

Taylor, T. (1992, November). *The needs of Native Americans*. Paper presented at the AAAS Right to Health Care Consultation Meeting, Washington, DC.

U.S. Bipartisan Commission on Comprehensive Health Care. (1990). *A call for action*. Washington, DC: U.S. Government Printing Office.

U.S. Congress Office of Technology Assessment. (1988). *Medical testing and health insurance* (OTA-H-384, No. 052-003-01113-1). Washington, DC: U.S. Government Printing Office.

U.S. Department of Commerce. (1993, October 4). Number of Americans in poverty up for third year, health care coverage drops, Census Bureau announces. *U.S. Department of Commerce News*. Washington, DC: Author.

U.S. Department of the Treasury. (1990). *Financing health and long-term care: Report to the President and to Congress*. Washington, DC: U.S. Government Printing Office.

U.S. General Accounting Office. (1993). *Rochester's community approach yields better access, lower costs. Report to the Committee on Government Operations, House of Representatives* (GAO/HRD-93-44, No. B-251507). Washington, DC: Author.

Weissman, J. S., Gatsonis, C., & Epstein, A. M. (1992). Rates of avoidable hospitalization by insurance status in Massachusetts and Maryland. *Journal of the American Medical Association, 268,* 2388–2394.

Willis, C. (1991, November). How to protect your retirement money. *Money, 20,* 90–97, 100.

WORK FORCE ISSUES IN PSYCHOLOGY AND HEALTH CARE

Introduction

Bruce Caplan

Part II examines work force issues in psychology and health care in an effort to determine "the adequacy of psychology's work force, that is, the size and characteristics of the psychological work force needed to provide services in . . . health care settings" (Glueckauf, 1993, p. 2). While we may have some idea of the number of licensed psychologists overall, we lack vital figures about the breadth of responsibilities and practices of working psychologists in health care and how these differ by setting, training, experience, and other relevant factors. We must discover who we are, how we have come to be where we are, what we currently do, and what we are capable of doing. In chapter 4, the authors observe that we seem to lack even an acceptable definition of the word, "psychologist." What are the key features? Training? Experience? Current roles? Eubanks et al. argue that after a consensus has been developed on the definition of "psychologist," surveys can then establish the size of the work force and the "scope of practice." From that would flow figures on the magnitude of need for various psychological services, recommended sizes for training programs, and all manner of estimates with practical and economic import.

A major impetus for this volume—and a point of consensus echoed in the two chapters that follow—is that substantial and increasing numbers of psychologists work in "nontraditional" (i.e., nonmental health) settings, providing health care services that merit respect and reimbursement at least equivalent to that afforded conventional mental health practitioners. A recent survey (Black & Holden, 1995) of psychologists practicing in medical schools found that, although most of these individuals were affiliated with departments of psychiatry, some 42% were employed by other departments, such as family medicine, neurology, rehabilitation, and pediatrics. This contingent of psychologists cannot be excluded from so central a venture as the formulation of a definition of their profession. Any definition will need to be somewhat elastic, as psychologists should and will continue to expand the boundaries of their work, developing new applications of existing skills and recognizing their capacity to fill new positions (e.g., program manager of a traumatic brain injury rehabilitation service).

Despite areas of potential expansion, these are precisely that—*potential* developments; it remains to be seen whether they become reality. In chapter 3, Frank and Johnstone offer no grounds for great optimism, noting the narrow view of psychological services held by much of the managed care monolith. Furthermore, we should recall that growth for its own sake is the philosophy of the cancer cell. Frank and Johnstone caution psychologists against emulating the ultimately counterproductive sequence that they describe in medicine: a burgeoning field creating an asymmetry in favor of specialists over generalists that produced ever-rising costs, straining the system to the breaking point, and causing a societal backlash embodied in the explosion of managed care. Reading their chapter, one is struck by the possibility of a future psychology profession that is ill defined, oversupplied, underemployed, and required to offer services at cut-rate prices to survive. One imagines new PhDs in psychology driving cabs, waiting tables, and buying lottery tickets. Those in the current psychology work force who wish to avoid this brave new world certainly have their work cut out for them.

REFERENCES

Black, M., & Holden, E. W. (1995). National survey of psychologists in medical schools. *The Medical School Psychologist, 3*(1), 4.

Glueckauf, R. L. (1993). Health care reform and psychological practice in rehabilitation and health care settings. *Rehabilitation Psychology News, 21*(2), 1–3.

Chapter 3

Changes in the Health Work Force: Implications for Psychologists

Robert G. Frank and Brick Johnstone

The prevailing need to contain health care costs has led to a critical examination of the composition of the health work force. Virtually every comprehensive health care reform proposal in the 103rd Congress, including the Health Security Act proposed by President Clinton, included provisions for reform in the recruitment, education, and composition of the health work force. As the health care reform debate lost steam in 1994, reform of the health work force became less central to many of the reform proposals. However, as Congress addresses this issue again, reform of the health work force will come to the fore. The centrality of health reform to health care reform is linked to the inextricable relationship between the health work force and health care costs.

Typically, free markets are considered the most efficient method for allocating resources in the economy. Free markets are most effective when consumers have useful information about the characteristics of the products and the price. Moreover, markets are effective when products are standardized, readily allowing comparisons among competing versions. When the market includes several competitors, no single vendor can control prices. Price competition among sellers lowers prices (Bingaman, Frank, & Billy, 1993). The effects of a large supply of health providers, especially physicians, defy typical supply-demand relationships. Unlike other commodities, when the supply of health providers increases, there is no lessening of demand. Indeed, increased supply increases demand as specialists refer to other specialists for more detailed analysis of medical systems.

The current health care market in the United States does not function as a "free market." Quality in the medical market is difficult to judge and is often judged from a personal perspective. Health care consumers rarely compare health products because they are not in a position to shop at the point of utilization of services. Health providers, especially physicians, function as intermediaries reducing the competition. The incentive to shop is reduced further because a large portion of health care expenditures is paid by private or public third-party payers. Health providers, especially physicians, play a critical role in the escalation of health care prices. It has been shown that specialists order more tests and provide more intensive care than generalists (Cooper, 1994).

The number of health care professions has grown because of the high demand for health care services. A significant factor in the escalation of health care costs has been the increase in the intensity of services provided. In addition to providing a higher volume of services, health service providers also are providing more intense, expensive services (Frank & VandenBos, 1994). This increase in intensity of services is a major factor in the escalation of health care costs and is related to several factors. Many argue that consumers are more educated regarding health care options and demand a broader array of more intense services. The increased incidence of chronic disease and disability in aging populations will increase the demand for health care services. The number of elderly (65 years and older) doubled between 1950 and 1984; in the same period, persons older than age 85 more than tripled to 2.6 million (Larson, Osterweis, & Rubin, 1994). By the year 2070, about 17% of the total U.S. population will be elderly.

GROWTH OF THE PHYSICIAN

In 1986, the Council on Graduate Medical Education (COGME) was authorized by Congress to provide an ongoing assessment of physician supply trends and to recommend appropriate efforts to address identified needs. Since it was inaugurated in 1986, COGME has issued a series of four reports addressing the physician, health care access, and rising costs (Rivo & Satcher, 1993). In 1961, one half of all U.S. physicians were generalists. Since then, the percentage has declined dramatically. In 1990, 33.5% of active allopathic physicians (MD) were generalists, with 13.9% in general medicine, 12.9% in family practice, and 6.7% in pediatrics. In 1990, 54.4% of active osteopathic physicians (DO) were in general practice (Rivo & Satcher, 1993). In the decade between 1980 and 1990, there were major increases in nonprimary care specialties and subspecialists. During this 10-year period, emergency medicine grew 150%; radiology, 118%; anesthesiology, 63%; and other pediatric subspecialists, 117%.

The increasing imbalance between generalists and specialists in the United States threatens the health care delivery system's ability to provide universal access to health care in urban and rural settings. Increasingly, primary care services are provided by specialists and subspecialists with little training in primary care. Such services are more costly and inefficient as specialists tend to use technology and procedures more than generalists. Moreover, specialists seek consultation more frequently, resulting in fragmented and duplicated care (Rivo & Satcher, 1993).

Despite a doubling of physicians in the past 25 years, there remains a significant geographic disparity in the distribution of physicians. Large metropolitan areas have three times the physician density of small metropolitan areas (Rivo & Satcher, 1993). Areas of primary care shortage actually increased during 1980 and 1990 despite a net gain of 150,000 physicians. In 1990, almost half a million people lived in 109 counties with no practicing physician (Rivo & Satcher, 1993).

During the 1980s managed care became prevalent in many health delivery marketplaces. Managed care, defined as an integrated delivery system that manages health services rather than simply financing or delivering services, grew rapidly in popularity (Weiner, 1994). HMOs represent a prototype managed care plan (controlled access to services and primary care emphasis). By 1990, conventional (i.e., unmanaged) indemnity health plans no longer covered most Americans (Weiner, 1994).

HMOs have managed costs by careful control of their health providers. Recognizing the relationships between specialty mix and use of services, HMOs have carefully controlled both the number and mix of physicians and other health professionals. The staffing patterns that have developed within these organizations have been recognized as one standard for national physician levels (Weiner, 1994). A recent survey of large staff and group HMO plans by the Group Health Association of America revealed that, on average, there were 119.1 full-time equivalent (FTE) nonadministrative physicians per 100,000 members or 840 enrollees per physician (Weiner, 1994). Weiner (1994) estimates that managed care settings use 124 physicians per 100,000 population or 1 physician for every 803 persons. These staffing standards contrast with the fee-for-services (FFS) sector, which has 180.1 FTEs per 100,000 or 1 physician per 555 individuals. Weiner (1994) found that 48% of the physicians in the plans surveyed were in primary care specialties (family/general practice, general internal medicine, and pediatrics). Weiner's finding that HMOs staffing levels routinely approximated 48% primary care specialties illustrates the substantial difference between managed care and FFS settings. Overall, only 36% of U.S. physicians are generalists.

In the same survey, the staff levels of nonphysician providers were found, on average, to be 14.1 nonphysician providers per 100,000 members, with a range from 0 to 36.9 (the survey did not include psychologists). Most of the plans surveyed had at least 21 primary care nurse practitioners (NPs) and physician assistants (PAs) per 100,000 enrollees.

Although NPs and PAs provided a significant portion of care in the primary care categories, Weiner also reported that these practitioners provided a large percentage of ambulatory obstetrics and gynecology contacts. Surprisingly, he also found that staff-model HMOs used NPs for a large percentage of ambulatory visits within both a medical subspecialty (dermatology) and a surgical subspecialty (orthopedics). Using NPs for ambulatory visits within medical subspecialties and surgical subspecialties heralds a new phase of composition in managed care settings. Although it has been widely acknowledged that NPs are useful in primary care settings, heretofore, it has not been recognized that NPs are being used routinely to provide subspecialty management. It is only a small leap to recognize the analogies of using NPs in specialty settings to using master's-level practitioners in psychology practice settings.

Weiner (1994) found that the number of nonphysician providers varies substantially across HMOs. Among the largest and oldest plans, the average was higher: 23 per 100,000 members, with approximately 60% of all NPs and PAs practicing in three primary care specialties. Differences in staffing among HMOs reflect organizational culture, which is not necessarily a function of cost differences. Current evidence suggests that differences between HMO structure (staff vs. Independent Practice Association vs. mixed, etc.) do not yield differences in HMO costs (Miller & Luft, 1994). In the same report, Miller and Luft failed to find differences among types of HMOs in cost or use of resources. HMOs, however, did cost significantly less than FFS plans (Miller & Luft, 1994).

After correcting for growth factors, Weiner (1994) predicts that by the year 2000, 40 to 60% of consumers in the market will be covered by managed care systems. When this occurs, there will be a surplus of 60 physicians per 100,000 individuals, or about 163,000 physicians overall. This surplus is equivalent to about 30% of all patient care physicians. The primary care physician supply would be close to equilibrium according to Weiner's predictions. Overall, the supply of specialists is estimated to range from 61% to 77% above demand for the year 2000 (Weiner, 1994).

The policies of the prepaid group practice plans have been designed to control costs (Weiner, 1994; Wennberg, Goodman, Nease, & Keller, 1993). Control of health care costs will dominate health policy in the coming decade. If costs are not controlled effectively, there will be a decrease in access to health care services. The intimate relationship between size and composition of the physician and health care costs will likely lead to interventions to alter the physician supply. Currently, medicine, through graduate medical education funds, spends $70,000 on each medical resident (Wennberg et al., 1993). In addition, the increasing excess of specialists creates further cost demands through the use of more costly procedures. The high cost of training too many physician specialists will encourage the public sector to adopt policies developed for managed care settings.

Implementation of managed care strategies will control costs in several ways. First, primary care systems are less costly. Second, restriction of physician access will reduce use, thereby diminishing the intensity of services, which further exacerbates costs. Currently, the available supply of specialty physicians is more than adequate to meet demand (Wennberg et al., 1993). For example, the supply of neurosurgeons exceeds the numbers required to perform all operations for brain tumors or head trauma. Wennberg et al. (1993) estimate that on a per-capita basis there are 2.5 times more neurosurgeons, 2.5 times more general surgeons, and 1.4 times more urologists in the nation than are needed on the basis of staffing for classic HMOs. Physician excess has subtle but major implications for costs. Wennberg and his colleagues (1993) report that a halving of the interval between returned visits to a physician (i.e., seeing a patient with mild congestive heart failure every 6 weeks instead of every 3 months) accommodates a doubling of the supply of internists.

The supply of physicians continues to grow at approximately 1.5 times the general population (COGME, 1994). Controlling the growth of the physician is complicated by the migration of international medical graduates (IMGs). Moreover, the number of 1st-year IMGs has been rising slowly (COGME, 1994). In 1992, IMGs accounted for 35% of the 1st-year residents (COGME, 1994). The use of IMGs to fill resident slots reflects the shortage of fully certified providers in many areas, as well as the need of training programs to maintain "actual mass."

Despite a net increase of 150,000 physicians over the past decade, the number of health provider shortage areas actually has increased. At the same time, the number of Americans lacking access to primary care physicians also has increased (COGME, 1994). Despite the increase in the number of physicians, minority groups are substantially underrepresented amid the vast increase in the number of physicians (COGME, 1994).

GRADUATE MEDICAL EDUCATION (GME) AND TRAINING CONSORTIA

Having recognized the implications of excess physicians in the health work force, many medical groups have lobbied to reduce the overall number of physicians educated in the United States. Overall, spending on graduate medical education exceeded $5.8 billion in fiscal year 1994. The role of excess physicians in exacerbating health care costs and the excessive cost of educating physicians argues that reduction in the physician is an inevitable target for future congressional considerations. Indeed, during the recent debates on health care, legislative initiatives to limit the number of resident physicians and to alter the specialty mix of physicians were common. Using the model endorsed in the "Fourth Report to Congress and the Department of Health and Human Services" (January 1994), COGME suggested that the formation of nonhospital based (GME) consortia offer a mechanism for implementing regulation of resident physician providers within a community (Whitcomb, 1994). Many proposals during the 1994 debate emphasized the use of these consortia that provided a method for enhancing community- and university-based medical education (Whitcomb, 1994).

GME consortia are seen as a way of reducing GME costs and providing a method of reducing the current emphasis on tertiary care. By moving physician training to ambulatory care settings, it is conjectured that there will be less emphasis on use of high-technology tertiary care of services. In addition, GME consortia provide a method for reducing the level of payments to hospitals that currently increase the number of physicians trained in hospital-based services.

The federal government currently spends more than $5.8 billion dollars annually on GME (Dunivin, 1994). This spending is divided between indirect medical education costs provided to training institutions for the costs associated with the education of medical residents and direct medical expenses that are provided to offset salary costs of residents. Funding for GME comes from the Medicare Program. As costs continue to escalate in Medicare, it is likely there will be increasing pressure to control both GME dollars and physician supply (Frank, 1993). Implementation of GME consortia is a likely solution to the control of health care costs.

During the 103rd Congress, proposals for GME consortia typically emphasized regulation of the physician and, occasionally, other health professions. Little attention was directed to the interaction of increased health capacity in related disciplines, such as medicine, psychology, nursing, and social work. Those in medicine and nursing, who currently enjoy a virtual monopoly on GME training dollars (Dunivin, 1994), have viewed efforts to include other health professions in GME consortia or other GME proposals as efforts to reduce their training revenues. It is likely that efforts to expand GME consortia to other health professions will be strongly resisted.

Physicians have been more attentive to the issue of oversupply in the work force. Surgical specialties have been controlling production since the 1970s. Using the residency review committee, which is required for approval of all residencies, surgeons have controlled the number of individuals entering the profession. Because the overall number of physicians has doubled since 1960, their efforts to control their growth have fallen short, and there is still an excess of surgeons. Federal funds are intimately involved in the training of physicians. Consequently, the federal government has a stronger role in the control and influence of the number of physicians trained. Although still difficult, it is easier for physicians to control access to the profession. Decisions can be made at the point of entry to medical school, residency selection, subspecialization, or fellowships.

PSYCHOLOGY AND THE HEALTH CARE SYSTEM

Although physicians have become increasingly aware of the relationship between work force size and the viability of medical practice, psychologists have paid less attention to this issue. Over the past 20 years, there has been a substantial increase in the production of psychologists. In 1974, there were 20,000 psychologists licensed to practice. By 1990, there were 63,000, a 300% increase in fifteen years (Shapiro & Wiggins, 1994). More than 70% of all psychologists are involved in health care services (Shapiro & Wiggins, 1994). Despite national policy strongly favoring psychiatrists, psychologists now substantially outnumber the 37,000 psychiatrists in the United States.

In 1993, there were about 180 physicians per 100,000 people in the United States. The ratio of physicians to patients is substantially lower in managed care settings. In managed care settings, the ratio is 119 physicians per 100,000 members (Weiner, 1994). Although much attention has been directed to determining appropriate numbers and mix of physicians in a managed care setting, examination of other disciplines in managed care settings is revealing. The number of psychologists, as well as a number of other nonphysician health specialties, is rarely monitored in managed care settings. It is difficult to obtain data on the perceived needs of psychologists in managed care organizations. Variations in staffing in managed care settings may reflect variations in practice domains among a range of subspecialties. Weiner also found a tremendous variation within medical subspecialties in managed care staffing. Average staffing for psychiatrists was 1.27 per 100,000 members (Weiner, 1994). The Group Health Association of America estimates the national staffing average for psychologists is .92 per 100,000.

Although psychologists have directed less attention to the composition of their work force than physicians and other health care practitioners, there has been some effort to project future needs. Most often these efforts have come under the rubric of "human resources" rather than as it is often described in the medical literature. The perceived need for additional psychologists and other mental health professionals has waxed and waned over the past 30 years. In 1959, Albee predicted a shortage of mental health professionals (Albee, 1959). This perception was held by institutions training mental health professionals. Between 1975 and 1985, there was an 80% increase in the number of psychologists (Robiner, 1991). The growth in psychology was accompanied by a similar growth in psychiatry, social work, and marriage and family counseling, resulting in a 109% overall increased percentage of these professions (Robiner, 1991).

Although recent estimates derived from managed care staffing levels have dominated considerations of needs, historically other methods have been used. A debate has raged on whether projections should be based on "market demand (i.e., service utilization and demographics), need (based on morbidity prevalence), or a combination of such factors" (Robiner, 1991, p. 428). In 1959, an estimated 14,794 psychologists, a ratio of 8.6 psychologists per 100,000 Americans, existed. As noted, these numbers were deemed inadequate, and a call for additional psychologists was issued. During the 1980s, a frequently cited estimate of psychology's need was one clinical psychologist for every 10,000 persons (Robiner, 1991). This estimate was thought to be derived from early models of HMO staffing estimating one medical specialist per 7,200 members (Dorken & Rodgers, 1976). This estimate did not compensate for overlap among mental health disciplines.

Most needs estimates in the mental health field have been estimates of the needs for psychiatrists. For example, COGME found a shortage of general surgeons, adult and child psychiatrists, and preventive medicine specialists (Rivo & Satcher, 1993). Given the growth of psychologists and other mental health professionals, it appears unlikely that there is a true shortage of psychiatrists in the United States (Robiner, 1991; Shapiro & Wiggins, 1994).

Difficulty estimating the number of psychologists reflects the lack of a systematic database describing the profession. Most counts of psychologists are tallies based on professional organization memberships (e.g.,

American Psychological Association; licensee of state boards) that include academics, recent graduates, and psychologists practicing in exempted settings—or combinations thereof (Robiner, 1991). These tallies are imprecise for several reasons. Psychologists practicing in settings exempt from licensure requirements may be omitted from such tallies. Psychologists in academic settings often have limited practices. In general, there is no method to estimate the number of psychologists involved in part-time employment, thereby creating overestimates of the numbers of practicing psychologists. Use of state licensing and professional associations membership lists may lead to overestimates when individuals hold more than one license or belong to multiple associations. Recent graduates awaiting licensure and nondoctoral-level practitioners may also be underestimated by tallies. Case loads may vary in different work settings, further confounding the estimates derived from tallies. In a 1993 survey, there were 44,580 doctoral-level psychologist practitioners (Robiner, 1991; Stapp, Tucker, & VandenBos, 1985). This number exceeded by 80% the original estimates of psychology needs made by Albee (1959). By 1988, an APA Practice Directorate study supplemented by state-licensing boards indicated there were 57,000 psychologists, an average of 23.12 psychologists per 100,000 persons (Robiner, 1991) . Between 1974 and 1990, the number of psychologists increased 300% (Shapiro & Wiggins, 1994). This increase in the absolute number of psychologists was accompanied by a dramatic increase in the number of training programs (72% increase between 1979 and 1990) (Robiner, 1991). Despite this huge growth in the number of psychologists, there was little unemployment among doctoral-level psychologists (Robiner, 1991).

The use of NPs and PAs in managed care settings has important implications for the staffing of psychologists in the future. Weiner (1994) found tremendous variation in the numbers of NPs and PAs in HMOs. He found that plans range from a low of zero to a high of 67, with an average of 23 per 100,000 members. Approximately 60% of all NPs and PAs practicing in managed care settings surveyed worked within three primary care specialties (i.e., pediatrics, family medicine, and adult medicine). Importantly, a significant minority of NPs and PAs were working in the subspecialties (i.e., dermatology and orthopedics).

Clearly, any staffing level can be appropriate depending on the design of the system. As reflected by the lack of national data on the psychology, psychologists are not perceived as critical to either managed care or organizations. A similar pattern exists in federal health policy where psychology rarely is viewed as critical to the health care system.

The increase in the use of NPs and PAs in managed care settings has implications for the use of doctorate-level psychologists. Although the analogy is slightly stretched, it is relevant to consider NPs and PAs as comparable with master's-level practitioners in psychology. Clearly, managed care settings will exploit the use of lower trained professionals as long as major decreases in quality are not noted. Overall production of master's-level psychologists vastly exceeds doctoral-level providers. During the past decade, 3,000 doctoral and 8,000 master's degrees were awarded annually in psychology (Robiner, 1991).

The low unemployment among psychologists led VandenBos, DeLeon, and Belar (1991) to argue that calls to curtail the production of psychologists were based on fears related to the rapid growth of the profession rather than true evidence of excess capacity of psychologists. VandenBos and colleagues argued that the low unemployment among psychologists reflected the flexibility of psychologists in the workplace. The proliferation of opportunities for psychologists in health sectors, as opposed to mental health, led these authors to argue that the growth of psychologists would continue unabated for the foreseeable future. In predicting continued growth for the profession, VandenBos et al. based their arguments on the rapid proliferation of new niches for psychologists rather than a systematic analysis of changes in the health market. These authors argue that calls to limit the production of psychologists as Robiner (1991) had urged were premature and did not reflect the increasing, diverse opportunities for psychologists.

VandenBos and colleagues (1991) did not consider changes in the health work force that were not yet apparent. The growth of managed care has exceeded projections—even those made a few years ago. It appears the growth of managed care exceeds even the growth of psychology. As managed care has infiltrated more markets, managed care planners have paid little heed to the diversified roles of psychologists. Indeed, when psychologists have been considered in projections in managed care settings, it typically has been only within the purview of mental health.

It is apparent that currently there are no accurate methods to estimate the number and types of psychologists needed in the future. The current production rate of psychologists appears to exceed demand. The rapid increase in managed care accompanied by the reduction of referrals to specialists, including psychologists, suggests that clinical demands for psychologists will diminish despite the diversity of settings in which psychologists are employed. It is likely that the physician surplus that is rapidly developing will further diminish opportunities for psychologists. If current projections prove accurate, and there is a surplus of approximately 165,000 physicians by the turn of the century, it is likely that many of these specialists will compete with psychologists in the niches that psychologists have moved into over the past decade. Given the advantage a medical license offers, psychologists will be severely challenged to succeed in this competition. It seems unlikely that the current rate of the production of psychologists, when combined with the rate of physicians, nurses, and other practitioners competing in the mental health field, can be sustained.

THE FUTURE

As efforts to control health care costs intensify, GME proposals and efforts to control the health work force are a virtual certainty. Psychology stands to lose many of its gains in professional autonomy, reimbursement, and influence if the profession is excluded from reform proposals. Exclusion from these proposals will prohibit psychology from enjoying the extensive federal support currently provided for physician training. Even if that support is reduced in future cost-containment initiatives, current federal commitments to physician training massively outweigh any support provided to graduate training for psychologists (Dunivin, 1994). GME consortia also are likely to define those professions that are designated as essential service providers or critical health professions. Simply put, if the federal government is committed to training members of a profession because of a perceived need for those professional services, it is likely that those services will be designated as reimbursable under any federal health benefits package. As pressures to control health care costs build, future debates are likely to center around the definition of essential health care benefits. Psychologists, as during the 1992 to 1993 debate, must be able to argue for the importance of psychological services in the benefit package.

SUMMARY

Escalating health costs demand reform of the health care system. A major component in escalating health care costs is the increase in the number of health care practitioners. Most emphasis has been directed toward the increasing number of physicians. It is estimated that there will be 165,000 excess physicians by the turn of the century. These specialists will compete with psychologists and other health professionals for a shrinking health care dollar. One method of controlling health care costs is to reduce the number of health care practitioners. Several proposals were discussed during the 103rd and 104th Congress to limit health care professionals by creating training consortia communities—instead of hospitals that would be responsible for training physicians. These consortia would place increased emphasis on primary care and less emphasis on tertiary centers or hospitals. Virtually all proposals discussed during the 103rd and 104th Congress excluded psychologists, an omission that has important implications for the future of the profession. As the debate over how to reform the health care system continues, cost-containment efforts will necessitate tighter controls of spending. Those disciplines in which the federal government invests training dollars are likely to be seen as the essential providers. In contrast, professions that have not been allotted federal spending are likely to be deemed as optional services. If psychologists are excluded from GME consortia, they are likely to be viewed as an optional service. Inclusion among professions viewed as critical to the health work force assures psychologists a role in the health delivery system. Inclusion in planning also suggests psychologists are likely to be included in any federal benefit plans developed in the future.

The Council on GME is not mandated to monitor psychologists or other health professionals. Consequently, there is no mechanism to assess the number of psychologists produced or practicing at this point in time. Crude estimates indicate a rapid proliferation in the number of psychology providers. Master's-level providers are counted in these data only if they are licensed at the state level. Lack of accurate information on the growth of the profession is a major limitation to those advocating the role of psychology in the U.S. health care system. To participate in the changing system accurately, psychologists must know the number and activities of those in their profession.

REFERENCES

Albee, G. W. (1959). *Mental health manpower trends.* New York: Basic Books.

Bingaman, J., Frank, R. G., & Billy C. L. (1993). Combining a global health budget with a market-driven delivery system: Can it be done? *American Psychologist, 48,* 270–277.

Cooper, R. A. (1994). Seeking a balanced physician for the 21st century. *Journal of the American Medical Association, 272,* 680–687.

Council on Graduate Medical Education. (1994, January). *Fourth report to Congress and the Department of Health and Human Services Secretary: Recommendations to improve access to health care through physician work force reform* (Council Report). Washington, DC: U.S. Department of Health and Human Services.

Dorken, H., & Rodgers, D. A. (1976). Issues facing professional psychology. In H. Dorken and Associates (Eds.), *The professional psychologist today: New developments in law, health insurance, and health practice* (pp. 264–292). San Francisco: Jossey-Bass.

Dunivin, D. L. (1994). Health professions education: The shaping of a discipline through federal funding. *American Psychologist, 49,* 868–878.

Frank, R. G. (1993). Health care reform: An introduction. *American Psychologist, 48,* 258–260.

Frank, R. G., & VandenBos, G. R. (1994). Health care reform: The 1993–94 evolution. *American Psychologist, 48,* 851–854.

Larson, P. F., Osterweis, M., & Rubin, E. R. (1994). *Health issues for the 21st century.* Washington, DC: American Association of Academic Health Centers.

Miller, R. H., & Luft, H. S. (1994). Managed care plan performance since 1980: A literature analysis. *Journal of the American Medical Association, 271,* 1512–1519.

Rivo, M. L., & Satcher, D. (1993). Improving access to health care through physician reform. *Journal of the American Medical Association, 270,* 1074–1078.

Robiner, W. N. (1991). How many psychologists are needed? A call for national psychology human resource agenda. *Professional Psychology: Research and Practice, 22*(6), 427–440.

Shapiro, A. E., & Wiggins, J. G. (1994). A PsyD degree for every practitioner: Truth in labeling. *American Psychologist, 49,* 207–210.

Stapp, J., Tucker, A. M., & VandenBos, G. R. (1985). Census of psychological personnel: 1983. *American Psychologist, 40,* 1317–1351.

VandenBos, G. R., DeLeon, P. H., & Belar, C. D. (1991). How many psychologists practitioners are needed? It's too early to know! *Professional Psychology: Research and Practice, 22,* 441–448.

Weiner, J. P. (1994). Forecasting the effects of health care reform on U.S. physician requirement: Evidence from HMO staffing patterns. *Journal of the American Medical Association, 272,* 222–229.

Wennberg, J. E., Goodman, D. C., Nease, R. F., & Keller, R. B. (1993). Finding equilibrium in the U.S. physician supply. *Health Affairs, 12*(2), 89–103.

Whitcomb, M. E. (1994). The role of graduate medical schools in graduate medical education. *Journal of the American Medical Association, 272,* 702–704.

Chapter 4

Work Force Issues in Professional Psychology

Joseph D. Eubanks, Alan L. Goldberg, and Ronald Fox

Underpinning any discussion of work force issues for psychology is the debate about the role of other providers who offer *some* overlapping services and the impact of these providers on the psychology work force. These providers include psychiatrists, social workers, and counselors.

This chapter constitutes a consensus statement from the group discussions concerning work force issues for psychologists in health care settings. Current issues, problems, and initial steps to determine solutions are highlighted.

IDENTIFICATION OF THE WORK FORCE

A definition of who is a psychological-service provider is clearly needed. Licensed psychologists constitute one group within the work force. In 1990, this group alone comprised approximately 63,000 individuals (Fox, 1990). If individuals with master's degrees, psychometrists, and other "extenders" are included, the ranks of psychological service providers swell by an estimated 80,000 to 100,000 (Saeman, 1994). Gehlmann (1994) has provided data on this latter group of providers. He reported that more than 800 institutions provide master's-level training in clinical and counseling psychology. He surveyed 410 such institutions and found that between July 1, 1991, and June 30, 1992, more than 5,000 individuals received their master's degrees in psychology. In some states, people with master's degrees in psychology practice under the authority of a psychology licensing board. Such individuals most often have a limited scope of practice and must practice under the supervision of a licensed doctoral-level psychologist for many aspects of practice. In Texas, 1,428 individuals are listed as "psychological associates" (Texas State Board of Examiners of Psychologists, 1994). It should be noted that administrators and researchers who hold doctoral degrees in psychology may not need to be licensed. Conversely, psychology licenses are often "generic" and do not designate clinical specialization.

The effectiveness of psychologists is at issue in settings other than mental health settings. This fact is often misunderstood by the public and by policy makers. Psychologists need to be seen as health care providers as opposed to *mental* health care providers. Changing the perception of the scope of the psychologist's practice from mental health care provider to health care provider parallels recent trends in medicine to practice more holistically. The strict dichotomy between physical health and mental health is blurring. It is now clear that mental health and behavior often have significant consequences for physical health and vice versa. Many of the leading causes of death in the United States include behavioral components in either treatment or etiology. Lifestyle choices involving smoking, drinking, exercise, diet, and compliance with treatment can clearly affect health. One has only to look at the work settings of psychologists to know that psychologists are inexorably tied to the provision of health care services in its broadest sense. Psychologists have integral roles in service provision and research in departments of medicine, neurology, neurosurgery, pediatrics, and physical medicine and rehabilitation. The growth in numbers of such service providers can be correlated with rapid increases in membership of the divisions of Rehabilitation Psychology, Health Psychology, and Neuropsychology of the American Psychological Association. Defining psychologists as health care providers in the broad sense, and demonstrating rigorous training needed to obtain skills necessary for licensing/specialty credentialing will help to show the uniqueness of the profession of psychology to consumers of services.

Once a broader definition of psychological service is in place, demographic data concerning practitioners will need to be assembled. This should include data on training, geographic distribution, service provision, and practice patterns. Some of this information is available through the Office of Demographic, Employment, and Educational Research of the Education Directorate of the APA (Kohut & Wicherski, 1993), but it will need to be updated to reflect the broader definition. Other important data that need to be collected include demographic information on patient populations and service-use patterns. Models for research in this arena can be found in Allison, Crawford, Echemendia, Robinson, and Knepp (1994), and Bernal and Castro (1994).

Although we struggle to define who is a psychological service provider, members of the public, government agencies, and insurance companies have similar difficulties. The public often equates psychologists with other licensed providers of mental health services (Murstein & Fontaine, 1993). Excluding physicians and nurses, these other providers commonly include social workers and licensed professional counselors. The latter may include marriage and family counselors, as well as drug and alcohol counselors. The American Counseling Association (1993) reported that as of December 1, 1993, there were more than 67,000 individuals in the United States who were credentialed counselors. According to the Bureau of Labor Statistics, there were 484,000 social workers in 1992, many of whom provide therapeutic services (U.S. Department of Labor, 1994).

Three issues need to be more clearly delineated: (a) the roles and scope of practice of psychologists, (b) the specific training requirements that differentiate psychologists from other service providers, and (c) the specific health care services provided by and *unique* to psychologists. Psychologists, for example, are uniquely qualified to provide assessment services. Use of such services should ultimately lead to more effective treatment planning, and therefore to enhanced outcomes. Research efforts in outcome research will need to be continued and intensified to demonstrate differential outcomes for psychological practice, strong correlational links with assessment expertise, and cost-effectiveness. For example, outcome research, such as that of Szymanski and Danek (1992), which showed outcome to be correlated with level of provider's education (more highly trained professionals had better client outcomes), needs to be replicated.

IDENTIFICATION OF THE NEED FOR PSYCHOLOGICAL SERVICES

One of the major problems facing psychology is that of precisely identifying the need for psychological services. This problem is a multidimensional one. Issues of identification of service types, potential patient populations, and identification of funders of services must be addressed. Consumer education concerning services is potentially confounded with current perceived service needs. The issue of work force size needed is dependent on perception of need for services.

DETERMINING SIZE OF THE WORK FORCE

The prior discussion of identification of the need for psychological services clearly impacts determination of the size of the work force. Although it is difficult to disentangle these areas, certain key issues are relevant to the question of determining the size of the work force. Training facilities, be they universities, professional schools, internship sites, or postdoctoral training programs, all have a vested interest in keeping their doors open. Fox (1994) has commented that ''a university is harder to reorganize than a cemetery'' (p. 206). He went on to suggest that the same may be true for psychology education. One issue that may need to be addressed is that of limiting the number of students accepted into training programs.

Employers of psychologists are in the position of wanting to find well-qualified candidates for positions, but the number of positions is decreasing. Because of the redistribution of scant health care dollars, it is increasingly becoming a ''buyers' market.''

Lastly, funders of psychological services have an interest in determining the size of the work force. The prevailing concerns of payers is about expedient service (i.e., quick outcome) and cost. Payers have set seemingly artificial limits on amount and type of services eligible for reimbursement. In short, there is a type of rationing of services. This has tremendous implications for the size of the work force. Frank (this volume) reported that one managed care company ''determined'' that the need for psychologists within their network was .92 per 100,000. Given this ratio, the total number of psychologists needed in the United States would be approximately 2,400.

Need or demand for services is also constrained by the cost of services and a person's ability to pay for services. Ability to pay may vary with type of provider, diagnosis, and insurance plan limits. Moreover, currently the burden for financial responsibility is often shuffled. Private insurers frequently have limited responsibility, so that payment moves from the private to the public sector. A payer may be responsible for only a set number of days. After such time, clients may need to ''spend down'' to become Medicaid eligible. Alternatively, in cases where disability is chronic, Medicare may pick up costs once the qualification period has been met. A single, accountable payer source may help to resolve this shifting of the burden of care, leading to more responsible decision making for the long term.

Again, it must be reiterated that only limited information is available about the size of the psychology work force. Studies are needed to determine the projected needs for psychologists under different models of service delivery and funding. Assembled data can be used to help in development and implementation of policy designed to meet the demand for services.

NEED FOR OUTCOME MEASURES

Another major issue that needs to be addressed concerns development and use of clinical outcome measures. Psychologists need to be able to document that provided services lead to *better* outcomes, with incremental utility over services provided by others. Psychotherapeutic services are offered by psychologists, psychiatrists, nurses, social workers, and counselors. Although psychologists were once looked to as the experts in assessment, even assessment services are now offered by others who have access to tests and interpretation programs. Assessment and treatment of school-aged children who have cognitive or emotional problems are often done by school psychologists, who may have MA, MS, or MEd degrees. Although published reports do exist concerning the effectiveness of psychological treatment (e.g., Lipsey and Wilson, 1993), to date, there is no compelling literature that empirically supports the belief that psychologists offer ''better'' services than other providers. Absence of such literature and hard data can cause payers to question the value of psychologist-provided services, as opposed to services provided by other, often less expensive, practitioners. The failure to show differential effectiveness may well result in payers not funding services. Fees may be reduced to the lowest rate accepted by any provider of psychological services. Even without hard data, fees are being reduced, and use of master's-level providers is being encouraged.

Given the high degree of training that psychologists receive in statistics and experimental design, psychologists may have too great a desire for elegance in outcome measures and research. Simple outcome measures must be developed immediately to examine effectiveness of services. Procedures, outcomes, and costs must all be investigated, with dissemination of information to referral sources. This is an urgent, priority issue.

WORKING WITH MANAGED CARE

A major area of concern, which has transcended others, is the impact of managed care on psychological services. Managed care is defined as an integrated delivery system that manages health services rather than simply financing or delivering services (Weiner, 1994). Iglehart (1991) states that managed care will continue to have a considerable influence in health care, including psychological services, and will continue to do so regardless of what happens (or does not happen) to federal legislation on national health insurance. Although there are multiple types of managed care plans (HMOs, PPOs, etc.), they have many similarities. These include an emphasis on primary care and controlled access to services. As managed care has infiltrated the marketplace, psychologists have found that there is impact on type of service reimbursed, amount of service reimbursed, and amount of reimbursement. Regional differences in the impact of managed care have been noted. The nature of psychological services has profoundly changed in states with greater infiltration of managed care (Thompson, Burns, Goldman, & Smith, 1992). Although some states have had little impact (yet), the momentum for change to managed care systems is growing.

Managed care systems are affecting psychologists in every level of health care systems. In hospital settings, for example, reimbursement is being set through contracted rates, per diem rates, and capitation. As dollars are reduced, changes are inevitable. More master's-level service providers are being used, middle managers are being displaced from the work force, and departmental structures are crumbling in favor of more "team-oriented" models, which often blur the boundaries between (and, uniqueness of) individual disciplines. Given reductions in staff, psychologists are more likely than ever to have full clinical caseloads. Moreover, psychologists may be viewed as too expensive (at this time) to be used for leadership positions (management, administration, team leadership, etc.). Psychologists must be creative in bringing skills to a newly emerging marketplace. For example, if skills can be used for prevention and stress management, and the case can be built for ultimate reduction in cost to payers, then psychologists must move quickly to build new systems of care.

Being "managed care friendly" does not mean passive acquiescence to the changes occurring. We must work cooperatively to expand the boundaries of the profession, while providing state-of-the art care in expedient, cost-effective, efficient ways. Psychology has not reached its maturity. By joining forces, psychologists practicing in disparate health care settings can work creatively to build model systems of care. Involvement of psychologists on boards that regulate and oversee managed care entities might be one way to help preserve the profession while meeting the needs of clientele.

SUMMARY AND RECOMMENDATIONS

Numerous concerns have been identified with respect to work force issues in psychology. These include identifying the work force, identifying the need for psychological services, development of outcome measures addressing treatment efficacy and cost, and working collaboratively with managed care entities.

Identification of the work force involves defining what psychological services are, determining the distribution of service providers, and identifying the types of services provided. Although some information is available, current information must be collected and disseminated. In general, psychological services must be more broadly defined to reflect the breadth of services provided by psychologists, particularly in areas separate from traditional mental health services.

Regarding identification of the need for psychological services, continued discussion and model development are necessary before firm recommendations can be advanced. Conversely, we already know that psychologists must take responsibility for increased public awareness of types of psychological services and their efficacy. Informed consumers are able to make better choices and can help to lobby for better services where needed.

Efficacy of service can be better determined when user-friendly outcome measures are developed and used. Funders and service consumers need information concerning efficacy in terms that are readily understandable and can help to guide the decision-making process. Customer satisfaction instruments must also be developed. Of immense importance will be research efforts that analyze empirical evidence regarding incremental value of services provided by doctoral-level psychologists compared with services provided by allied psychological service providers.

Clearly our health care systems are evolving rapidly. Managed care systems are here to stay, and collaboration with these systems is necessary to ensure professional survival. Efforts should be taken to expand input of psychologists in policy making and management, in addition to providing professional services.

Given the rapid changes in health care delivery and funding, attention to the future of psychology is urgently needed. Modification and flexibility in accepting changes in traditional ways of conducting research, collecting data, publishing results, and providing services is sorely needed. Psychological services are vital to the well-being of our population. Concerted efforts now will prolong the viability of the field.

REFERENCES

Allison, K. W., Crawford, I., Echemendia, R., Robinson, L., & Knepp, D. (1994). Human diversity and professional competence: Training in clinical and counseling psychology revisited. *American Psychologist, 49*, 792–796.

American Counseling Association (1993). *Number of Credentialed Counselors in States with Counselor Credentialing Laws.* Alexander, VA: Author.

Bernal, M. A., & Castro, F. G. (1994). Are clinical psychologists prepared for service and research with ethnic minorities? Report of a decade of progress. *American Psychologist, 49*, 797–805.

Fox, R. E. (1990). Increasing state association support and influence: An interview with Ron Fox. *Bulletin of Division 31: State Psychological Associations Affairs, 22(4)*, 1, 3.

Fox, R. E. (1994). Training professional psychologists for the twenty-first century. *American Psychologist, 49*, 200–206.

Frank, R. G. (1994). Work force issues: Where do we go from here? In R. L. Glueckauf, R. G. Frank, G. R. Bond, & J. H. McGrew (Eds.), *Psychological Practice in a Changing Health Care System.* Springer: New York.

Gehlmann, S. H. (1994). *1993 Employment survey: Psychology graduates with master's, specialist's, and related degrees.* Washington, DC: Office of Demographic, Employment, and Educational Research, APA Education Directorate.

Iglehart, J. K. (1992). The American health care system: Managed care. *New England Journal of Medicine, 327*, 742–747.

Kohout, J., & Wicherski, M. (1993). *1991 doctorate employment survey.* Washington, DC: Office of Demographic, Employment, and Educational Research, APA Education Directorate.

Lipsey, M. W., & Wilson, D. B. (1994). The efficacy of psychological, educational, and behavioral treatment: Confirmation from meta-analysis. *American Psychologist, 48*, 1181–1209.

Murstein, B. I., & Fontaine, P. A. (1993). The public's knowledge and other mental health providers. *American Psychologist, 48*, 839–845.

Saeman, H. (1994, September-October). Dilemma that won't go away: The master's degree issue. *National Psychologist, 3(5)*, 1, 4, 5.

Shapiro, A. E., & Wigging, J. G. (1994). A PsyD degree for every practitioner: Truth in labeling. *American Psychologist, 49*, 207–210.

Sznamski, E., & Danek, M. (1992). The relationship of rehabilitation counselor education to rehabilitation client outcome: A replication and extension. *Journal of Rehabilitation, 58*, 49–56.

Texas State Board of Examiners of Psychologists. (1994). *1994 roster.* Austin, TX: Author.

Thompson, J. W., Burns, B. J., Goldman, H. H., & Smith, J. (1992). Initial level of care and clinical status in a managed mental health program. *Hospital and Community Psychiatry*, *43*, 599–603.

U.S. Department of Labor. (1994). *Occupational Outlook Handbook 94–95* (Bureau of Labor Statistics Bulletin No. 2450-6). Washington, DC: U.S. Government Printing Office.

VandenBos, G. R., DeLeon, P. H., & Belar, C. D. (1992). How many psychological practitioners are needed? It's too early to know! *Professional Psychology: Research and Practice*, *22*, 441–448.

Weiner, J. P. (1994). Forecasting the effects of health care reform on U.S. physician workforce requirements: Evidence from HMO staffing patterns. *Journal of the American Medical Association*, *272*, 222–229.

ACCESS ISSUES IN PSYCHOLOGY AND HEALTH CARE

Introduction

Lee Hersch

The following section focuses on access issues in relation to health and rehabilitation psychology in a reformed health care environment.

In chapter 5, Hofschire and Foote present their views on access. Hofschire and Foote begin by emphasizing that the health care reform discussion is, in the final analysis, not about underinsured and uninsured populations. They emphasize that the debate is driven by concerns about *money*. In the context of a $1 trillion annual price tag for health care, 40% of which is paid for with government funds, the deficit and financing of health care is the underlying pressure that has brought health care reform into the national spotlight. They also points out that with the cost of health care spiraling upward toward 20% of the GNP, cost is also having a significant negative impact on productivity and the economy as a whole. With respect to access, Hofschire and Foote detail the dilemma faced in attempting to manage cost, while preserving choice in the types of services and the providers who deliver those services.

Hofschire and Foote examine the political forces that are at play in the access debate. Although there is general consensus that universal health care is a socially desirable goal, they outline the difficulties in achieving this goal (now or in the future). They suggest that access will ultimately take a secondary role to cost management. They predict that Congress will decrease benefits and access to Medicaid recipients and the economically poor segment of our population in an attempt to control the federal deficit. They also point out that managed care of this population has become the standard in most states. Although there has been some experience with managed care for physical illness, there is not significant data regarding mental health care in either the private or public arena.

They then note that a central challenge to psychologists is to show the value of their services in "cost-based outcomes." They argue that psychologists have failed to document the validity and efficacy of their work. They call for critical nationally standardized outcome techniques that can be applied in a systematic manner in assessing the efficacy of these services.

Armed with meaningful outcomes data, Hofschire and Foote contend that these services can be effectively marketed to policy makers, purchasers, payers, and consumers. They advocate for the development of integrated service delivery systems as vehicles for more efficient service delivery. They also suggest that capitation will represent a necessary reimbursement mechanism in a reformed health care system. With these modifications in place, Hofschire and Foote conclude that access, to both services and the providers who deliver them, can be preserved.

Using the preceding discussion as a springboard for debate, chapter 6 examines access issues that emerge as most salient to the delivery of psychological services in the areas of health and rehabilitation. Participants concluded that access in its broadest context relates to both the availability of psychological services as well as the inclusion of psychologists as fully enfranchised providers of these services in a reformed health care environment. They also argue that the legitimate domain of psychological services must be defined in terms of primary health care and not subjected to the traditional restriction of the rehabilitation of nervous and mental disorders only.

The issues of financing and organizational structures for the delivery system are then reviewed. Capitation and risk-sharing arrangements between purchasers, payers, and providers need to be developed to create broad-based incentives for the stable financing of a reformed system. To accommodate these requirements, conference participants agreed that integrated delivery systems were essential for the delivery of clinical services and the evaluation of their efficacy. Managed care is viewed as a realistic form of health care delivery to be included in this context.

With respect to specific recommendations and action steps pursuant to these conclusions, chapter 6 asserts that enhanced marketing efforts predicated on improved communication, both within and outside the psychological community, were of critical importance. Communication within the psychological community needed to involve practice divisions, the practice directorate, as well as the other APA directorates. Communication and linkage outside the psychological community were recommended with the following types of organizations: other professional provider groups (e.g., physicians and allied health professionals), consumer advocacy groups, disease prevention associations (e.g., the American Diabetes Association and American Heart Association), payers and purchasers, legislators and policy makers at the federal and state levels, and the public at large. Through the successful pursuit of these strategies and linkages, access to psychological services in a reformed health care system will be optimized.

Chapter 5

Access to Psychological Services

Philip J. Hofschire and Rebecca C. Foote

Rising health care costs in the United States have affected access to quality medical and mental health care. Although the care of 39 million uninsured Americans concerns both providers and the government, the debate regarding access is now dominated by the size of the federal budget deficit and growing health care costs (Frank & VandenBos, 1994). Psychological services tend to be viewed as having only limited impact on cost and access, and thus are largely ignored in most states' health reform programs (Frank, Sullivan, & DeLeon, 1994). It is critical for mental health providers to assure both governmental and private insurers that they can produce good outcomes at a reasonable cost. Psychologists are uniquely suited to provide such data, and have much to contribute in the redesigning of our country's health and mental health delivery systems. No other professional group is in a better position to influence the use of psychological knowledge and increase attention to psychological and behavioral health needs (Frank & VandenBos, 1994). Failure to accept this challenge will have serious implications for psychology as a profession.

Despite the fact that mental illness is highly prevalent in the general population, most individuals with mental disorders do not receive mental health care (Shapiro et al., 1984). Even if mental health care is broadly defined to include a single visit to a general medical provider or a mental health specialist for a mental health reason, fewer than one in five persons with a mental disorder is found to have received care during the past 6 months (Klerman, Olfson, Leon, & Weissman, 1992). Over a 6-month period, approximately 30 million adult Americans with a mental disorder do not receive any mental health care, of whom approximately 5.5 million suffer from schizophrenia, bipolar affective disorder, and major depression.

As discussed in part II, given the influx of mental health professionals into the work force over the past 20 years, one must question why people are not receiving needed services. In identifying barriers that serve to prevent the use of services by individuals who would be recognized as in need of treatment, it is important to examine factors that influence health care seeking behavior. Health seeking is influenced both by clinical factors, such as symptoms and level of subjective distress, as well as predisposing factors, such as sociodemographic, geographic, economic, and attitudinal variables (Anderson & Newman, 1973).

Financial barriers are well known to decrease access. The demand for mental health services appears to be more price sensitive than is the demand for outpatient general medical services (Shapiro et al., 1985). Those who do not have Medicaid whose household incomes are below 150% of the federal poverty level are at higher risk than other groups of having their needs for mental health services unmet (Keeler, Wells, & Manning, 1986).

Financial access is necessary but not sufficient in guaranteeing that patients will seek service. Research findings by Leaf and colleagues (1988) suggest that sociodemographic factors significantly influence use of mental health services. They found that being white, female, of higher educational status, and between the ages of 24 and 65 increase the likelihood of making a mental health visit. They suggest that males, the young and elderly, nonwhites, and those of lower educational status are at increased risk for not receiving care.

In addition, geographic barriers prevent access to care. Psychologists and other mental health professionals are disproportionately concentrated in urban areas. As a consequence, most U.S. counties have either few or no psychiatrists, psychologists, or social workers (Knesper, Wheeler, & Pagnucco, 1984).

Finally, personal and public attitudes may also influence the use of mental health services. Social stigmatization of mental illness is likely to lead to an avoidance of necessary treatment. However, it should be noted that the American public appears to believe in the importance of mental health. A *U.S. News and World Report* survey conducted in March of 1994 revealed that 75% of those polled would favor mental health benefits similar to those offered for physical illness. Sixty percent favored full mental health coverage and claimed to be willing to pay up to $100 for such coverage (Good, 1994).

Each of the aforementioned access barriers have important implications for both health and mental health providers, as well as for the overall health of the general population. Certainly, these barriers require further attention and study. Still, removing financial barriers remains a critical first step in making mental health services available to all Americans who are in need of treatment. Significantly, only the Clinton health care plan advocated specific mental health coverage. Other plans reflected concern over the potential for mental health benefits to lead to uncontrolled costs.

This skepticism can be traced back to the 1963 Community Mental Health Centers Act, which deinstitutionalized hundreds of thousands of hospitalized mentally ill patients across the country. This huge volume of uncared-for patients greatly increased the costs of mandated, chronic mental health care benefits. The problem is complicated by the fact that many of the individuals with persistent mental illness require long-term care and tend to be resistant to any type of medical care.

The challenges involved with caring for people with serious mental illness are not unique to the United States. Even the Canadian health system, which is highly regarded by its consumers and appears to work well for those patients who can benefit from office or general hospital intervention, is having difficulty providing adequate services for those who suffer from serious mental illness (Freeman, 1994). Although the Canadian system is beginning to show the effects of increased utilization, it remains superior to the U.S. system because of its single funding source and unified governmental philosophy regarding the mental health of its citizens.

Private insurance in the United States has historically stigmatized patients requiring treatment for mental illness and substance abuse in comparison with those in need of general medical care (Tommasini, 1994). This inequity can be attributed, in part, to the assumption that liberal mental health benefits result in unnecessary and excessive use. Although there is no scientific literature to justify this assumption, insurers simply note that $54 billion were spent on alcohol/drug abuse and mental health treatment in 1990 (Frank, McGuire, Regier, Manderscheid, & Woodward, 1994). These expenditures were grossly skewed toward inpatient psychiatric care, severe mental illness, and substance abuse. Research has shown that even though inpatient psychiatric episodes account for only 36% of total psychiatric episodes, they account for more than 82% of total expenditures (Kiesler & Simpkins, 1993). Although there has been a significant decrease in the use of hospital beds for mental health treatment, the chronic care of those with the severest disorders remains expensive.

Concern over the expense of treating persons with serious mental illness is legitimate, and it is unclear how this population will be served by the new health care delivery systems. The question remains: How will costs be contained? Although access to health care services continues to be a real concern for both providers and legislators, little in the debate of the 103rd Congress related to access to health or mental health services.

Health care reform efforts during the 103rd Congress were driven largely by economic and political agendas. Health reform was based on money and the growing cost of the federal deficit. Without control of the federal entitlement programs, Medicare and Medicaid, the deficit is likely to grow. Social Security, Medicare, and Medicaid accounted for 57%, or $521 billion, of the total entitlement program in 1993. There is little political chance that Social Security and Medicare will be modified because of the powerful presence of the senior citizen lobby in Washington. Consequently, only Medicaid is available for discussion.

The 104th Republican Congress believes that transferring federal funds by means of block grants will allow greater local control of the money and services needed. States view such grants as a mixed blessing. On the one hand, they have control of the money but, on the other hand, have little control over the number of recipients in times of economic downturn. Even the balanced budget amendment was met with skepticism by many governors as they realized the potential for the federal government simply to shift the costs to the states to balance the federal budget. Medicaid patients are overwhelmingly poor, underserved, and frequently persons of color. Although low-income adults and children accounted for most Medicaid beneficiaries, 73% of the 32.1 million in 1993, their health care costs accounted for only a third of total program spending. The other two thirds of the Medicaid costs were consumed by long-term care of the elderly.

Since its inception, Medicaid has averaged double-digit inflation, with the exception of a brief period in the 1980s. Moreover, Medicaid enrollment has continued to grow. By 1992, Medicaid enrollment had grown to 31 million and had experienced an average annual increase of 8.3% (Merlis, 1993). For these and numerous other reasons, states are experimenting with innovative, cost-effective ways of delivering care to this population.

Mental health providers must include themselves in these laboratories for new delivery experiments. The surviving providers will be those that offer innovative, cost-effective services. Capitated mental health programs are spreading across the country rapidly (Dangerfield & Betit, 1993) and hold great promise for community mental health centers and providers who are willing to assess their costs and benefits to the patient population served. The potential for these pilot Medicaid mental health programs to increase access and control cost is unlimited. Their failure, conversely, will assuredly decrease access in this day of limited public funding.

Mental health utilization in a managed care environment is similar to the pattern of usage for physical illness. That is, as the illness becomes severer, mental health utilization within the HMO increases. Outside usage of mental health services seems to be related to sociodemographic factors (Simon, VonKorff, & Durham, 1994). Increasing copayment levels progressively reduce the demand for services without respect to the severity of the illness. Such self-imposed restrictions are going to affect both the providers and the poorest recipients, whether Medicaid or privately insured.

Because there will be no comprehensive reform legislation, what will be the impact on access and services for providers? The marketplace changes that accelerated in 1994 will continue to escalate and dramatically reform health care delivery. The American public has become much more concerned about the deficit and any requirements for mandated future funding. The crux of the problem for state and federal government is that any attempt to shift costs to the taxpayer is largely being rejected by the electorate.

Currently, the federal and state governments are hoping that managed care will control health care costs. This is despite a recent Congressional Budget Office report (Reischcauer, 1994) that suggested that managed care may only be marginally successful.

As a response to this governmental interest, we have seen emphasis on managed care and integration of health delivery sporadically, but effectively, moving across the medical landscape. These systems are far reaching and include hospitals, providers, and insurers. Accepting that managed care can control cost, both the state and federal government will encourage such movement.

Insurers, such as Cigna and Aetna, have recognized this move to managed care and have hired groups of primary care providers in metropolitan areas potentially to serve those federal entitlement patients, particularly those on Medicaid. Private insurers, however, are also faced with the near-impossible task of developing a nationwide program of integrated care. The costs for such nationwide access are enormous and probably beyond the scope of all insurers. Regional success in well-chosen markets will be the rule rather than the exception. The absence of a comprehensive program, such as that seen in Canada, will preclude nationwide standards of care. Decreasing mental health benefits will be easy prey for those who choose payment for physical illness while avoiding costly, poorly defined mental health diagnoses. Already we see most private- and public-sector payments for inpatient treatment of mental health being dramatically reduced. Although this may manage those who are less ill and be cost-effective, less is known about how those who suffer from chronic mental illness will be impacted. Several states, including Massachusettes, Vermont, and Washington, have developed specific initiatives to ensure that vulnerable populations receive needed services within managed care systems.

Although some have criticized the movement of the private and public patient to managed care, there is little question that such care does decrease emergency room visits for physical illness. Managed care is rapidly changing the face of Medicaid. Nearly 25% of the Medicaid eligible, or 34 million people, are currently in managed care plans, up from 12% in 1992 (French, 1995). By the turn of the century, it is projected that as much as 65% of the U.S. population will receive care through managed systems (Weiner, 1994). The success of capitated care in mental health is largely unknown and is clouded by the lack of historical perspective.

The importance of the move to managed care lies in the implication that the successful systems will be those that can deliver care at low cost. The issue of quality of care appears only an afterthought in Washington. Policy makers incorrectly assume that most health care professionals will continue to deliver quality care despite dwindling reimbursement. However, not all companies or states deliver managed care effectively because there is wide variation in quality and cost of services.

Managed care delivery systems will continue to center on the primary care provider. These individuals will become gatekeepers to specialty services and technology usage. This emphasis will change the current problem of overusage of technology and specialty services to the potential problem of underusage of those services because both systems are based on perverse financial incentives. Managed care also enables insurers to divest themselves of risk. It is easy to understand why major health insurance companies are hiring large groups of primary care physicians. They are effectively shifting the risk of care to the providers with little loss of company profit.

This movement to primary care occurs despite technology that is increasingly sophisticated and difficult for the generalist to understand. Not only will primary care control much of technology, but also will control access to psychology and mental health services. Prager and Scallet (1992) have suggested that mental health professionals develop effective mechanisms for bringing mental health expertise to a range of health care settings to assure greater access to competent mental health care.

If managed care is not successful, how will costs be contained? Initially, there will be federal attempts to decrease physician and hospital reimbursement for Medicare and Medicaid. It will be necessary to control access to services as well as to reduce the actual services provided. Such reduction means ''a reduction in specialty services and services that are difficult to quantify.'' Psychology services are among those ''specialty services that would be difficult to quantify.''

Fortunately, the administration and Congress realize that mental health is relatively inexpensive because technological support is rarely necessary in providing services. Most services are not performed in hospitals and are relatively inexpensive in comparison with other medical procedures. These advantages are balanced by congressional concern regarding the potential for overusage and unlimited encounters, creating a "black hole" in which mental health costs would be neither accountable nor controllable.

The issue of overusage is valid because mental health services have always been difficult to quantify in identifying success. Psychologists are partly responsible for this. Many professional societies have claimed that success or cure is difficult to quantify. This claim will not be satisfactory in the future. In fact, psychologists quantify success clinically all of the time by releasing patients from their care. That physicians quantify outcomes in coronary artery surgery does not imply that people are cured. Rather, it means there is an expectation of hospitalization, prescription, and professional fee costs. Psychologists must do the same within their societies.

There is significant scientific literature detailing the financial and societal benefits of mental health. Mental health professionals need to show outcomes that will give satisfactory results in a reasonable time and at a reasonable cost. To accomplish these goals, psychologists must develop and justify economically outcomes measures and critical pathways.

A convincing scientific base has developed in relation to mental health treatment and how it causes sharp reductions in medical care utilization and encourages more appropriate use when services are needed, among both the patients themselves and their family members (Langenbucher, 1994). For example, in cost-offset research on patients who have received alcohol and other drug abuse treatment, their use of health care in the posttreatment period falls dramatically, immediately, and converges over time to near the utilization level of the normal population (Langenbucher, 1994). Studies have shown impressive cost-savings (Becker & Sanders, 1984; Blose & Holder, 1991), which pay for addictions treatment within 2 to 3 years (NIAAA, 1985).

Similarly, the Hawaii Medicaid Project, conducted by Cummings, Pallack, and Dorken and funded by the Health Care Finance Administration, found that the delivery of targeted, focused psychological treatment interventions can have a dramatic effect on reducing the medical needs of patients in Medicaid and federal employee patient groups (Cummings, Pallack, Dorken, & Henke, 1993). The author concluded that by actively encouraging patients from Medicaid and federal employee populations to seek appropriate mental health treatment, the federal and state governments have an opportunity to decrease their overall health care program costs significantly. However, there are still many unanswered questions about medical offsets, especially where the treatment of severe mental illness is concerned. Some have cautioned that offsets are more commonly associated with people with less severe mental or substance disorders (G. Bond, personal communication, May 31, 1995).

As more research is conducted on "cost-offsets" of mental health care, psychologists will be more convincing in their assertions that mental health represents an integral part of the overall health system. Indeed, defining psychology narrowly in terms of "mental health" is likely to limit access. A broad definition, which acknowledges the role of mental state in the maintenance and deterioration of good physical health, and in the treatment and recovery of physical illness, is more accurate and will likely expand access. To this end, describing the services provided by psychologists as psychological services instead of mental health services seems important.

Psychologists must quantify and define outcomes for another reason. Although there are frequently differences regarding diagnoses and treatment programs, there are also varying levels of providers who wish to provide psychological services. While realizing there are considerable "turf" issues, professional groups need to collaborate to set standards of care instead of leaving this important task to untrained politicians in Washington or the state houses.

Another challenge lies in the fact that universities and professional schools continue to graduate many doctoral- and master's-level psychologists, and social workers (see Frank and Johnstone, chapter 3). This unlimited entry of workers has the potential to dilute the ability of the profession to monitor quality and obtain reasonable compensation from insurance companies and managed care groups. Recent professional reports from New York detail the draconian methods of insurers that have dramatically reduced the reimbursement and quality control of mental health professionals.

To ensure access to psychologists, both local and state societies must work aggressively with insurance companies and managed care firms to include adequate professionals in their plans. Success will depend on the field's ability to remain banded together to ensure a collective benefit.

Once professional criteria for mental health and rehabilitative services, the outcome measures, and critical pathways have been established, this information can be disseminated to societies, state and local governments, and legislative offices. Although Washington, DC, is important to the total profession, there are advantages to working with state offices and legislators. State legislators frequently have more time, smaller staffs, and are not as heavily lobbied. They are likely to be receptive to advice on a variety of issues if approached in an honest and unbiased manner.

Lobbying can be effective at the state level. Virtually every state has a health care reform package as they realize that Congress and the administration in Washington are going to have a difficult time coming to a consensus.

It remains important to influence Congress, both by means of direct contact and through the education of the general public. Nothing influences congressional leaders more than a constituent coming to their office and telling them what they know is the best policy. The more psychologists can influence public opinion in the various constituencies, the greater the likelihood that significant legislative support for psychological services will be obtained.

The fact remains that if professionals do not become involved in accessing our governmental officials, then we as a profession will fail to influence policy. Congress does not intentionally want to do wrong; more often, Congress simply does not know the right course to follow. In 1992, when the attempt to quantify the work and value of physician activities was performed by the Congress, all physicians were given a substantial ability to respond. Fewer than 20% voiced any opinion to their elected representatives. If professionals do not respond when their ability to deliver care is threatened, Congress will assume that psychologists are not important in influencing individual congressional votes.

There are several specific actions that can begin locally. First, psychologists can ensure that they are not excluded from "willing provider" laws. Managed care companies and many insurance companies have passage of such legislation in most states, allowing them to exclude, without cause, unwanted providers. Under the guise that such laws enable them to control cost, these companies can dictate costs, reimbursement, and access to patients. Providers have no recourse with such legislation in place. Although this is intended to control providers within an integrated network, the effect is to limit both provider access and patient choice. Unfortunately, many insured citizens have only cursory knowledge of their health care benefits. People who are newly insured in physician networks or HMOs seem uncertain about what services their plan covers (Garnick et al., 1993). This legislation can exclude providers, barring any opportunity for inclusion in the delivery system.

There appear to be ethical or perhaps even constitutional issues raised when insurers exclude providers purely on an economic basis (i.e., economic credentialing) without knowing whether or not psychologists are willing or able to comply with their plans. Although such bills tend to protect insurers, they do little to improve the quality of care or the freedom of choice for our patients. If economic credentialing is prevented, psychologists must establish relationships with hospitals or an integrated system. Failure to do so may allow psychologists to be omitted from the system as insurers selectively exclude providers at their own discretion.

Psychologists must develop an effective package of services that includes quality assurance and cost guarantees. Integration of provider groups will allow psychologists to market their group to employers, as well as to insurers. Standards and outcomes measures that are specific to psychologists' locality must also be developed.

Although it is important to have national guidelines and follow national constructs, psychologists must also be guided by their local or state society. Local input is crucial because all health care is locally influenced. Finally, psychologists must examine the potential for capitating their services. This factor includes the development of a reasonable fee structure and the ability to justify it.

Psychologists have a unique opportunity to play an important role in these changing times. Not only do they have the opportunity to be reimbursed at greater levels but also to help in establishing the higher quality health care package for all Americans. To do this, the profession must move in a coordinated direction toward the common goal of improving the mental health of Americans and thus, general health, of all Americans. Kissinger said, "If you don't know where you're going, any road is going to take you." Psychologists need to find the best road to take. The spoils will go to those who are the best organized and who stress quality care at a low cost.

SUMMARY

National health care reform legislation in today's political milieu is highly unlikely. Factors influencing the lack of governmental reform on a national level center on Republican control of the Congress, the high cost of such a national program, and the desire to downsize the influence of government in the private lives of citizens.

Although many would subscribe to such ideas, the likelihood of excluding significant numbers of poorly paid and economically endangered citizens from health and mental treatment benefits is probable. In an attempt to control the federal deficit, Congress is going to decrease the benefits and access to the Medicaid recipients and the economically poor segment of our population.

Because President's Clinton health plan did not receive either public or congressional approval, mental health benefits will remain the domain of the state or local government or the private insurer. As Congress works to control Medicaid costs, managed care of this population has become the standard in most states. Even though there has been some experience with managed care for physical illness, there is not significant data regarding mental health care in either the private or public arena.

Psychologists need to form provider groups that can assure both governmental and private insurers that quality mental health care can be given at a reasonable cost. This will require such groups to establish quality assurance mechanisms and an ability to review utilization on an outpatient basis, as well as within the hospital setting.

Psychologists must assure quality and outcomes, and inform Congress and the public about their success. The absence of effective dissemination and notification of that information will allow other caregivers and insurance providers to assume that psychologists do not have such data.

Finally, psychology must continue to educate those in public office, both at the state and local level. Too often professionals do not wish to be seen as lobbyists; yet valid information needs to be seen by our elected officials, and we are the best messengers of our story.

REFERENCES

Anderson, R., & Newman, J. F. (1973). Societal and individual determinants of medical care utilization. *Milbank Memorial Fund Quarterly, 51*, 95–103.

Becker, F. W., & Sanders, B. K. (1984). *The Illinois Medicare/Medicaid Alcoholism Services Demonstration: Medicaid cost trends and utilization patterns* (Managerial Report). Springfield: Sangamon State University, Center for Policy Studies and Program Evaluation.

Blose, J. O., & Holder, H. D. (1991). The utilization of medical care by treated alcoholics: Longitudinal patterns by age, gender, and type of care. *Journal of Substance Abuse, 3*, 13–27.

Cummings, N. A., Pallack, M. S., Dorken, H., & Henke, C. J. (1993). Medicaid, managed mental healthcare and medical cost offset. *Behavioral Healthcare Tomorrow, 2*, 15–20.

Dangerfield, D., & Betit, R. L. (1993). Managed mental health care in the public sector. *New Directions in Mental Health Services, 59*, 67–80.

Frank, R. G., & Johnstone, B. (1996). Changes in the health work force: Implications for psychologists. In R. L. Glueckauf, R. G. Frank, G. R. Bond, & J.

H. McGrew (Eds.), *Psychological practice in a changing health care system: Issues and new directions*. New York: Springer.

Frank, R. G., McGuire, T. G., Regier, D. A., Manderscheid, R., & Woodward, A. (1994). Paying for mental health and substance abuse care. *Health Affairs Millwood, 13*, 337–342.

Frank, R. G., Sullivan, M. J., & DeLeon, P. H. (1994). Health care reform in the states. *American Psychologist, 49*, 855–867.

Frank, R. G., & VandenBos, G. R. (1994). Health Care Reform. *American Psychologist, 49*, 851–854.

Freeman, S. J. (1994). An overview of Canada's mental health system. *New Directions in Mental Health Services, 61*, 11–20.

French, B. (1995). The urgent care crunch. *Hospitals and Health Networks, 69*, 34–38.

Garnick, D. W., Hendricks, A. M., Thorpe, K. E., Newhouse, J. P., Donelan, K., & Blendon, R. J. (1993). How well do Americans understand their health coverage? *Health Affairs Millwood, 12*, 204–212.

Good, E. E. (1994). How much coverage for mental illness? *U.S. News and World Report, 116*, 56–57.

Keeler, E. B., Wells, K. B., & Manning, W. G. (1986). *The demand for episodes of mental health services* (RAND Report No. R-3432-NIMH). Santa Monica, CA: The RAND Corporation.

Kiesler, C. A., & Simpkins, C. G. (1993). *The unnoticed majority in psychiatric inpatient care*. New York: Plenum Press.

Klerman, G. L., Olfson, M., Leon, A. C., & Weissman, M. M. (1992). Measuring the need for mental health care. *Health Affairs, 11*, 24–33.

Knesper, D. J., Wheeler, J. R. C., & Pagnucco, D. J. (1984). Mental health services providers' distribution across counties in the United States. *American Psychologist, 39*, 1424–1434.

Langenbucher, J. (1994). Offsets are not add-ons: The place of addictions treatment in American Health Care Reform. *Journal Substance Abuse, 6*, 117–122.

Leaf, P. J., Bruce, M. L., Tischler, G. L., Freeman, P. H., Weissman, M. M., & Myers, J. K. (1988). Factors affecting the utilization of specialty and general medical mental health services. *Medical Care, 26*, 9–26.

Merlis, M. (1993, January 22). *Medicaid: An overview* (Congressional Research Service Report for Congress).

National Institute on Alcohol Abuse and Alcoholism. (1985). *Alcoholism treatment impact on total health care utilization and costs: Analysis of the Federal Employee Health Benefit Program with Aetna Life Insurance Company* (DHHS Publication No. [ADM] 281-83-001). Rockville, MD: U.S. Department of Health and Human Services.

Padgett, D. K., Patrick, C., Burns, B. J., & Schlesinger, H. J. (1994). Ethnicity and the use of outpatient mental health services in a national insured population. *American Journal of Public Health, 84*, 222–226.

Prager, D. J., & Scallet, L. J. (1992). Promoting and sustaining the health of the mind. *Health Affairs, 11,* 118–124.

Reischcauer, R. D. (1994, April). *An analysis of the managed competition act* (A CBO Study).

Shapiro, S., Skinner, E. A., Kessler, L. G., Von Korff, M., German, P. S., Tischler, G. L., Leaf, P. G., Benham, L., Cottler, L., & Regier, D. A. (1984). Utilization of health and mental health services: Three epidemiologic catchment sites. *Archives of General Psychiatry, 41,* 971–978.

Shapiro, S., Skinner, E. A., Kramer, M., Steinwachs, D. M., & Regier, D. A. (1985). Measuring need for mental health services in the general population. *Medical Care, 23,* 1033–1043.

Simon, G. E., VonKorff, M., & Durham, M. L. (1994). Predictors of outpatient mental health utilization by primary care patients in a health maintenance organization. *American Journal of Psychiatry, 151,* 908–913.

Tommasini, N. R. (1994). Private insurance coverage for the treatment of mental illness versus general medical care: A policy of inequity. *Archives of Psychiatric Nursing, 8,* 9–13.

Weiner, J. P. (1994). Forecasting the effects of health care reform on U.S. physician workforce requirements: Evidence from HMO staffing patterns. *Journal of American Medical Association, 272,* 222–229.

Chapter 6

Access Issues in a Changing Health Care System

Lee Hersch and Donald Kewman

OVERVIEW

Discussions regarding health care reform generally focus on the following three key variables: cost, quality, and access. The access issue addresses the following central questions: who will be able to use the system, which services will be available, which providers will deliver the services, and under what circumstances will services be delivered. This chapter focuses on both access to psychological services and to psychologists as health care providers. After examining these core issues, funding for psychological services and outcome assessment is discussed. Finally, specific recommendations and action steps for enhancing access to psychological services are provided.

ACCESS TO SERVICES

The statistics regarding the access limitations of the current health care system have been widely disseminated. Forty-one million individuals are uninsured at any given time, and more then 13 million individuals are temporarily uninsured during the course of a year (see Hofschire et al.'s and O'Keeffe's chapter in this volume). Twenty percent of the U.S. population is without health insurance at some point during the course of each year. Yet these statistics obscure other important facts about access. First, there is great disparity in the definition of the word, "insured." In

some cases insured refers
cases insured refers to con
sured does not necessaril
rather, it may mean indige
at taxpayers' expense. Fi
preventive and early inte
results in more complic
improving access to the
factor in its developmen
coverage is highly desir
climate can bear ("Hea
Contemporary efforts
age as the ideal goal.
coverage by 2005 (He
modest goals, there is n

80

(ADA, 1990). It remains, h
and advocacy.
The difficulties faced
compounded for indiv
long-standing social
gists and other he
number of indi
whose benef
adequate m
compani
many
in

Minorities and Handicapped Populations

Minorities and handicapped populations are likely to face several obstacles in gaining access to health care services (Mays & Albee, 1992). To the extent that minority groups in our society are employed in lower paying jobs lacking health care benefits, their access to the health care system is differentially impacted (Wallen, 1992). A reformed health care system needs to address this issue as a central matter of social policy. The costs of not providing reasonable health care to minority populations may ultimately prove to be greater than the cost of providing it (APA, 1992).

Regardless of minority or disability status, persons with emotional or interpersonal problems may experience difficulties in obtaining adequate mental health services (Santiago, 1992). A prior medical condition or disability is often an impediment to employment, as well as to obtaining medical insurance. Ironically, an individual with a major disability may have better access to medical insurance then an individual with a partial disability. Private disability benefits (which include medical benefits) or public benefits with government-sponsored health care through Medicaid are generally available to totally disabled individual. In contrast, individuals with less severe disabilities may be limited to minimal employment opportunities, which have few or no health benefits, or be forced to remain in their present job to maintain their current benefits. Changing jobs or seeking training for a better job could jeopardize the benefits they do have. Fortunately, the Americans with Disabilities Act appears to be a starting place to redress this aspect of the access problem for this population

wever, an area that requires monitoring

by persons with disabilities in our society are
uals with mental health problems because of the
stigma associated with these conditions. Psycholo-
lth professionals have become painfully aware of the
iduals who do not have any mental health benefits or
s are so restrictive as to prohibit meaningful access to
ntal health care. Although some states do mandate insurance
s to offer mental health benefits as part of their benefits packages,
states do not. Psychologists receive reimbursement under Medicaid
nly 22 states (Glueckauf, Frank, Bond, & McGrew, 1994). This
rtling fact has received relatively little attention by the profession.

Insurance companies and benefits managers for employers have incorporated numerous strategies for limiting access to mental health care benefits (Bak & Weiner, 1993). The most arcane and inefficient is the historical bias toward funding for costly inpatient care without collateral outpatient benefits (Frank, Salkever, & Sharfstein, 1991). While this pattern is now beginning to be reversed, it remains problematic in many insurance policies. Additionally, increased deductibles, higher co-payments, annual benefits caps and lifetime benefits caps, which selectively target mental health benefits, have been common trends during the course of the past decade (VandenBos, Cummings, & DeLeon, 1992). Businesses and insurance companies have also selectively ''carved out'' mental health benefits by subcontracting distribution of these benefits to managed care organizations under a capitation agreement or predetermined cost for the population of persons served (Berney, 1992). Services delivered then receive greater scrutiny through active preauthorization and interval case review, both in inpatient and outpatient settings. The application of the ''medical necessity'' criterion represents both another mechanism for limiting benefits and obscuring the essential linkage between physical and mental health (Bianchi, Edmiston, & Strasser, 1988). The medical necessity criterion requires that treatment be contingent on the presence of an identifiable medical risk which would be exacerbated, if treatment were discontinued. The issue of mental health care ''parity'' is of major concern as the reform process proceeds (Beckman-Brindley et al., 1993). There remains a general lack of appreciation of the medical ''cost-offsets'' in terms of increased physical health care costs, when access to bona fide mental health services is not available (VandenBos & DeLeon, 1988).

Specific Services

As noted earlier, access to psychologists has been limited in many ways by insurance benefits designs and by managed care case management. In addition, there have been arbitrary limitations on a variety of modalities including biofeedback, marital and family therapy, neuropsychological assessment, neurobehavioral treatments, and other valuable approaches. These limitations would appear to derive from the medical model orientation, which does not yet fully recognize nor value many of the newer treatments developed by psychologists. Treatment techniques, such as biofeedback and hypnosis, are frequently disqualified as unapproved techniques even when the research literature identifies them as legitimate treatments and in some cases the "treatment of choice" (Basmajian, 1989). Finally, exclusions of various diagnoses for reimbursement, such as the DSM III-R diagnosis of "psychological factors affecting physical condition," dramatically limit the availability of necessary psychological interventions (Spitzer, 1987). This diagnosis reflects the essential nature of the interactive processes between psychological and physiological functioning. Nevertheless, the linkage between physical and psychological functioning is still generally not appreciated by purchasers nor payers of health benefits, and therefore are not included in many benefits packages.

Settings

An additional access consideration relates to the settings where psychological services are delivered. Traditionally, psychologists have worked in either private practices or hospital settings under some form of supervision by physicians. The availability of psychological services in other health care settings, such as extended care/geriatric facilities, rehabilitation facilities, schools, and business all represent potential opportunities for increasing access to services that can promote health. Such issues as hospital privileges and autonomous professional functioning across settings are important variables in the assurance of access to psychological services.

A further consideration regarding access that relates to settings involves rural health care services. Given the tendency for health care providers to be more densely distributed in urban areas, the individual residing in a rural area at a significant distance from a major city may have difficulty in accessing psychological services (Richards & Gottfredson, 1987). This fact can be particularly problematic to the extent that psychological services usually require repeated contacts through the course of treatment. The logistics can be prohibitive, unless a reformed health care system includes incentives to encourage psychological services to be offered in remote rural locations.

Still another concern with respect to settings and access is the historical boundary between public- and private-sector service delivery systems.

These systems have traditionally been segregated with the public system tending to focus on persons with severe mental illness (especially those who are low income, uninsured, or indigent), whereas the private system has served persons with emotional difficulties or lifestyle problems, who were insured through their work. As health care reform progresses, greater coordination between these settings will be required to ensure continuity of care, as well as access to services for persons with severe mental illness (Greene, 1994).

A final issue relates to the fact that most of the research and outcomes assessment resources have been localized in university settings. Whether the research is privately or publicly funded, it generally has not used data from the private sector. Given the magnitude and relevance of data from the private sector, facilitating the provision of private-sector data for publicly funded outcome research would appear desirable. The development of a "practice research network," where public and private resources are shared, represents an important opportunity to improve both research and clinical practice (APA Board of Professional Affairs, 1994).

ACCESS TO PROVIDERS

The second overarching access issue relates to the issue of access by consumers to various types of providers. This is also an issue of concern to the professionals providing these services. Enhancing the choice of providers for the consumer and guaranteeing that "any willing provider" can participate in a reformed health care system are central access issues. Current managed care strategies frequently attempt to limit their provider panels to individuals who use "brief psychotherapy" models and whose "provider profiles" reflect fewer treatment sessions per treatment episode (Bennett, 1994). In so doing, individuals who have difficulties not amenable to brief therapy do not have access to providers trained to treat these disorders. Three categories of providers are examined, including doctoral-level psychologists, master's-level psychologists, and other providers.

Doctoral-Level Psychologists

To the extent that the doctoral level represents the terminal degree of the profession, all doctorally trained psychologists, including PsyDs and PhDs in clinical, counseling, health, rehabilitation psychology, and neuropsychology should be considered eligible providers. Doctoral-level psychologists are required to show proficiency in a broader range and greater depth of assessment and intervention skills than is possible to achieve in a master's-level training program. At the present time, there is no nationally recognized licensing authority. Individual states vary significantly in their licensing requirements. Insurance companies also vary considerably with respect to their recognition and reimbursement of professional degrees and competencies. The universal caveat is that they only undertake interventions or applications for which they are qualified by their training and experience.

Master's-Level Psychologists

A related issue is the designation of master's-level psychologists to function in the health care system, albeit perhaps in an adjunctive or affiliative role. Current regulations in many states limit the roles of master's-level psychologists or preclude them from practicing entirely. It is notable, however, that master's-level individuals make up most providers of psychological services in some managed care settings. Many settings do not see any advantage to hiring doctoral-level psychologists compared with less costly and more plentiful bachelor's- and master's-trained mental health practitioners (see Hofschire's and Foote's chapter in this volume).

Nonpsychologist Providers

From the viewpoint of developing an integrated health care system, professionals from all mental health disciplines (i.e., psychology, psychiatry, social work, counseling, and nursing) need to be included in a reformed health care system so that the unique perspectives and contributions of each discipline are available to the public. Team work and coordination are the best ways to ensure efficient and effective care. Inpatient psychiatric settings have relied on interdisciplinary teams as the standard of care for many years. The emergence of partial hospital, intensive outpatient programs, and integrated outpatient practices with interdisciplinary mental health teams has been a relatively recent development.

REIMBURSEMENT

A difficult issue in the access discussion relates to the funding of psychological services. The traditional FFS model, predicated on indemnity insurance plans, is rapidly being replaced by managed care models. Risk sharing among purchasers, payers, and providers is becoming increasingly common. Although reasonable arguments can be made for both funding mechanisms, each approach has significantly limited access to psychological services in distinct ways. The indemnity system has traditionally provided relatively high levels of service to the limited numbers of individuals covered by comprehensive mental health benefits (Bennett, 1994). In contrast, the managed care approach has been to offer a limited benefit to the entire ''population'' covered by the plan. In these cases, the problem is that individuals with significantly greater needs for services because of diagnosis, severity, and comorbidity may be left without adequate benefits (Bennett, 1994). Other reimbursement policies that negatively impact access include the disqualification of various diagnostic categories, noninclusion of various types of services, and exclusion of various provider groups. As the health care system is reformed, alternative reimbursement and incentive systems need to be explored. As business and industry become more aware of the implications of failing to provide psychological services and recognize the cost of reduced productivity associated with behavioral and lifestyle difficulties, they may be more willing to reimburse psychological services as a way to manage health care costs.

CHANGES NEEDED IN HEALTH CARE SYSTEM

The process of facilitating change in the health care system, which will enhance access, requires initiatives in at least four areas. These areas include legislative and regulatory, purchasers and payers, and consumers and providers. Initiatives in these areas will require a combination of both education and marketing efforts.

Legislative and Regulatory Initiatives

First, policy makers at the federal and state levels need to be educated about the importance of including psychological services in comprehensive health insurance. It is also important that they understand the variety of psychological services offered by a range of health care providers, including psychologists. As health care reform continues, increasing pressure to reduce costs lessens the feasibility of mandating comprehensive benefits. The case must be made that real value for the health care dollar is gained by addressing the psychological component of medical illness, as well as treating psychological illness per se.

Marketing to Purchasers and Payers

Second, business and insurance companies that offer benefits packages have historically been unreceptive to including psychological services into their benefits packages for a variety of reasons. Mental illness is "difficult to see." People look at a depressed person and cannot identify the impairment. It is easy to react to the individual as unmotivated or self-defeating rather than disabled. Further, there is the perception that there are no reliable "tests" analogous to "lab tests" to document either the presence of a mental illness nor to measure the improvement from these diseases in ways which employer/payers can relate to in functional terms (e.g., productivity). Also, the limited availability of adequate and relevant outcome research creates a situation where purchasers have had to accept the value of psychological services on "faith." While "doing the right thing" may have had appeal, there is a perception that "hand holding and indulgence" does not represent "good business." This is particularly true when purchasers perceive their mental health dollars as going toward "personal growth" rather than what they recognize as real health care. The traditional mental health care benefit package included in many indemnity health insurance products was acceptable when the costs were minimal, but now that services for mental illness and chemical dependency represent 16% of a rapidly accelerating health care budget, faith alone is not sufficient to motivate these individuals (APA, 1992).

Marketing to Consumers

Third, consumers of health care services need to understand the linkage between physical and mental health care so that they are better able to make educated choices about which services they need. The public at large does not yet generally appreciate the degree to which psychologically influenced factors, such as stress and behavior, directly impact on both the development of disease states and outcome of treatment. They may not understand that major physical illness is frequently accompanied by significant psychological illness. This degree of comorbidity exacerbates both types of conditions, impeding a speedy recovery. Addressing physical symptoms without adequate attention to psychological factors cannot result in the most effective treatment strategy. Discussions regarding health care partnerships typically address purchasers, payers, and providers. A comprehensive strategy for an integrated health care system must also actively recruit the public as partners in the health care endeavor. A consumer who is a knowledgeable participant in their health care will be more likely to request concurrent psychological intervention along with their physical care.

Marketing to Psychologists

Finally, providers need information about how to adapt their practices to ongoing changes in the health care system. Psychologists and other mental health providers are showing predictable but counterproductive resistance to current changes in the health care delivery system. They have become used to the FFS–"solo practice" system because its rewards include autonomy, status, and good incomes. Psychologists need to be educated regarding the opportunities to apply their theory and techniques to the whole spectrum of health-related difficulties. Working with physicians and allied health professionals in a variety of health settings represents new challenges. The training of psychologists in the areas of health care psychology will be an important direction for psychology to pursue. Provisions for the retraining of the existing professional work force will also be necessary. Psychologists will also have to be educated regarding structural adaptations to their practices administratively and organizationally, if they are going to function more efficiently in an integrated health care system. Educating psychologists and motivating them to change will require significant efforts.

CONCLUSION

There is general agreement on several recommendations for action steps both within and outside the profession. Psychologists should continue to pursue opportunities to provide services in mental health vigorously, but also seek to expand opportunities to provide service in a broader range of health settings. Furthermore, APA advocacy efforts are strengthened by recognizing that psychology is a health care profession with equal emphasis placed on the application of psychological services to treat aspects of physical problems as well as mental health.

Action Steps Within Psychology

It is widely recognized that there are important, ongoing efforts to address concerns related to access to mental health by many branches of APA.

However, the broader range of psychological services, particularly those delivered in health care settings, have not been routinely included in these advocacy efforts. The Health and Behavior Task Force, chaired by Dr. Joseph Matarazzo, should be reactivated as a vehicle to coordinate health and behavioral issues within the APA structures. An alternative is the formation of a new interdivisional task force composed of representatives of divisions with particular health care psychology interests to interface with the APA Practice Directorate, and to field candidates for the APA Practice boards and committees, such as the Committee for the Advance of Professional Practice and the Board of Professional Affairs. Existing interdivisional initiatives, such as Stan Moldawski's Health Care Reform Task Force and Jack Wiggins's effort toward a coordinated approach to disability policy, are examples of this type of interdivisional effort. The APA should also establish an electronic bulletin board as a mechanism to facilitate communication between directorates and between APA and its membership. These are action steps that are strongly recommended for implementation.

Actions Steps Outside of Psychology

An additional area of importance is the establishment of linkages with other professions and organizations within the health care system. Whenever possible, psychologists should work with other professionals who provide psychological services, including psychiatrists, social workers, counselors, rehabilitation specialists, and psychiatric nurses to improve access to our services.

Psychologists should develop professional relationships with primary care and specialist physicians. There are many areas in which care could be coordinated, such as with physician specialists (e.g., oncologists in the management of the side effects of chemotherapy; anesthesiologists in the treatment of pain; and gynecologists in the management of phase-of-life difficulties, such as menopause). Similarly, communicating actively with groups of allied health professionals (e.g., dentists and physical therapists) represents still another way of integrating psychological services into the total health care system.

There is also agreement on the desirability of working with consumer advocacy groups. Organizations, such as the American Diabetes Association, could represent important opportunities for collaboration, mutual education, and marketing. Historically, organized psychology has not had active relationships with this type of organization in the same manner that physician groups have.

Finally, continuing changes in the health care system are likely to occur for the next decade regardless of legislative initiatives at the federal level. Barring a crisis of access, health care reform will be an incremental and developmental process that will evolve as new reimbursement and delivery systems mature. Strong national leadership by APA and by state psychological associations are needed, but must be supplemented by individual psychologists at the grassroots level to shape public policy.

REFERENCES

American Psychological Association. (1992, August). *Medical cost offsets* (Practice Directorate). Washington, DC: Author.

American Psychological Association Board of Professional Affairs. (1994, March). *Unapproved minutes of March 18–20 meeting*. Washington, DC: Author.

Americans With Disabilities Act of 1990. 42 U.S.C. 12101. Public Law 101-336.

Bak, J. S., & Weiner, R. H. (1993). Practice potpourri: Issues affecting psychologists as health care service providers in the national health insurance debate: 1. *Independent Practitioner, 13(1)*, 30–38.

Basmajian, J. V. (1989). *Biofeedback principles and practice for clinicians* (pp. 317–318). Baltimore, MD: Williams & Wilkins.

Beckman-Brindley, S., DeMaio, T., Hersch, L., Koch-Sheras, P., Sheras, P., & Stewart, H. (1993). *Mental health care for Virginians: Combining quality and cost containment: A position paper of Virginians for Mental Health Equity: Health care for Virginians*. Unpublished manuscript.

Bennett, J. M. (1994, May). *Assessment, diagnosis, and effective treatment planning: Working successfully within managed care systems*. Presentation for the Consortia for Clinical Excellence, Charlottesville, VA.

Berney, K. (1992, October). Carve-outs: The next generation. *Risk and Insurance*, 37–40.

Bianchi, S., Edmiston, R., & Strasser, A. (1988, July). Directing cost controls with medical necessity. *Business and Health*, 22–27.

Frank, R., Salkever, D., & Sharfstein, S. (1991, Summer). A new look at rising mental health costs. *Health Affairs*, 116–123.

Frank, R. G. (1994, August). *Health care reform and rehabilitation in health care settings: An update from the Indianapolis conference*. Paper presented at the annual convention of the American Psychological Association, Los Angeles.

Glueckauf, R. L., Bond, G. R., McGrew, J., & Frank, R. G. (1994, summer). National conference on health care reform and psychological practice in rehabilitation and health care settings. *Rehabilitation Psychology News, 21*, 1–5.

Greene, J. L. (Ed.). (1994, September). States move to manage Medicaid: H.H.S. says there may be 45 demos by year-end 1994. *Managed Care Law Outlook*, 10–11.

Health care bargaining: Congress must forget that the point of health care reform is to reduce the number of people who are currently uninsured. (1994, August, 17). *The Washington Post*, p. A18.

Health Security Act, H. R. 103rd Cong., First Sess. (1993).

Hofschire, P., & Foote, R. C. (in press). Access to psychological services. In R. L. Glueckauf, R. G. Frank, G. R. Bond, & J. H. McGrew (Eds.), *Psychological practice in a changing health care system: Issues and new directions*. New York: Springer.

Mays, V. M., & Albee, G. W. (1992). Psychotherapy and ethnic minorities. In D. K. Friedheim (Ed.), *History of psychotherapy: A century of change* (pp. 65–107). Washington, DC: American Psychological Association.

O'Keeffe, J. (1996). The American health care system. In R. L. Glueckauf, R. G. Frank, G. R. Bond, & J. H. McGrew (Eds.), *Psychological practice in a changing health care system: Issues and new directions*. New York: Springer.

Richards, J. M., & Gottfredson, G. D. (1987). Geographic distribution of U.S. psychologists: A human ecological analysis. *American Psychologist, 33*, 1–99.

Santiago, J. M. (1992). The fate of mental health services in health care reform: 1. A system in crisis. *Hospital & Community Psychiatry, 43*, 1091–1094.

Spitzer, R. L. (1987). *Diagnostic and statistical manual of mental disorders*. Washington, DC: American Psychiatric Association.

VandenBos, G. R., Cummings, N. A., & DeLeon, P. H. (1992). Economic and environmental influences. In D. K. Friedheim (Ed.), *History of psychotherapy: A century of change* (pp. 65–107). Washington, DC: American Psychological Association.

VandenBos, G. R., & DeLeon, P. H. (1988). The use of psychotherapy to improve physical health. *Psychotherapy, 25*, 335–343.

Wiggins, J. (1994). Would you want your child to be a psychologist? *American Psychologist, 49*, 485–492.

Wallen, J. Providing culturally appropriate mental health services for minorities. Multicultural mental health and substance abuse services [Special issue]. *Journal of Mental Health Administration, 19*, 288–295.

Part IV

QUALITY AND OUTCOME ISSUES IN PSYCHOLOGY AND HEALTH CARE

Introduction

Barbara G. Melamed

Less than 20% of all medical interventions are estimated to be effective. Yet, there is optimism on the horizon. Although this statistic is distressing on the one hand, on the other hand, it points to the potential opportunities available for complementary approaches, such as psychological interventions. Between 60% and 90% of visits to physicians are prompted by conditions that are related to stress and are poorly treated by drugs and surgery (Cummings & VandenBos, 1981). Strong placebo effects have been estimated to yield up to 70% improvement in patients who believe in their physician, regardless of the proven efficacy of the intervention (Roberts, 1995). The major risk factors for most of the leading causes of death are behavioral (e.g., smoking, exercise, and how and what we eat). As psychologists, we must take ourselves, our scientific methodology, and our services more seriously. The evaluation of medical technology, including drugs, surgical procedures, and diagnostic tools, has been controlled by specialty boards and federal agencies. Psychological interventions have not warranted such scrutiny, perhaps because our technology is not seen as a threat to "safety." Is this because we do not make much of a difference, or because we have, in fact, undervalued or undermarketed our contributions? This section of the book clearly makes a strong case for the latter. In fact, many existing studies show cost-offsets (reduced use of other services) following psychological interventions (Cummings, Pallak, Dorken, & Benke, 1992). In such areas as prevention, compliance with medical and health regimens, and psychological factors affecting decision making and rehabilitation, the data presented in chapter 8 (O'Keeffe, Quittner, & Melamed) suggest that by integrating psychological and medical factors, patients achieve and maintain better health at less expense than by pursuing purely medical treatment.

The two chapters that follow in this section provide us with a road map by which we can venture into the "brave new world." O'Keeffe and colleagues (chapter 8) outline the requirements for proving clinical effectiveness by the Office of Technology Assessment and, to this end, recommend establishing an Academy of Health Psychologists within the APA to define clinical practice guidelines for psychologists in health care settings. This section specifies issues that still need to be addressed and examines how to disseminate our findings to consumers, policy makers, and colleagues from other health-related disciplines. In chapter 7, Dr. Robert Kaplan, an internationally well-respected health psychologist, provides us with a prototype for evaluating psychological and medical interventions on an equal footing. By defining quality-of-life adjustment by factors influencing both mortality and functioning, Kaplan provides a metric common to both physical and psychological disorders. In this modern time of increased longevity resulting from technological breakthroughs, such as transplanted organs and psychoneuroimmunology, we are simultaneously confronting escalating costs and greater variations in consumer demands and physician practices. The health care system is not working well, as attested to by the higher costs and marginal increases in life expectancy. This circumstance provides psychologists with a window of opportunity. Rather than viewing the access to health care (both as patients and providers) as a political, economic, or ethnic issue, we can view the rationing of resources through a multifaceted question: For whom does which procedure (intervention) work, for how long, and under what contextual circumstances? Moreover, for policy makers to be sure they are getting their money's worth, they require answers to the following questions:

1. Why should psychological outcomes be considered?
2. How much impact have psychological approaches made on the reduction of health care costs?
3. How effective are psychologists and their methods relative to less expensive providers of these or alternative services?
4. Can psychologists make contributions outside of the traditional mental health areas?

In addressing these questions, we will have, indeed, rediscovered what makes psychologists unique. Moreover, we have theory and scientific traditions to evaluate what we do and do not know. O'Keeffe and colleagues (chapter 8) conclude that outcomes research and quality assurance must be viewed as integrated processes. Three major methods are highlighted: (a) the use of instruments to measure health status and health outcomes; (b) the conduct of primary studies, such as clinical trials; and (c) the use of statistical methods, such as metaanalyses, to synthesize the results of primary studies to produce new insights or stronger conclusions.

Although suggesting that we maintain an interdisciplinary approach in learning about and delivering quality health care, O'Keeffe and colleagues recommend that we must first put our own house in order. By promoting an academy of psychologists who do, in fact, work in health care settings, estimated to be as many as 42% of all psychologists practicing in medical schools (see Caplan, Introduction to Part II), we can coordinate a database of how we function and how well we compare with alternative practices and providers. This should serve as a foundation for our own clinical practice guidelines. Because there are more than 1,500 guidelines promulgated by other interest groups, our guidelines must be framed so that they are compatible with the tools of other providers and assist in reducing costs and improving healthy functioning. This effort aims to not only provide the best care for the most people, but also maintains our visibility in the system, by disseminating our empirically based interventions to consumers and policy advocates alike.

In answering question 1 (Why psychological outcomes should be included?), it is clear that operationalizing health outcomes in terms of both psychological adjustment and physical functioning has led to better prediction of mortality and morbidity. For example, optimistic individuals are likely to live longer even with severe disease states compared with those who repress or express their frustration in a hostile manner (Williams & Williams, 1994). What these predispositions mean in terms of practicing healthy lifestyles, accessing supportive social networks, or conserving energy for needed tasks is still under investigation. In the words of Dr. Kaplan, it is critical to ''build a comprehensive theoretical model of health status.'' He suggests that in addition to understanding disease, we must understand illness, which is defined by patient's mobility and physical and social activity. O'Keeffe and colleagues further extend the concept of adjustment to the system level. Thus, psychological contributions must be viewed within a context that includes (a) community values with quality-of-life scores based on peer values, (b) current medical knowledge, and (c) the providers' capabilities in knowing how to use this technology. Even if the techniques and medications for enhancing quality of life exist, a skilled practitioner must know how to motivate the patient, family, and involved medical providers to initiate and maintain the new behavior by incorporating it into their lifestyle. Whether we are trying to get the patient to take a new drug, increase the amount of activity level, or change his or her diet, more than just knowledge about its effectiveness is required to make the changes. The family must find the changes compatible with their way of daily living.

Data now show with certainty that mental health problems escalate medical costs. However, primary care physicians seriously underdiagnose or fail to refer individuals with psychological conditions concurrent with physical problems. Psychological factors undoubtedly influence how patients manifest their physical conditions. Medical practices that ignore how psychiatric factors influence patient care and compromise adherence to medical regimens risk increased costs and ineffective treatments. The PRIME-MD, a timesaving and readily usable 8-minute interview protocol, has been developed for primary care physicians to assist in recognizing mental problems, and associated moods and behaviors (Spitzer et al., 1994). Psychologists must show that attention to these factors can lead to a more informed decision process regarding what type of service intervention is required and who can best maintain its effectiveness (e.g., patient, family supports, religious values, or health care network providers). To assume a primary care provider role, we must indicate how our intervention prevents entrance into the expensive remediative arm of health care or enhances use of the preventive branch. Thus, it may be far more economical to assure that a patient maintains health care behaviors (e.g., vaccinations, prophylactic dental visits, or screening for disease precursors of treatable or preventable problems) than to perform potentially unnecessary diagnostic or surgical procedures. For example, Kaplan uses controversial recommendations regarding mammography screening to illustrate how research can lead to economical decisions. However, emotional responses (e.g., denial) and failure to follow through on these recommendations remain problems with both legal and psychological ramifications.

Question 2 asks to what extent our services reduce costs. Recent findings have shown that the inclusion of mental health counseling for patients with disabling diseases, such as coronary heart disease, diabetes, and obstructive pulmonary diseases, have significantly reduced overall medical costs (Pallak, Cummings, Dorken, & Henke, 1994, 1995). Thus, it is not necessary to wait until the problems are diagnosable in terms of DSM IV criteria (American Psychiatric Association, 1994) before introducing psychological interventions. Psychologists have also identified high-risk groups, (e.g., persons at risk for heart disease or lung cancer) for whom behavioral factors have been shown to influence the age of onset and susceptibility to morbidity. The cost-effectiveness of our procedures may be enhanced by modifying our approaches to consider the differential effectiveness within these groups. Thus, individuals who smoke or abuse drugs, individuals with obesity, and those with sedentary lifestyles within disease groups may need to be approached more vigorously or paired with paraprofessionals (or family members) who can provide adjunctive supervision. We need to undertake more system analyses of relationships between patients, family members, health care providers, and institutions to promote better outcomes, as discussed in chapter 8. Measures of psychological functioning and perception of self-control need to be routinely evaluated as potential mediators of the therapeutic change processes.

A special section of a recent volume of *Health Psychology*, the official journal of Division 38 of the APA, devoted to the comorbidity of physical and mental disorders provides some useful insights into question 2. Conceptual models were presented that clearly link moods underlying mental disorders with physical disease parameters, such as biological pathways (sympathetic adrenal-medullary system and hypothalamic-pituitary-adrenocortical axis); behavioral pathways (health practices, inappropriate health care use, and poor adherence); and cognitive pathways (biased interpretation of physical stimuli) (Cohen & Rodriguez, 1995). The reciprocal pathways by which physical disease may result in emotions that interfere with patient's response to medications and treatment and may actually cause affective disturbances also are addressed. Prospective studies clearly link negative affect (especially depression and anxiety) to heart disease, asthma, diabetes, and mortality (Frasure-Smith, Lesperance, & Talafjic, 1995; Martin et al., 1995). Clinical studies have shown that cognitive factors, such as disease-specific panic-fear (catastrophizing about illness), can lead to overuse of expensive emergency room care, unnecessary hospitalization, and increased average length of stay. This adds in excess of $4 billion to the annual costs associated with the treatment of chronic obstructive lung diseases. Similarly, the cost of treatment for low back disability, which is approximately $16 billion annually, is escalating at a rate 14 times as fast as the population growth (Frymoyer, 1991). In prospective research examining predictors of the return to work within 6 months of an acute low back injury, Gatchel, Polatin, and Kinney (1995) showed that individuals with personality disorders or a tendency to somatize emotional problems were far more likely not to return to work. Thus, the progression from prechronicity to chronicity may be short-circuited by identifying individuals at most risk and developing treatments to facilitate their capacity to deal with the pain and discomfort and to prevent unnecessary surgical intervention.

Question 3 regarding comparative effectiveness with other alternative treatments has only just begun to be addressed. Seventy percent improvement is often noted in patients who believe in their provider (physician, psychologist, priest, or healer) or who follow nonmedical alternative treatments, even when there is no scientific validity (Roberts, 1995). This provides psychologists with an added obligation to apply our scientific method to understanding what influences the treatment process, including powerful placebo or nonspecific effects. As O'Keeffe and colleagues suggest, it may not be either/or but the combination of psychological treatments in conjunction with medical practices that is required to secure the most cost-effective approaches. In addition, even the most powerful pill will not prove effective if it sits in the bottle. For example, it has been long known that although hypertensive medications are effective in reducing the possibilities of stroke, as many as 85% of those who receive such prescriptions are noncompliant. Similarly, elderly depressed heart patients are more likely to fail to take their medication (Carney, Freedland, Eisen, & Jaffe, 1994). Furthermore, the failure of mothers to continue to give penicillin for the full course, once symptoms of fever and discomfort have abated, reduces the effective properties of the drug (Korsch & Negrete, 1972). In a longitudinal study of school-aged children with insulin-dependent diabetes mellitus, it was found that pervasive noncompliance with the health regimen accounts for greater metabolic instability than disease-specific factors of disease, duration, onset, or severity (Goldston, Kovacs, Obrosky, & Iyengar, 1995). Each of these cases of failure to comply with the medical solutions necessitated an understanding of the life-span relevance (old age, motherhood, and adolescence) and the failure to see a relationship between adherence and wellness.

In preparing for routine elective surgery, chemotherapy, or lumbar punctures, therapeutic packages that include attention to psychological stressors in the patient and family have led to reduced treatment time, fewer postoperative complications, and less time in the hospital, as discussed by O'Keeffe and colleagues. Thus, as Dr. Kaplan has noted, there is merit in examining both physical and psychological factors related to quality of well-being. His health policy model has been used in clinical trials evaluating a wide range of medical and surgical conditions and in studies involving decisions of health resource allocation. As these examples clearly show, we must abandon the artificial dichotomy between medical and psychological practice. In this regard, it is perhaps better to label psychological treatments as complementary, rather than alternative treatments.

In response to question 4 regarding the generalizability of psychological interventions outside of traditional mental health settings, Dr. Kaplan's model provides a common measurement unit for comparing both medical and mental health problems. The cost utility ratio demands that we look not only at the current costs but also at duration of wellness. In the innovative Oregon experiment described in Kaplan's chapter, the quality of adjustment measures used in determining reimbursement for Medicaid include such psychological symptoms as depression, pain, and anxiety. Thus, in quantifying effectiveness criteria, it is not the presence or absence of disease that should regulate health care expenditures, but the process by which individuals or communities maintain wellness functioning and propagate more societal resources.

Our world is rapidly expanding beyond our formerly narrow focus on the patient. No doubt we have a long way to travel to equip ourselves for this brave new world in which ethical and legal influences coexist with health decision making. For example, psychologists have shown that social support networks may enhance functioning or impede illness exacerbation. Thus, in the future the clinical trials must include not only the patient with the disease but also significant others (caretakers, religious mentors, employers, and coworkers) to provide the empirical database by which decisions concerning health resource allocations can be made. Our journey into the brave new world is just beginning.

REFERENCES

American Psychiatric Association. (1994). *Diagnostic and statistical manual of mental disorders* (4th ed.). Washington, DC: American Psychiatric Association.

Caplan, B. (1996). Introduction. In R. L. Glueckauf, R. G. Frank, G. R. Bond, & J. H. McGrew (Eds.), *Psychological practice in a changing health care system: Issues and new directions.* New York: Springer.

Carney, R. M., Freedland, S. A., Eisen, M. R., & Jaffe, A. S. (1994). Major depression and medication adherence in elderly patients with coronary artery disease. *Health Psychology, 14,* 88–90.

Cohen, S., & Rodriguez, M. (1995). Pathways linking psychological and physical disorders. *Health Psychology, 14,* 374–380.

Cummings, N. A., Pallak, M. S., Dorken, H., & Henke, C. J. (1992). *The impact of psychological services on medical utilization and costs* (HCFA Contract Number 11-C-98344/9 report). Baltimore, MD: Health Care Financing Administration.

Cummings, N. A., & VandenBos, G. R. (1981). The twenty year Kaiser-Permanente experience with psychotherapy and medical utilization: Implications for national health policy and national insurance. *Health Policy Quarterly, 1,* 59–87.

Frasure-Smith, N., Lesperance, F., & Talajic, M. (1995). The impact of negative emotions on prognosis following myocardial infarction: Is it more than depression? *Health Psychology, 14,* 388–398.

Frymoyer, J. (1991). Epidemiology of spinal disease. In T. G. Mayer, V. Mooney, & R. J. Gatchel (Eds.), *Contemporary conservative care for painful spinal disorders.* Philadelphia: Lea & Febiger.

Gatchel, R. J., Polatin, P., & Kinney, P. (in press). Predicting outcome of chronic back pain using clinical predictors of psychopathology: A prospective analysis. *Health Psychology.*

Goldston, D. B., Kovacs, M., Obrosky, D. S., & Iyengar, S. (1995). A longitudinal study of life events and metabolic control among youths with insulin dependent diabetes mellitus. *Health Psychology.*

Kaplan, R. M. (1996). Measuring health outcome for resource allocation. In R. L. Glueckauf, R. G. Frank, G. R. Bond, & J. H. McGrew (Eds.), *Psychological practice in a changing health care system: Issues and new directions.* New York: Springer.

Korsch, B. M., & Negrete, V. F. (1972). Doctor-patient communication. *Scientific American, 227,* 66–74.

Martin, L. R., Friedman, H. S., Tucker, J. S., Schwartz, J., Criqui, M. H., Wingard, D., & Tomlinson-Keasey, C. (in press). An archival prospective study of mental health and longevity. *Health Psychology.*

O'Keeffe, J., Quittner, A., & Melamed, B. G. (1996). Health outcomes consensus chapter. In R. L. Glueckauf, R. G. Frank, G. R. Bond, & J. H. McGrew (Eds.), *Psychological practice in a changing health care system: Issues and new directions.* New York: Springer.

Pallak, M. S., Cummings, N. A., Dorken, H., & Henke, C. J. (1994). Medical costs, Medicaid and managed mental health treatment: The Hawaii study. *Managed Care Quarterly, 2,* 64–70.

Pallak, M. S., Cummings, N. A., Dorken, H., & Henke, C. J. (1995). Effect of mental health treatment on medical costs. *Mind/Body Medicine, 1,* 7–12.

Roberts, N. H. (1995). The powerful placebo revisited: Magnitude of nonspecific effects. *Mind/Body Medicine, 1,* 35–44.

Spitzer, R. L., Williams, J., Kroenke, D., de Gruy III, F., Hahn, S., Brody, D., & Johnson, J. (1994). Utility of a new procedure for diagnosing mental disorders in primary care. *Journal of the American Medical Association, 272,* 1749–1756.

Williams, R. B. Jr., & Williams, V. (1994). *Anger kills.* New York: Wiley.

Chapter 7

Measuring Health Outcomes for Resource Allocation

Robert M. Kaplan

The Health Care debate has been naively conceptualized as a simple struggle between "good guys and bad guys." When President Clinton addressed Congress in September 1993, he suggested that the good guys were physicians, nurses, and hospitals. The bad people were lawyers, insurance companies, and holders of MBA degrees. I argue that the distinctions are not so clear. To place this in context, we must examine the problems in health care.

THE THREE As

Some people argue that there is no health care crisis. For example, some elected representatives have suggested that we need only minor changes in our current system. Yet their constituents frequently testify with challenging stories. For example, a family with a sick child may not be able to get health insurance because the illness is too expensive. Testimony on health care reform produced countless stories of families seriously distressed because they could not obtain health care. When Hillary Clinton headed the task force on health care reform, she received literally thousands of letters describing personal complications in relation to the health care system. One case was that of a family in Cleveland who had three daughters. The first was healthy, but the other two were born with serious chronic illnesses that required constant care. The parents were employed but were unable to purchase private health insurance. In a communication to Mrs. Clinton, the mother noted, "I finally realized how futile it was when I was talking to an insurance agent explaining our medical problems with our daughters and he looked at me and he said, you don't understand; we don't insure burning houses'' (from remarks by the president and the first lady, Health Care Forum, Century Village East, Deerfield Beach, Florida, distributed over Internet, March 24, 1994). There are countless cases in which people in need of help are unable to get basic services. Some of the issues in health care might be described by the ''Three As'' (Kaplan, 1993a, 1993b). The first is affordability—health care costs too much. A second issue is *access*. We have too many people who do not have a regular source of health care. They are either uninsured or underinsured. In addition, there are other barriers to health care. For example, some people do not have transportation. The third is *accountability*. Despite the fact that we spend more on health care than any other country, we have failed to document that the care that we provide makes a difference (Eddy, 1994; Kaplan, 1993b; Wennberg, 1994).

The three As are connected. For example, providing access to everyone will resolve the problem of access but may make the problem of affordability severer because costs will go up. To solve the health care crisis, the three As must be addressed simultaneously. We have to find ways to reimburse for services that make people better and not to use resources for services that do not work. Refusing to spend money on nonefficacious services may save enough money to expand access to basic care for people who were currently underinsured and uninsured. To explore these issues in more detail, each of the three As will be addressed briefly.

Affordability

Some people argue that we do not have to worry about expanding health care costs. Reinhardt (1993) has questioned whether we need to limit health care spending. Spending more money on health care in relation to other public services, such as education, defense, and so forth, may be our way of making resource allocation decisions. However, it is important to recognize that if we care about other services, we must also address the health care problem. As more resources are used for health care, fewer are available to improve schools, support a national defense, and so on.

The exponential growth in health care costs over the last 50 years is shown graphically in Figure 7.1. However, it is important to focus attention on the two right-hand bars of the figure. Health care costs have risen exponentially since 1940. Between 1990 and today, there has been substantial de facto health care reform. In the last few years, there have been significant reductions in hospital admissions and lengths of hospital stay.

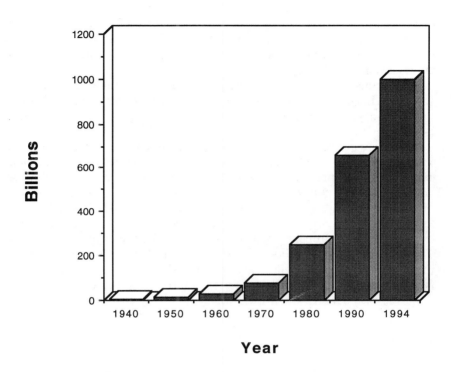

FIGURE 7.1 Costs of health care in the United States, 1940–1994.

Nevertheless, health care costs in the United States have risen an estimated $350 billion since 1990. In 1990, experts estimated that health care costs would reach $1 trillion by the turn of the century. Current estimates indicate that we may hit $1 trillion by 1997.

To put these expenditures in other terms, consider an agency like the National Heart Lung and Blood Institute, one of the best funded institutes in the National Institutes of Health. If we had capped our health care expenditures in 1990, the savings each day would pay for the entire National Heart Lung and Blood Institute for an entire year. As we spend more and more of our gross domestic product on health care, we have less for other sectors of the economy. In particular, the purchase of consumer goods may be slowed (Warshawsky, 1994). Yet the purchase of these goods drives the rest of the economy (Fuchs, 1990). So, for example, as our expenditures in health care have increased relative to other countries, our balance of trade has gone in the negative direction (Levit et al., 1994). As an increasing percentage of the economy is devoted to health care, the rest of the economy will be starved for capital, and there may be economic decline and a reduction in the standard of living (Warshawsky, 1994).

To summarize my first argument, we cannot continue to spend this way. We have to set some sort of expenditure ceiling. This will most likely be accomplished by government intervention or through a regulated competition.

In some ways our problems are not that different from other countries. We are spending about 14.5% of our gross domestic product on health care while most other countries are below 10%. However, no country can do all the things that they want to do in health care. All of them face difficult decisions. Rich countries may be able to set their allocation thresholds higher, but all countries face choices (Williams, 1988). For example, many European countries have formal policies to control costs. The United Kingdom accomplishes cost control through a government-run system with explicit policies on what services will be covered. The Netherlands restricts growth in health care to a fixed portion of the gross domestic product (Kirkman-Liff, 1991).

Access

Despite these high expenditures, the United States is unique among developed countries because we have large numbers of people who are uninsured or underinsured. An estimated 38 million people in the United States have no health insurance, and 58 million are uninsured for at least part of each year (Health Care Financing Administration, 1994). Most of the uninsured are employed, and the poor and minority group members are disproportionately represented among those without coverage.

Opportunity Cost.

Opportunity costs are the foregone opportunities that are surrendered as a result of using resources to support a particular decision. To put it in other terms, if we spend a lot of money in one sector of health care, we necessarily spend less money elsewhere. This problem is heightened by the tendency to follow a "rule of rescue." The rule of rescue, in the words of philosophers, is a moral obligation to provide rescue services whenever saving a life is a possibility (Hadorn, 1991). However, the decision to invest in rescue may necessarily mean two decisions have been made. With limited resources, a decision to perform an expensive liver transplantation surgery for one person often means giving up the opportunity to perform less expensive services for many people. Sometimes a liver transplant has extremely limited potential for producing a health benefit, while the preventive services that are neglected have substantial potential to help other people. Indeed, the U.S. health care system is rich with applications of the rule of rescue. Large investments in dramatic and often futile care have resulted in the unfunding or underfunding of substantial opportunities in primary care, mental health, and prevention. For example, the state of Illinois passed a 1985 bill that guaranteed reimbursement of up to $200,000 for any citizen who needed an organ transplant. At the same time, more than 60% of black children in Chicago's inner cities did not receive routine medical care and were not even immunized against common diseases, such as polio. In 1990, Florida's Governor Martinez committed $100,000 to a heroic attempt to save the life of a single child who had nearly drowned in a swimming pool accident. All experts agreed that the case was futile. While the governor received great acclaim for his compassion, thousands of Florida children were denied basic services through Florida's underfunded Medicaid program (Kitzhaber, 1990). When funds are directed toward rescue, prevention programs are typically the first victim of the revenue shortfall.

Cost Shifting.

Some members of our society feel that we should not care about the uninsured. They believe that the uninsured are typically poor people who do not take care of themselves and their failure to plan should not be our problem. However, it is not necessarily true that people without insurance do not get care. In fact, they do get health care by going to emergency rooms, but they are often unable to pay for their services. When a patient is unable to pay, the hospital still has to reimburse its nurses, it still has to support its pathology laboratories, and so forth. Someone also has to pay for the surgeons and other physicians.

It is not necessarily true that patients who are uninsured get free care. In fact, the costs are just shifted. When an uninsured patient comes to the hospital and cannot pay, his or her charges are shifted to insured patients. When the insured patients get charged, insurance rates go up. There are a whole series of shifts. As a result, charges in fancy suburban clinics, where most patients are insured, may be lower than they are in inner-city hospitals, where a high percentage of patients are uninsured.

The reason is that the people who are able to pay in inner-city hospitals are subsidizing a larger number of patients who are uninsured. A corollary is that insurance rates should be higher in areas of the country where there are high rates of people who are medically uninsured. In fact, this seems to be so. For example, in cities, such as Los Angeles and Miami, where the rates of medical insurance are low, charges to businesses for health insurance are higher than in cities, such as Minneapolis and Seattle, where the rates of uninsurance are lower (Kaplan, 1993b).

In summary, cost shifting suggests that costs are not avoided; they are just charged to someone else. However, the uninsured obtain services in a costly way, because they are often more seriously ill at entry to the system and are cared for inefficiently through emergency rooms. In Hawaii, providing universal coverage has actually decreased health care costs (Lewin & Sybinsky, 1993). The following sections explore the accountability problem in more detail. Specifically, it will be suggested that better accountability can contribute to the solution to the health policy crisis. Accountability is focused on using resources to make people healthier. By using resources more efficiently, it may be possible to achieve better health outcomes, to save money, and to use the savings to expand access.

Accountability

Health care must achieve greater accountability. Part of the problem in producing greater accountability has been that the health care system has not quantified its major product. The health status benefit of most of the services delivered by the system is rarely measured or reported.

To understand health outcomes, it is necessary to build a comprehensive theoretical model of health status. This model includes several components. The major aspects of the model include mortality (death) and morbidity (health-related quality of life). We have suggested elsewhere that diseases and disabilities are important for two reasons. First, illness may cause the life expectancy to be shortened. Second, illness may make life less desirable at times before death (health-related quality of life) (Kaplan & Anderson, 1988a, 1988b, 1990).

A GENERAL HEALTH POLICY MODEL (GHPM)

Over the last two decades, a group of investigators at the University of California, San Diego, has developed the GHPM. Central to the General

Health Policy Model is a general conceptualization of quality of life. The model separates aspects of health status and life quality into distinct components. These are life expectancy (mortality), functioning and symptoms (morbidity), preference for observed functional states (utility), and duration of stay in health states (prognosis).

Components of GHPM

Mortality.

A model of health outcomes necessarily includes a component for mortality. Indeed, many public health statistics focus exclusively on mortality through estimations of crude mortality rates, age-adjusted mortality rates, and infant mortality rates. Death is an important outcome that must be included in any comprehensive conceptualization of health.

Morbidity.

In addition to death, quality of life is also an important outcome. The GHPM considers functioning in three areas: mobility, physical activity, and social activity. Descriptions of the measures of these aspects of function are given in many different publications (Kaplan & Anderson, 1988a, 1988b). Most public health indicators are relatively insensitive to variations toward the well end of the continuum. Measures of infant mortality, to give an extreme example, ignore all individuals capable of reading this chapter because they have lived beyond 1 year following their births. Disability measures often ignore those in relatively well states. For example, the RAND Health Insurance Study reported that about 80% of the general populations have no dysfunction. Thus, they would estimate that 80% of the population is well. Our method asks about symptoms or problems in addition to behavioral dysfunction (Kaplan et al., 1976). In these studies, only about 12% of the general population report no symptoms on a particular day. In other words, health symptoms or problems are a common aspect of the human experience. Some might argue that symptoms are unimportant because they are subjective and unobservable. However, symptoms are highly correlated with the demand for medical services, expenditures on health care, and motivations to alter lifestyles. Thus, we believe that the quantification of symptoms is important.

Utility (Relative Importance).

Given that various components of morbidity and mortality can be tabulated, it is important to consider their relative importance. For example, it is possible to develop measures that detect minor symptoms. Yet, because these symptoms are measurable, it does not necessarily mean they are important. A patient may experience side effects of a medication but be willing to tolerate them because the side effects are less important than the probable benefit that would be obtained if the medication is consumed. Not all outcomes are equally important. A treatment in which 20 of 100 patients die is not equivalent to one in which 20 of 100 patients develop nausea. An important component of the GHPM attempts to scale the various health outcomes according to their relative importance. This exercise adds the "quality" dimensions to health status. In the preceding example, the relative importance of dying would be weighted more than developing nausea. The weighting is accomplished by rating all states on a quality continuum ranging from 0 (for dead) to 1.0 (for optimum functioning). These ratings are typically provided by independent judges who are representative of the general population (Kaplan et al., 1978). Using this system, it is possible to express the relative importance of states in relation to the life-death continuum. A point halfway on the scale (0.5) is regarded as halfway between optimum function and death. The quality-of-life weighting system has been described in several different publications (Kaplan et al., 1976, 1978, 1979). Although there are differences between cultures and religious groups on the definition of wellness, preferences for health states are remarkably constant across demographic and cultural groups (Kaplan, 1994)

Prognosis.

Another dimension of health status is the duration of a condition. A headache that lasts 1 hour is not equivalent to a headache that lasts 1 month. A cough that lasts 3 days is not equivalent to a cough that lasts 3 years. In considering the severity of illness, duration of the problem is central. As basic as this concept is, most contemporary models of health outcome measurement completely disregard the duration component. In the GHPM, the term *prognosis* refers to the probability of transition among health states over the course of time. In addition to consideration of duration of problems, the model considers the point at which the problem begins. A person may have no symptoms or dysfunction currently, but may have a high probability of health problems in the future. The prognosis component of the model takes these transitions into consideration and applies a discount rate for events that occur in the future. Discount rates are used to value resources and health outcomes differently if the onset is delayed as opposed to immediate. A headache that will begin a year from now may be less of a concern than a headache that will start immediately.

Quality of Well-Being Scale (QWB)

The QWB is one of several different approaches for computing quality-adjusted life years (QALY) (Kaplan & Anderson, 1988b). Using this method, patients are classified according to objective levels of functioning. These levels are represented by scales of mobility, physical activity, and social activity (see Table 7.1). In addition to classification into these observable levels of function, individuals are also classified by the symptom or problem that they found to be most undesirable (see Table 7.2). On any particular day, nearly 80% of the general population is optimally functional. However, fewer than half of the population experience no symptoms. Symptoms or problems may be severe, such as serious chest pain, or minor, such as having to take medication or adhering to a prescribed diet for health reasons.

Human value studies have been conducted to place the observable states of health and functioning onto a preference continuum for the desirability of various conditions, giving a ''quality'' rating between 0 for death and 1.0 for completely well. These weights are shown in Tables 7.1 and 7.2. A QALY is defined as the equivalent of a completely well year of life, or a year of life free of any symptoms, problems, or health-related disabilities. The well-life expectancy is the current life expectancy adjusted for diminished quality of life associated with dysfunctional states and the durations of stay in each state. It is possible to consider mortality, morbidity, and the preference weights for the various observable states of function. Table 7.3 gives formulas and an example of the calculation of the QWB for a patient with chronic lung disease. The model quantifies the health activity or treatment program in terms of the years that it produces or saves.

A mathematical model integrates components of the model to express outcomes in a common measurement unit. Using information on current functioning and duration, it is possible to express the health outcomes in terms of equivalents of well years of life. The model for point in time QWB is

QWB = 1   (observed morbidity × morbidity weight)
          (observed physical activity × physical activity weight)
          (observed social activity and social activity weight)
          (observed symptom/problem × symptom/problem weight)

The net cost/utility ratio is defined as

TABLE 7.1 Quality of Well-Being/General Health Policy Model: Elements and Calculating Formulas (Function Scales, With Step Definitions and Calculating Weights)

Step no.	Step definition	Weight
	Mobility Scale	
5	No limitations for health reasons	−.000
4	Did not drive a car, health related; did not ride in a car as usual for age (younger than 15 years), health related, or did not use public transportation, health related; or had or would have usedmore help than usual for age to use public transportation, health related	−.062
2	In hospital, health related	−.090
	Physical Activity Scale	
4	No limitations for health reasons	−.000
3	In wheelchair, moved or controlled movement of wheelchair without help from someone else; or had trouble or did not try to lift, stoop, bend over, or use stairs or inclines, health related; or limped, used a cane, crutches, or walker, health related; or had any other physical limitation in walking, or did not try to walk as far as or as fast as other the same age are able, health related	−.060
1	In wheelchair, did not move or control the movement of wheelchair without help from someone else, or in bed, chair, or couch for most or all of the day, health related	−.077
	Social Activity Scale	
5	No limitations for health reasons	−.000
4	Limited in other (e.g., recreational) role activity, health related	−.061
3	Limited in major (primary) role activity, health related	−.061
2	Performed no major role activity, health related, but did perform self-care activities	−.061
1	Performed no major role activity, health related, and did not perform or had more help than usual in performance of one or more self-care activities, health related	−.106

$$\frac{\text{Net cost}}{\text{Net QWB} \times \text{duration in years}} = \frac{\text{Cost of treatment} - \text{cost of alternative}}{[\text{QWB}_2 - \text{QWB}_1] \times \text{duration in years}}$$

Where QWB_2 and QWB_1 are measures of quality of well-being taken before and after treatment.

TABLE 7.2 Quality of Well-Being/General Health Policy Model: Symptom/Problem Complexes (CPX) With Calculating Weights

CPX No.	CPX Description	Weights
1	Death (not on respondent's card)	−.727
2	Loss of consciousness such as seizure (fits), fainting, or coma (out cold or knocked out)	−.407
3	Burn over large areas of face, body, arms, or legs	−.387
4	Pain, bleeding, itching, or discharge (drainage) from sexual organs—does not include normal menstrual (monthly) bleeding	−.349
5	Trouble learning, remembering, or thinking clearly	−.340
6	Any combination of one or more hands, feet, arms, or legs either missing, deformed (crooked), paralyzed (unable to move), or broken—includes wearing artificial limbs or braces	−.333
7	Pain, stiffness, weakness, numbness, or other discomfort in chest, stomach (including hernia or rupture), side, neck, back, hips, or any joints or hands, feet, arms, or legs	−.299
8	Pain, burning, bleeding, itching, or other difficulty with rectum, bowel movements, or urination (passing water)	−.292
9	Sick or upset stomach, vomiting or loose bowel movement, with or without chills, or aching all over	−.290
10	General tiredness, weakness, or weight loss	−.259
11	Cough, wheezing, or shortness of breath, *with* or *without* fever, chills, or aching all over	−.257
12	Spells of feeling, upset, being depressed, or of crying	−.257
13	Headache, or dizziness, or ringing in ears, or spells of feeling hot, nervous or shaky	−.244
14	Burning or itching rash on large areas of face, body, arms, or legs	−.240
15	Trouble talking, such as lisp, stuttering, hoarseness, or being unable to speak	−.237
16	Pain or discomfort in one or both eyes (such as burning or itching or any trouble seeing after correction	−.230
17	Overweight for age and height or skin defect of face, body, arms, or legs, such as scars, pimples, warts, bruises, or changes in color	−.188
18	Pain in ear, tooth, jaw throat, lips, tongue; several missing or crooked permanent teeth—includes wearing bridges or false teeth; stuffy, runny nose; or any trouble hearing—includes wearing a hearing aid	−.170
19	Taking medication or staying on a prescribed diet for health reasons	−.144
20	Wore eyeglasses or contact lenses	−.101
21	Breathing smog or unpleasant air	−.101
22	No symptoms or problem (not on respondent's card)	−.000
23	Standard symptom/problem	−.257
X24	Trouble sleeping	−.257
X25	Intoxication	−.257
X26	Problems with sexual interest or performance	−.257
X27	Excessive worry or anxiety	−.257

TABLE 7.3 Calculating Formulas and Example of QWB for Patient With Lung Disease

Calculating formulas

Formula 1. Point-in-time well-being score for an individual (W):

$$W = 1 + (CPXwt) + (MOBwt) + (PACwt) + (SACwt)$$

where "wt" is the preference-weighted measure for each factor, and CPX is symptom/ problem complex. For example, the W score for a person with the following description profile may be calculated for one day as follows:

CPX-11	Cough, wheezing or shortness of breath, with or without fever, chills, or aching all over	−.257
MOB-5	No limitations	−.000
PAC-1	In bed, chair, or couch for most or all of the day, health related	−.077
SAC-2	Performed no major role activity, health related but did perform self-care	−.061

$$W = 1 + (-.257) + (-.000) + (-.077) + (-.061) = .605$$

Formula 2. Well years (WY) as an output measure:

$$WY = [\text{No. of persons} \times (CPXwt + MOBwt + PACwt + SACwt) \times Time]$$

Consider, for example, a person who is in an objective state of functioning that is rated by community peers as 0.5 on a 0 to 1.0 scale. If the person remains in that state for 1 year, he or she would have lost the equivalent of one half of 1 year of life. Thus, a person limited in activities who requires a cane or walker to get around the community would be hypothetically rated at 0.50. If they remained in that state for an entire year, such an individual would lose the equivalent of one-half year of life. However, a person who has the flu may also be rated as 0.50. In this case, the illness might only last 3 days, and the total loss in well years might be $3/365 \times 0.50$, which is equal to 0.004 well years. This may not appear as significant an outcome as a permanent disability. But suppose that 5,000 people in a community get the flu. The well years lost would then be $5,000 \times 0.004$, which is equal to 20 years. Now suppose that a vaccination has become available and that the threat of the flu can be eliminated by vaccinating the 25,000 people in the community. The cost of the vaccine is $5 per person, or $125,000. The cost/utility of the program would be

$$\frac{\$125,000 \text{ (cost)}}{20 \text{ years (utility)}} = \$6,250/\text{well year}$$

Ideally, the outcomes are assessed in systematic clinical studies. For example, patients might be randomly assigned to a treatment or to a control group and followed at regular intervals. Well-designed studies take both outcome and duration into consideration and the benefit is shown in QALYs. Although the model does not depend on any particular experimental design, the weight given to a particular finding might be lower for nonsystematic experiments.

The GHPM has been used in a wide variety of population studies (Anderson et al., 1989; Erickson et al., 1989). In addition, the methods have been used in clinical trials and studies to evaluate therapeutic interventions in a wide range of medical and surgical conditions. These include chronic obstructive pulmonary disease (Kaplan et al., 1984), acquired immunodeficiency disorder (Kaplan et al., 1995), cystic fibrosis (Orenstein et al., 1989), diabetes mellitus (Kaplan et al., 1987), atrial fibrillation (Ganiats et al., 1993), lung transplantation (Squier et al., 1994), arthritis (Bombardier et al., 1986; Kaplan et al., 1988), cancer (Kaplan, 1993c), Alzheimer's disease (Kerner et al., 1996), Sinus disease (Hodgkin, 1994), and a wide variety of other conditions (Kaplan, 1993b). Further, the method has been used for health resource allocation modeling and has served as the basis for an innovative experiment on rationing of health care by the state of Oregon.

Is the Model Applicable to Mental Health?

Despite widespread interest in the model among practitioners in many different specialties, the concept of a QALY has received little attention in the mental health fields. We believe that this reflects the widespread belief that mental health and physical health outcomes are conceptually distinct. Ware and Sherbourne (1992) emphasized that mental and physical health are different constructs, and that attempts to measure them using a common measurement strategy is like comparing apples to oranges. We recognize the distinction between mental health and physical health outcomes, and acknowledge the need to measure the effects of treatment using different units. However, we also suggest that a common measurement strategy is required so that the productivity of mental and physical health providers can be compared directly.

Several years ago, Kaplan and Anderson (1988a) argued that there are many similarities in mental and physical health outcomes. The QWB system includes the basic dimensions of observable functioning, symptoms, and duration. Mental health problems, like physical health problems, can be represented by symptoms and disrupted role functioning. Consider some examples. Suppose that a patient has the primary symptom of a cough. If the cough does not disrupt role function, the QWB score might show a small deviation from 1.0. If the cough is more serious and keeps the person at home, the QWB score will be lower. If the cough is severe, it might limit the person to a hospital and may have serious disruptive effects on role functioning. This would necessitate an even lower QWB score. Coughs can be of different duration. A cough associated with an acute respiratory infection may have a serious impact on functioning that may last only a short period. This would be indicated by a minor deviation in well years. A chronic cough associated with obstructive lung disease would be associated with significant loss of QALY because duration is a major component of the calculation.

Now consider the case of a person with depression. Depression may be a symptom reported by a patient just as a cough is reported by other patients. Depression without disruption of role function would cause a minor variation of wellness. If the depression caused the person to stay at home, the QWB score would be lower. Severe depression might require the person to be in a hospital or special facility, and would result in a lower QWB score. Depressions, like coughs, are of different durations. Depression of long duration would cause the loss of more QALYs than would depression of short duration.

Some evidence supports the validity of the QWB in studies of mental health. One recent study evaluated the validity of the QWB as an outcome measure for older psychotic patients. Seventy-two psychotic patients and 28 matched controls from the San Diego Veterans Affairs Medical Center completed the QWB, the Structured Clinical Interview for the DSM-III-R patient version (SCID-P), Scales for the Assessment of Positive and Negative Symptoms (SAPS and SANS), and the Global Severity Index (GSI) from the Brief Symptom Inventory (BSI) were administered to all subjects. The QWB correlated with the SANS $-.52$ ($p<.001$) with the SAPS $-.57$ ($p<.001$) and the GSI $-.62$ ($p<.001$). Patients and controls were significantly different on the QWB. We also identified a linear relationship between QWB and severity of illness (as classified by the SANS and the SAPS). In addition, component scores of the QWB (i.e., mobility, physical activity, social activity, and worst symptom) were significantly lower among patients compared with controls and declined systematically as psychiatric symptoms increased (Patterson et al., 1996).

Using the GHPM, it is possible to estimate the benefit of any health care intervention in terms of the QALY the treatment produces. Suppose, for example, that a treatment for anxiety elevates patients from a level of .65 to a level of .75. Suppose, further, that this treatment benefit lasted for 1 year. Each patient would gain .1 QALY (.75 − .65 = .10 × 1 year = .1 QALY) for each year the benefit was observed. The treatment benefit would be expressed in terms of general QALY units. The productivity of the providers could be compared with providers in other areas of health care. All providers in health care use resources. Dividing the cost of a treatment by the QALY productivity provides the cost-utility ratio. Measuring mental health productivity in QALY units would allow the assessment of investments in mental health services to be compared directly with those in other aspects of health care.

In summary, the general QWB measure has evidence for validity in a variety of different specific diseases. It has been shown to be responsive to change, and its application has been found to be feasible in a wide variety of different populations. We will now turn to applications of the measure in clinical studies and public policy making.

Applications of the GHPM: Potential and Problems

Resource Allocation Decisions.

One of the advantages of the GHPM is that it allows for comparison between different types of services. QALY are a common metric, and all providers in the health care system have the common objectives of increasing length of life and improving quality of life. The general model allows evaluations of the production function for each of these specialties in comparison with the resources that they use. Allocating resources based on systematic data has been proposed by several different governments (Neumann & Johannesson, 1994). For example, the Australian government now requires evidence on effectiveness, as do a variety of European governments (Freund, Evans, Henry & Dittus, 1992). Canada has officially proposed the QALY as a basis for making decisions about which drugs will be purchased by the different provinces (Detsky, 1991). This approach has also been considered in the United Kingdom (Williams, 1988). Perhaps the most interesting experience in the United States has been in the state of Oregon. Oregon attempted to prioritize the cost/utility of different health services in an experiment with their Medicaid Program. One of the innovative features of the Oregon experiment was the attempt to put mental health services and other health services into the same prioritization. In an earlier version of the list, the cutoff for funding was roughly 600. At the top of the list were services, such as treatment for rumination disorder of infancy, treatment for delirium resulting from the use of psychoactive substance, or treatment for a single episode of major depression. In the middle of the list were services, such as psychotherapy for anxiety disorders and panic disorders, and treatment for conversion disorders in childhood. These services would clearly be funded by the program. However, at the bottom of the list were services, such as psychotherapy for antisocial personality disorder, psychotherapy for transsexualism, and psychotherapy for pica (see Table 7.4).

Black Hats and White Hats.

It is popular to conceptualize the health care debate as a fight between the good and bad people. For example, the American Medical Association funded a series of ads in *Time, Newsweek,* and elsewhere saying, "Who should make medical decisions, M.D.s or M.B.A.s?" All readers are supposed to know the answer: The former wear white hats and the latter wear black hats. However, this situation is somewhat more complicated. In the early days of the Medicare Program, physicians were reimbursed for essentially any service they wanted to deliver. Although this has changed somewhat in the last decade, most of the history of the Medicare Program provided physicians opportunities to bill for expensive services with little external review. There is overwhelming evidence that providing rich reimbursement for high expense medical treatments led to the overuse of some services (Hillman, 1994). For example, Figure 7.2 compares the rate of use for several services in the United States, Germany, and Canada. For a wide variety of services including magnetic resonance imaging, lithotrypses, radiation therapies, organ transplantations, cardiac catheterizations, and open heart surgeries, the United States performs more of these services than the other two countries. Yet despite this, we have no evidence that Americans live longer than people in other industrialized countries. In fact, our infant mortality rate is not lower, but it is somewhat higher than other Westernized countries.

Once again, the real challenge is linking the three As together. The U.S. system is expensive (affordability), and it is assumed that we are buying more services to obtain better outcomes. In fact, we have been unable to show that there has been greater value for the money we have spent (accountablility). Further, so much is spent on services, resources are not available to care for those who are less advantaged (access). For

TABLE 7.4 Examples of Mental Health Items From Oregon Integrated List

Rank	Item
76	Rumination Disorder of Infancy
99	Delirium from Psychoactive Substance Use
108	Major Depression, Single Episode
152	Youth Abuse of Hallucinogen, Amphetamine, or Alcohol
347	Anxiety Disorder
348	Panic Disorder
353	Conversion Disorder, Child
760	Antisocial Personality Disorder
761	Transsexualism
763	Pica

example, the costs of Medicaid in most states have escalated in recent years. Financially strapped states have had no choice but to restrict services for Medicaid recipients.

As mentioned earlier, one of the common arguments is that doctors (white hats) are offering too many unnecessary services, but it is really the fault of the lawyers (black hats). Doctors know that many of the services and tests are unnecessary, but, if they did not perform them, they would be at risk of being sued by lawyers. This practice is often called "defensive medicine" because the doctors are defending themselves against lawyers. Certainly, defensive medicine is practiced in the United States. However, there are also reasons to believe that financial interest in offering unnecessary services has also contributed to overuse. One example comes from a study by Hillman and colleagues (1990). This study considered the cost of an episode of care provided by family practitioners. This study was an observational analysis of patients cared for by family doctors who were carefully matched on a variety of different variables. The independent variable in the study was whether or not the doctor owned his or her own X-ray equipment. The results of the study are summarized in Figure 7.3. As the figure shows, the cost per episode of care for upper respiratory infections, pregnancy, back pain, or difficulty urinating, were all significantly higher for patients whose attending doctors owned their own X-ray machines (self-referred) in comparison with family doctors who referred their patients to radiologists to receive these exact same services. In these cases, the risk of being sued should have been the same. What differs is the pecuniary interest in using X-ray tests.

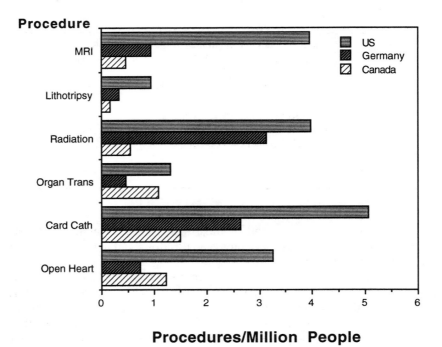

FIGURE 7.2 Rates of various medical procedures in the United States, Germany, and Canada.

Source: Adapted from *Health Care in the Nineties,* Blue Cross, 1990, p. 18—Canada data, 1989; German and U.S. data, 1987

   It is widely believed that malpractice lawsuits are a major component in total health care costs. Analyses suggest that malpractice costs are not a big piece of total health care expenditures. For example, malpractice premiums are about 1% of total health care costs. Thus, paying all practice premiums from some other source would reduce health care costs by only 1%. Providers often counterargue that, in fact, it is really not malpractice premiums that cause costs to be high. Instead, it is all the tests, some of which are unnecessary, that are required to protect oneself from litigation. Although experts disagree on the exact costs (Hudson, 1990), one estimate

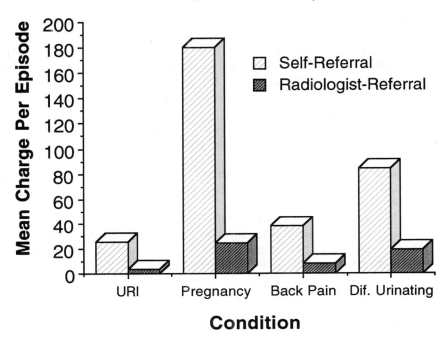

FIGURE 7.3 **Comparison of cost per episode of care for patients cared for by family physicians who owned their own X-ray equipment (self-referred) or those who referred to radiologists, for four diagnoses. (Adapted from Hillman et al., 1989)**

Source: From Hillman et al., *NEJM*, 1990.

is that for each $1 spent on malpractice premiums, $5 are spent on defensive medicine. Multiplying the estimated $9 billion spent on malpractice premiums by 5 yields $45 billion. Although, this is a substantial amount of money, it is still less than 5% of total health care costs. In contrast, consider expenditures on services for which there is no efficacy data. This has been analyzed by investigators at the RAND Corporation. They suggest that we are spending between $280 billion and $450 billion per year (adjusting for inflation) for services for which there is no evidence in the literature that the treatment works. In other words, as many as 30% to 50% of all health care services might be eliminated with no consequent effect on health status (Brook & Lohr, 1987). These procedures may benefit patients in theory, but there is no current documentation that they make people better.

The Gray Hats.

Many professional groups have an interest in health care reform. Literally, billions of dollars are at stake. Various professional organizations and public charities have prepared communications and testified on the value of their contribution. Psychology is not unlike other groups. APA, like other organizations, met with the first lady, who chaired the president's task force on health, to offer evidence of the value of psychology. Virtually every professional health care organization argued that their activities should not be neglected, but few organizations have considered the needs of their competitors or the needs of the nation as a whole.

To place this in prospective, consider the lobbying efforts of private nonprofit charities. These are particularly important because, by virtually every standard, these organizations would be considered the good guys (white hats). The Arthritis Foundation has publicly stated that health care reform must improve outcomes research, effectiveness research, and related activities. However, the Arthritis Foundation also argues that health care reform must make rheumatologic and orthopedic surgical care available regardless of economic considerations (Arthritis Foundation, 1992). In other words, they are arguing that rheumatologists and orthopedic surgeons should be reimbursed for everything that they do. The Arthritis Foundation provides a template for people to write to Congress and offers instructions for people to testify on their behalf. Here the foundation's statement becomes ambiguous. In their public statements, the foundation urges more outcomes research. However, in the template for testimony they suggest that the Clinton Plan overemphasizes outcomes, effectiveness, and clinical trials research. Instead, they argue that the plan does not recognize the cost-saving potential of basic science research. In particular, they worry about the support of molecular biology with the hope it will someday produce a total cure for arthritis.

The American Cancer Society (ACS) argued their guidelines for mammography every 1 to 2 years for women age 40 to 49 must be taken more seriously by providers and insurers. The organization takes issue with early statements by the Clinton administration health task force suggesting that screening begin at age 50. According to the ACS, the Clinton administration health task force proposals were based on "economic considerations rather than good science" (ACS, 1994). The ACS does acknowledge that there should be practice guidelines and emphasizes that these guidelines should be created by the ACS, not by any other group. The difficulty is that the ACS guidelines most clearly favor services offered by oncologists and other ACS-affiliated providers.

A few examples may clarify why the suggestions by these charitable organizations may be problematic. First, consider the Arthritis Foundation suggestion that we should reimburse orthopedic surgeons without challenge. Table 7.5 summarizes findings by Deyo and colleagues based on an observational trial of patients receiving spinal fusion for back pain. Spinal fusion is a complex surgical procedure that requires the fusion of vertebrae in the back. There has been a significant increase in the use of this procedure in recent years. The Deyo Study shows that, in comparison with patients not receiving spinal fusion, those undergoing the procedure are 4 times as likely to have a reoperation, twice likely to die, 2.2 times more likely to end up in a nursing home, and 5.8 times as likely to have a transfusion. In comparison with controls, those undergoing surgery are twice as likely to have complications. Because this is an observational study rather than a randomized trial the ordinary precautions in interpreting the data are necessary. For example, there is no assurance that those who received surgery had the same risk factors for bad outcomes as those who did not get surgery. Nevertheless, these results significantly challenge the idea that orthopedic surgeons should be reimbursed without question (Deyo et al., 1994).

The ACS argument about mammography is a particularly interesting one. It is emotionally arousing, and it does highlight some important problems in public decision making. Two viewpoints must be considered. First, a variety of advocacy groups have become almost exclusively focused on mammography as a center point for women's health policy. They are infuriated by suggestions that there be any limitation whatsoever in the use of this cancer screening procedure. Another constituency includes providers who have made significant profit providing these tests. As we will see shortly, there is controversy over whether a screening mammography should be offered to women less than 49 years of age who do not have other risk factors for breast cancer. The medical establishment's position is best exemplified in statements by Paul Goldfarb, who is the past president of the ACS of California. According to the *San Diego Union*, Dr. Goldfarb has stated, "I don't know if mammograms are effective under the age 50, but I don't see any reason not to have them. Nobody is going to get hurt by them" (*San Diego Union*, April 24, 1994). I will argue that, in fact, women are hurt by these policies. This is not because mammograms are dangerous. Rather, the problem is one of opportunity cost. Devoting resources to mammography is harmful when it detracts from the opportunity to use the resources for other services that may be necessary to enhance the health of other women.

Within these last few years, there has been an extensive campaign designed to increase the use of screening mammography. Virtually all magazines targeted for female readerships have produced articles on the need for greater use of mammography. *McCalls Magazine* entitled their

TABLE 7.5 Ratios of Complications for Patients Undergoing Spinal Fusion in Comparision With Controls

Complication	Ratio
Blood transfusion	5.8
Nursing home placement	2.2
Reoperation	4.0
Mortality (6 weeks)	2.0

Based on cohort study of 27,111 Medicare recipients of whom 1518 had fusions. (Adapted from Deyo et al., 1994.)

article: "Breast Cancer Alert" and the cover of *Self* displayed "Saving Your Breasts." These magazines are marketed to a younger readership. In most cases, it is suggested that failure to provide mammography for all women is a political scandal. The article went on to say that breast cancer is the leading cause of death for younger women, and that breast cancer is the most common cancer diagnosis for women between the ages of 35 and 50. The article suggested that younger women should insist on mammograms and demand further examinations when the mammograms are negative because denser breast tissue (characteristic of young women) may obscure the visualization of a tumor.

The difficulty is that scientific evidence tends not to support the use of screening mammography for women younger than age 50. Various countries around the world have examined the evidence. Virtually all countries, except Sweden, have recommended that screening mammography begin at age 50. The United States is somewhat unique because we have recommended screening mammography begin at age 35. Last year the ACS and the National Cancer Institute (NCI) were split in their opinions. The NCI, after reviewing the evidence, suggested that screening begin at age 50, and the ACS still insists that screening begin at age 35 to 40 (Fletcher, 1993).

Part of the controversy is in the way outcomes are examined. If we consider a narrow outcome, such as the number of tumors detected, more mammography will find more cases. However, if we consider an outcome, such as deaths resulting from breast cancer, screening women younger than age 50 appears to have little or no benefit. The reasons for this are complex and poorly understood, and it may be valuable to review them briefly.

Figure 7.4 shows the rates of breast cancer detected between 1970 and 1990. Figure 7.4 shows that there was an increase in cases of breast cancer

Breast Cancer Cases for White and Black Women: 1973-1987

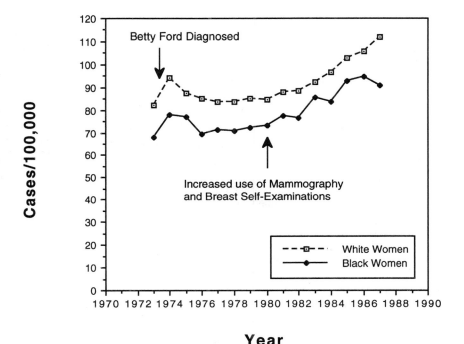

FIGURE 7.4 Breast cancer cases for White and Black women: 1973–1987.

for both White and Black women in the early 1970s. This coincides with the diagnosis of both Happy Rockefeller and Betty Ford. The diagnoses of breast cancer in these prominent women led to significantly more breast cancer screening. However, within a few years the rates of new cases declined. The 1980s were associated with a greater awareness of breast cancer and mass-scale mammography began in the mid-1980s. At that point, cases of breast cancer rose significantly.

If there is a public health benefit of early detection, then we should see a decrease in the rate of death due to breast cancer. Figure 7.5 summarizes the mortality experience during this same period. Interestingly, there has been no change at all in the rate of death because of breast cancer. In fact, the rate of death from breast cancer has been approximately the same over the last 50 years. Figure 7.5 marks the beginning of President Nixon's war on cancer, breakthroughs in surgical techniques, and the introduction of adjuvant chemotherapy for breast

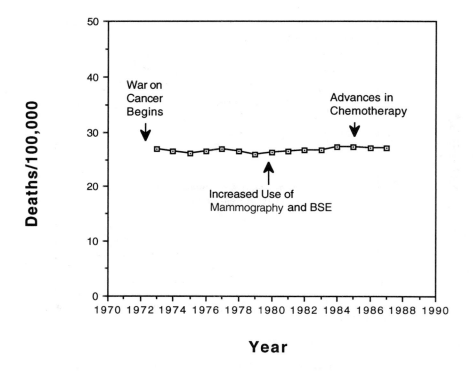

FIGURE 7.5 Change in breast cancer mortality, 1973–1987.

cancer. Each of these was announced as a major advance in breast cancer care. Nevertheless, the mortality rate associated with breast cancer has remained unchanged over this era.

The studies on breast cancer screening have also produced some confusion. There is no inconsistency across studies about the advantages of screening women past age 50. For post-menopausal women, the studies consistently show that breast cancer screening detects cases and results in significant reductions in mortality (Miller, 1994). The confusing aspect is for women 40 to 49 years of age. The most controversial study was the large-scale trial done in the Canadian National Breast Cancer Screening Study (Miller, 1993). In this randomized trial, women in the ages 40 to 49 years were more likely to die of breast cancer if they were regularly screened. A later reanalysis suggested that breast cancer screening may not have been harmful, but there was certainly no evidence that it was helpful.

We have performed a metaanalysis of these studies and shown that the risk ratio for women in the 40- to 49-year age bracket is higher than 1.0. In other words, averaged across studies, women screened regularly have a slightly (although not statistically significantly) *higher chance of dying* (Navarro & Kaplan, 1997, in press). Figure 7.6 summarizes an example of one of these studies. This is the Swedish Two-Countries Study, which compared the effect of screening for breast cancer by age. Risk ratios less than 1.0 imply a protective effect, whereas those greater than 1.0 suggest a damaging effect. Figure 7.6 shows that for women 50 to 59 and 60 to 69 years, there is a significant survival advantage of screening mammography. However, for women 40 to 49 years and those older than 70 years, there appears to be no advantage. In fact, eight out of eight studies in the literature fail to show any advantage of screening mammography for women 40 to 49 years of age. It is important to emphasize that these studies deal with asymptomatic women. Women with a family history of breast cancer or those who experience lumps are well advised to use mammography. Further, we do not want to suggest that these findings are conclusive. For example, it has been suggested that the failure to detect benefit for 40- to 49-year-old women might result from low power because of insufficient sample size or biases in older studies. However, most reviewers fail to find justification for population screening of women younger than the age of 50 (Kerikowski, Grady, Rubin, Sandrock, & Ernster, 1995).

The ACS is disturbed by the suggestions that women younger than age 50 do not need mammography. They argue that screening mammography is good for women. Clearly, it is also good for health care providers. But what about the argument that screening mammography will not hurt anybody? According to the opportunity cost argument, screening mammography may cause harm because it uses resources that could have been better spent elsewhere. Table 7.6 summarizes the cost per tumor detected for women of different ages. The most extreme case would involve screening women 20 years old. For 20-year-olds, the probability of having a breast tumor is about 1 in 100,000. If we assign mammography a cost of $100, approximately $10 million would be spent to detect a single case. Some may consider this expenditure would be worthwhile if it resulted in saving the life of that 20-year-old. However, the question of cost is mute. According to the available evidence, the woman would have no greater chance of survival than women who are unscreened. Considering the evidence, there is no reason to believe that screening before age 50 produces any significant public health benefit.

Analyses by Eddy (1989) also raise significant questions about the regular use of mammography. For example, a woman between ages 35

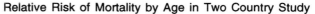

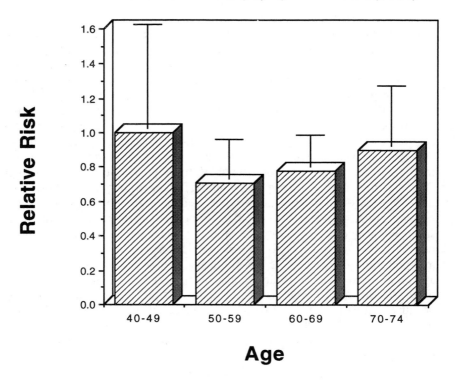

FIGURE 7.6 Relative risk of mortality by age in two-country study.

and 50 who obtains yearly screening mammography has either little or no probability of benefiting from the screening. However, in about one third of these women, findings will emerge that will require additional workup, including biopsy. These workups are not without consequence because they cause significant anxiety and can be costly.

Some of the implications of screening policies have recently been evaluated. Eddy (1994) used data from the Kaiser-Permanente Medical Group of Southern California. Currently, this HMO performs about 300,000 mammograms each year. About one half of these mammograms are completed on women between the ages 50 and 75 years, and about 45% are done for women younger than 50 years. The remaining 5% are done for women who are older than 75 years. Among the population of women that Kaiser serves, mammograms are given to about 22% of the women between the ages of 30 and 40 years, 60% of women between

TABLE 7.6 Cost per Tumor Detected by Age

Age (years)	Cost/Tumor
20	10,000,000
30	416,66 6
40	112,000
50	54,000
60	38,167
70	31,645

(Adapted from Kaplan, 1993a.)

40 and 50 years, and 69% of women between 50 to 75 years. In addition, Kaiser screens about 57% of the women between 75 and 85 years.

Using computer simulation, Eddy estimated that the current policy will prevent approximately 909 women from dying of breast cancer by the year 2010 at a cost of $707 million. There are alternative uses of the mammogram budget. One policy might be to discourage strongly the use of mammography for women younger than 50 years and older than 75 years. Instead, the policy might aggressively recruit women for mammography between ages 50 and 75 years, and those with risk factors for breast cancer (Eddy, 1994). In the 1990 National Health Interview Survey, less than 40% of women older than 50 years report screening mammography in the last year. An aggressive education program might significantly increase use of mammography in this group. Eddy (1994) estimated that if this program were successful in attracting 95% of the women in the 50- to 75-year age group, the number of breast cancer deaths prevented would increase to 1206 from 909 (a net increase in 297 lives). Further, the program would cost $210 million less than the current program. In other words, a cost-saving maneuver might result in about a 33% reduction in breast cancer deaths.

There could be biases in the studies. For example, let us assume that we are incorrect about the lack of benefit of mammography for younger women. Considering the most optimistic studies in the literature, screening mammography may reduce breast cancer mortality by 13% for women younger than 50 years of age (Nystrom et al., 1993). In Eddy's analysis, this would mean that the screening program would prevent 1045 premature deaths instead of 909. However, this is still significantly short of the 1206 deaths prevented by an age-targeted screening program. On the basis of a detailed review, of the literature, a group of policy analysts from the

RAND Corporation suggested that basic benefit packages in health insurance include screening mammography only for women 50 to 69 years of age (Kattlove, Liberate, Keeler, & Brook, 1995).

Opportunities Costs in the Mammography Example.

The real consequences of screening all women may accrue to the pool of women who cannot afford services. An estimated 17% of the U.S. population do not have health insurance. Today, public programs, such as Medicaid, cannot afford to support basic services for large numbers of people. In part, this results because public funds have been used to support some unnecessary services. Restricting the use of unnecessary services will free resources that could be used by others who are seriously in need of basic health care.

There are many potential alternative uses of the funds. For example, in a program like Kaiser of Southern California, restriction of mammograpy to women between the ages of 50 to 74 would save about $300 million each year (Eddy, 1994). What could be done with the savings? It is important to emphasize that many programs are not currently available within systems, such as Kaiser. For example, Eddy's analysis estimates that antismoking education programs for pregnant women may add 3,700 years of life that would have been lost to tobacco-related diseases. Other areas in which prevention programs could improve health status and prevent premature death include immunizations for children, prenatal care, and programs to reduce risk factors for cardiovascular diseases that kill more than 300 per 100,000 American women each year and remains the most common cause of death for both men and women in the United States (U.S. Department of Health and Human Services, 1991). These programs could be funded from the savings that would accrue from more effectively targeted mammography screening. The issue is not only to save money but also to use it more wisely (Navarro & Kaplan, 1997, in press).

CONCLUSION

Problems in health care are interconnected. Some of the problems might be characterized by the three words beginning with *A*. *Affordability* is linked to *access*, because creating greater access will use more resources. *Accountability* may help resolve some of these problems, because much of what makes health care unaffordable is the use of resources on services that provide little or no benefit. By changing reimbursement patterns to emphasize value for money, we may save enough to significantly expand access without raising cost.

Because of the growing expense of health care, there are significant consequences of not doing anything. Health care reform advocates must attend to all parts of the problem. The opportunity cost problem emphasizes that decisions necessarily involve choices between competing alternatives. Psychology is part of a larger health care network. A decision to reimburse psychologists for their efforts may displace the opportunity to spend resources on other services. If we allow orthopedic surgeons to be reimbursed for whatever they do, there may be little money left to provide mental health services. At some level, we are all part of the same system.

Competition for health care resources will require mental health providers to compete with other health care professionals. A general conceptualization of health outcome will allow direct comparisons between the productivity of mental health providers and the productivity of other health care providers.

REFERENCES

American Cancer Society. (1994). American Cancer Society Position: Clinton Health Reform Plan. New York: American Cancer Society.

Anderson, J. P., Kaplan, R. M., Berry, C. C., Bush, J. W., & Rumbaut, R. G. (1989). Interday reliability of function assessment for a health status measure: The Quality of Well-Being scale. *Medical Care, 27*, 1076–1083.

Arthritis Foundation. (1992). *Briefing paper for government affairs: Reforming access to health care.* Atlanta: Arthritis Foundation.

Bombardier, C., Ware, J., Russell, I. J., et al. (1986). Auranofin therapy and quality of life for patients with rheumatoid arthritis: Results of a multicenter trial. *American Journal of Medicine, 81*, 565–578.

Brook, R. H., & Lohr, K. (1986). Will we need to ration effective health care? *Issues in Science and Technology, 3*, 68–77.

Detsky, A. (1991). Guidelines for economic analysis of pharmaceutical products. Ontario Ministry of Health. Toronto: Drug Programme Branch, Ministry of Health.

Deyo, R. A., Ciol, M. A., Cherkin, D. C., Loeser, J. D., & Bigos, S. J. (1993). Lumbar spinal fusion: A cohort study of complications, reoperations, and resource use in the Medicare population. *Spine, 18*, 1463–1470.

Eddy, D. M. (1994). Clinical decision making: From theory to practice. Rationing resources while improving quality: How to get more for less. *Journal of the American Medical Association, 272*, 817–824.

Eddy, D. M. (1989). Screening for Breast Cancer, *Annals of Internal Medicine, 111*, 389–399.

Erickson, P., Kendall, E. A., Anderson, J. P., & Kaplan, R. M. (1989). Using composite health status measures to assess the nation's health. *Medical Care, 27* (Suppl. 3), S66–S76.

Fletcher, S. W., Black, W., Harris, R., Rimer, B. K., & Shapiro, S. (1993). Report of the International Workshop on Screening for Breast Cancer. *Journal of the National Cancer Institute, 85*, 1644–1656.

Freund, D. A., Evans, D., Henry, D., & Dittus, R. (1992). Implications of the Australian guidelines for the United States. *Health Affairs, 11*, 202–206.

Fuchs, V. R. (1990). The health sector's share of the gross national product. *Science, 247*, 534–538.

Ganiats, T. G., Palinkas, L. A., & Kaplan, R. M. (1992). Comparison of Quality of Well-being scale and functional status index in patients with atrial fibrillation. *Medical Care, 30*, 958–964.

Hadorn, D. C. (1991). Setting health care priorities in Oregon: Cost-effectiveness meets the rule of rescue. *Journal of the American Medical Association, 265*, 2218–2225.

Health Care Financing Administration. (1994). *Office of the Actuary report.* Washington, DC: US Government Printing Office.

Hillman, B. J. (1994). New imaging technology and cost containment. *American Journal of Roentgenology, 162*, 503–506.

Hillman, B. J., Joseph, C. A., Mabry, M. R., Sunshine, J. H., Kennedy, S. D., & Noether, M. (1990). Frequency and costs of diagnostic imaging in office practice: A comparison of self-referring and radiologist-referring physicians. *New England Journal of Medicine, 323*, 1604–1608.

Hodgkin, P. S. (1994). Health impact of endoscopic sinus surgery assessed by the Quality of Well-Being (QWB) Scale. Unpublished paper, University of California, San Diego.

Hudson, T. (1990). Experts disagree over the cost of defensive medicine. *Hospitals, 64*, 74.

Kaplan, R. M. (1993a). Application of a general health policy model in the American health care crisis. *Journal of the Royal Society of Medicine, 86*, 277–281.

Kaplan, R. M. (1993b). *Hippocratic predicament: Affordability, access, and accountability in health care.* San Diego: Academic Press.

Kaplan, R. M. (1993c). Quality of Life Assessment for Cost/Utility Studies in Cancer. *Cancer Treatment Reviews, 19* (Suppl. A), 85–96.

Kaplan, R. M., & Anderson, J. P. (1988a). A general health policy model: Update and applications. *Health Services Research, 23*, 203–234.

Kaplan, R. M., & Anderson, J. P. (1988b). The Quality of Well-Being Scale: Rationale for a single quality of life index. In S. R. Walker & R. Rosser

(Eds.), *Quality of life: Assessment and application* (pp. 51–77). London: MTP Press.

Kaplan, R. M., & Anderson, J. P. (1990). An integrated approach to quality of life assessment: The general health policy model. In B. Spilker (Ed.), *Quality of life in clinical studies* (pp. 131–149). New York: Raven.

Kaplan, R. M., Anderson, J. P., Patterson, T. L., McCutchan, J. A., Weinrich, J. D., Heaton, R. H., Atkinson, J. H., Thal, L., Chandler, J., & Grant, I. (1995). Validity of the Quality of Well-Being Scale for Persons with human immunodeficiency virus infection. *Psychosomatic Medicine, 57,* 138–147.

Kaplan, R. M., Atkins, C. J., & Timms, R. (1984). Validity of a quality of well-being scale as an outcome measure in chronic obstructive pulmonary disease. *Journal of Chronic Diseases, 37,* 85–95.

Kaplan, R. M., Bush, J. W., & Berry, C. C. (1978). The reliability, stability, and generalizability of a health status index (pp. 704–709). *Proceedings of the American Statistical Association, Social Status Section.* Washington DC.Kaplan, R. M., Bush, J. W., & Berry, C. C. (1979). Health Status Index: Category rating versus magnitude estimation for measuring levels of well-being. *Medical Care, 17,* 501–525.

Kaplan, R. M., Bush, J. W., & Berry, C. C. (1976). Health status: Types of validity and the index of well-being. *Health Services Research, 11,* 478–507.

Kaplan, R. M., Hartwell, S. L., Wilson, D. K., & Wallace, J. P. (1987). Effects of diet and exercise interventions on control and quality of life in non-insulin-dependent diabetes mellitus. *Journal of General Internal Medicine, 2,* 220–228.

Kaplan, R. M., Kozin, F., & Anderson, J.P. (1988). Measuring quality of life in arthritis patients (including discussion of a general health-decision model). *Quality of Life and Cardiovascular Care, 4,* 131–139.

Kattlove, H., Alessandro, L., Keeler, E., & Brook, R. H. (1995). Benefits and costs of screening and treatment for early breast cancer. *Journal of the American Medical Association, 273,* 142–148.

Kerlikowske, K., Grady, D., Rubin, S. M., Sandrock, C., & Ernster, V. L. (1995). Efficacy of screening mammography: A meta-analysis. *Journal of the American Medical Association, 273,* 149–154.

Kerner, D., Patterson, T. L., & Kaplan, R. M. (1996). Validity of the Quality of Well-being Scale in Alzheimer's disease. Manuscript submitted for publication.

Kirkman-Liff, B. L. (1991). Health insurance values and implementation in The Netherlands and the Federal Republic of Germany: An alternative path to universal coverage. *Journal of the American Medical Association, 265,* 2496–2502.

Kitzhaber, J. (1990). The Oregon Basic Health Services Act. Salem: Oregon State Senate.

Levit, K. R., Cowan, C. A., Lazenby, H. C., McDonnell, P. A., Sensenig, A. L., Stiller, J. M., & Won, D. K. (1994). National health spending trends, 1960–1993. *Health Affairs*, *13*, 14–31.

Lewin, J. C., & Sybinsky, P. A. (1993). Hawaii's employer mandate and its contribution to universal access. *Journal of the American Medical Association*, *269*, 2538–2543.

Miller, A. B. (1993). Canadian National Breast Screening Study: Public health implications. *Canadian Journal of Public Health*. (Revue Canadienne de Sante Publique), *84*, 14–16.

Miller, A. B. (1994). Mammography screening guidelines for women 40 to 49 and over 65 years old. *Annals of Epidemiology*, *4*, 96–101.

Navarro, A. M., & Kaplan, R. M. (1997, in press). Mammography screening: Prospects and Opportunity Costs. *Women and Health*.

Neumann, P. J., & Johannesson, M. (1994). From principle to public policy: Using cost-effectiveness analysis. *Health Affairs*, *13(3)*, 206–221.

Nystrom, L., Rutqvist, L. E., Wall, S., Lindgren, A., Lindqvist, M., Ryden, S., Andersson, I., Bjurstam, N., Fagerberg, G., Frisell, J., et al. (1993). Breast cancer screening with mammography: Overview of Swedish randomised trials. *Lancet*, *341*, 973–978.

Orenstein, D. M., Nixon, P. A., Ross, E. A., & Kaplan, R. M. (1989). The quality of of well-being in cystic fibrosis: 1. *95*, 344–347.

Patterson, T. L., Kaplan, R. M., Grant, I., Semple, S. J., Moscona, S., Koch, W. L., Harris, M. J., & Jeste, D. V. (1996, in press). Quality of Well-being in late-life psychosis. *Psychiatry Research*.

Reinhardt, U. E. (1993). Do global budgets make sense for the U.S. health system? *Internist*, *34*, 9–11.

Squier, H., Kaplan, R. M., Ries, A. L., Prewitt, L. M., Smith, C. M., Kriett, J. M., & Jamieson, S. W. (1995). Quality of well-being predicts survival in lung transplantation candidates. *American Journal of Respiratory and Critical Care Medicine*, *152*, 2032–2036.

U.S. Department of Health and Human Services, Public Health Service. (1991). Healthy people 2000: National health promotion and disease prevention objectives (DHHS publication No. [PHS] 91-50213). Washington, DC: US Government Printing Office.

Ware, J. E., & Sherbourne, C. D. (1992). The MOS 36-item short-form health survey (SF-36): Conceptual framework and items selection. *Medical Care*, *30*, 473–483.

Wenneberg, J. E. (1994). Health care reform and professionalism. *Inquiry, 31*, 296–302.

Warshawsky, M. J. (1994). Projections of health care expenditures as a share of the GDP: Actuarial and macroeconomic approaches. *Health Services Research, 29*, 293–313.

Williams, A. (1988). The importance of quality of life in policy decisions. In S. Walker and R. Rosser (Eds.), *Quality of life: assessment and application* (pp. 279–290). London: MTP Press.

Chapter 8

Quality and Outcome Indicators

Janet O'Keeffe, Alexandra L. Quittner, and Barbara Melamed

Concerns about health care outcomes have a long history, going back at least to the early 1900s when a Boston surgeon stated that improving the quality of medical care would require a detailed documentation of the long-term outcomes of various treatments (Neuhauser, 1990). More recently, the tremendous growth in new medical technologies with their attendant high costs, coupled with large variations in practice patterns among physicians, have led to increased concerns about both the quality and cost of health care interventions. In both the public and the private sector, third-party insurers are increasingly relying on assessments of treatment efficacy to make decisions about coverage (U.S. Office of Technology Assessment [OTA], 1994).

Given the projected increases in the cost of health care, there is likely to be increased interest in determining which health care interventions achieve not only effective outcomes but also cost-effective outcomes. Because this information will be used to influence many components of our health care system, from individual practice patterns to reimbursement policies, it is essential that psychologists become more knowledgeable about activities in this area.

This chapter provides an overview of a framework for research and other activities aimed at increasing the benefits and the economic value of health care. This framework is drawn from the recent report by the OTA on identifying health care technologies that work (OTA, 1994). Although the research reviewed in the OTA report focuses primarily on physician-initiated interventions, the question the report seeks to answer—how can we identify health care interventions that work—has enormous relevance and major implications for psychological practice. The chapter closes with recommendations for the professional involvement of psychologists in efforts to document the effectiveness and cost-effectiveness of psychological services.

SUMMARY OF CONSENSUS STATEMENT BASED ON CONFERENCE DISCUSSIONS

The discussion groups that dealt with the topic of quality and outcomes indicators recognized at the outset that, although outcomes research and quality assurance activities are often treated as separate fields of endeavor, their overall purpose is to assure the effectiveness and appropriateness of care, and to identify the lowest cost care that produces the highest quality outcome. There was considerable concern that some efforts to contain costs, such as managed care practices in the mental health field, might have a negative impact on the quality of care in some instances. However, there was general agreement that cost concerns warranted further research on treatment outcomes, and that clear indicators are needed for the type, duration, and intensity of treatments. Additionally, the groups agreed that psychologists—as part of the health care system—need to become knowledgeable about outcomes research and its increasingly important role in rationalizing treatment decisions and justifying reimbursement for services.

Another area of consensus was that appropriate psychosocial indicators should be used to measure health outcomes and quality of care. The groups did not discuss quality indicators for health plans and health delivery systems, but focused instead on indicators for measuring the outcomes of specific treatments. There was general concern that indicators currently used or being developed might fail to measure important dimensions of health and well-being, particularly the concept of ''functioning,'' including physical, mental, and emotional function. The importance of mental and emotional factors was emphasized because of the role they play in determining health-related behaviors, in increasing vulnerability to various physical illnesses, and influencing treatment compliance. There was also strong agreement that the functioning of an individual's informal support system should be considered when appropriate, particularly as it relates to an individual's ability to deal with the demands of a serious illness or permanent disability.

WHAT ARE OUTCOMES RESEARCH AND QUALITY ASSURANCE ACTIVITIES?

The OTA report (1994) notes that the many and varied uses of the term *outcomes research* has caused confusion among both policy makers and the public. One area of confusion is

> between activities to improve the quality of care and those primarily aimed at identifying and improving its effectiveness. Although the concepts of quality and effectiveness are closely related—both are aimed at making health care "work" better—they are not identical. Activities to improve *quality* generally focus on improving the process by which an activity is performed, or the capabilities of those performing it, in order to improve outcomes. In contrast, research to investigate *effectiveness* focuses on what outcomes are associated with a given technology (or clinical management strategy, or any other health care intervention), and whether and under what circumstances that technology is better than alternatives. The relative effectiveness of a technology does indeed depend in part on how well providers perform it. Policy interventions to address problems in the quality of care, however, may be different from those interventions that address the overall effectiveness of care. (p. 123)

For example, the quality of care delivered by a particular HMO may be measured by such indicators as the number of preschoolers who are fully immunized, the number of pregnant women who receive prenatal care, and reductions in the number of preventable hospitalizations for childhood asthma. Research and policy interventions to correct deficits in these areas would likely address process variables in the delivery of care and outreach services; for example, the type of administrative mechanisms aimed at assuring that HMO members with children are not only aware of the need for immunizations but are encouraged to have their children immunized according to the recommended schedule. In contrast, research seeking to evaluate the effectiveness of a health care technology or intervention, for example, a new drug, will focus on efficacy and safety (i.e., whether it provides a health benefit that outweighs any attendant risks), a crucial component of quality care (OTA, 1994).

At the systems level, improvements in the quality of health care can be achieved through the acquisition, dissemination, and application of knowledge about which interventions work better than others, for which patients, and under which circumstances. OTA (1994) identifies four overlapping components of this knowledge: the efficacy and safety of an intervention, the effectiveness of an intervention, the cost-effectiveness of an intervention, and the overall impact of an intervention. A description of each follows.

Efficacy and Safety

The efficacy and safety of a given health care intervention is determined on the basis of whether it can improve people's health *under ideal circumstances* and does not pose an unacceptable level of risk for the person being treated (OTA, 1994). Although there is considerable regulation and testing of certain interventions, such as drugs and medical devices, most health interventions are not similarly evaluated. In fact, it is estimated that only 10% to 20% of interventions have ever been formally evaluated for safety and efficacy (Eddy, 1992; White, 1968). This is due to several factors. First, much of medical practice predates the use of rigorous testing for efficacy. Randomized, controlled trials have been widely used only since the 1970s. Second, apart from drugs and medical devices, there are no legal requirements for most newly introduced interventions to demonstrate their efficacy. The OTA report (1994, p. 21) notes that "therapies such as psychological counseling and surgical procedures are subject to no regulatory requirements at all." Third, interventions are frequently used in circumstances that are different from those in which efficacy was first demonstrated (e.g., the use of drugs approved for a specific condition to treat other unrelated conditions, often termed "off-label" uses) (OTA, 1994).

Safety concerns are mostly restricted to the use of drugs and devices used in invasive surgical procedures. Although the safety of psychological services is not generally a concern, the clinical practice guidelines recently published by the Agency for Health Care Policy and Research (1993, p. 25) list several disadvantages of using psychotherapy *alone* to treat major depressive disorders. The concern expressed in the guidelines is that because there is insufficient research showing the effectiveness of psychotherapy alone, the patient may not only fail to improve, but may deteriorate during expensive treatments, whereas the patient may have improved if given medications. Although the safety of psychological services is rarely, if ever, a concern for third-party payers and consumers, their efficacy is.

Many psychologists believe that the lack of parity for insurance coverage of psychological services is evidence of the application of a different standard of proof of efficacy than is applied to medical interventions. Although this may be true to some extent, the lack of parity in coverage for mental health services is related to several factors, including a lack

of understanding about mental disorders and an unwillingness by employers to pay for more comprehensive coverage for their employees. Convention also plays a major role, in that when health insurance was first
developed in the 1930s, it covered only hospital and physician services.
Although psychological treatments have been available for decades, insurance coverage for mental health and other nonphysician services is a
relatively recent development, brought about primarily by state legislation
mandating insurers to cover particular services. As the cost of health care
continues to grow, insurers and other third-party payers are requiring that
effectiveness be shown before they cover ''new'' services.

Effectiveness

Whereas efficacy is concerned with the performance of a given health
care intervention under ideal circumstances in controlled settings, effectiveness is concerned with whether an intervention will generally improve
health under ordinary circumstances and in ordinary settings. Effectiveness
research is aimed at "identifying effective care and developing and refin-
ing methods to support the identification of effective care." The concept
of effectiveness includes a determination of both a given effect and whether
an intervention is more effective than alternatives (comparative effectiveness) (OTA, 1994).

There are three major methods for measuring the effect of a given
intervention: (a) the use of instruments to measure health status and health
outcomes (e.g., measurements of blood pressure before and after treatment,
and questionnaires measuring perceived health status at a given point);
(b) the conduct of primary studies, such as clinical trials and administrative
database analyses (e.g., insurance company records on utilization); and
(c) the use of secondary techniques, including statistical analyses, to
synthesize the results of primary studies to produce new insights or stronger
conclusions (e.g., metaanalysis) (OTA, 1994, p. 140).

Instruments to measure health status and outcomes can be subjective
or objective and can be condition specific or generic measures of health
(OTA, 1994). Examples include various Activities of Daily Living Scales
and health-related quality of life measures (Bowling, 1991; Kaplan, chapter
7, this volume; McDowell & Newell, 1987). A major concern identified
by discussants at the IUPUI Conference was whether researchers who
assess the effectiveness of psychological services use appropriate and
adequate outcomes measures. Because quality of life measures assess
functional ability, perceived health, psychological well-being, and role
functioning, they would seem to be appropriate measures for assessing

the effectiveness of psychological services. They are also particularly useful because they can measure both physical and mental health outcomes, including psychosocial functioning (Kaplan, chapter 7). However, there is a need to develop and evaluate these measures further, particularly as they apply to children.

Cost-Effectiveness

Cost-effectiveness analyses combine the results of effectiveness research with detailed cost information to evaluate the relative costs and effects of two or more health care interventions to determine whether an intervention's combined economic and health value makes it worth doing compared with alternatives (OTA, 1994). These analyses can also be used to evaluate the relative costs and effects of different types of health care practitioners providing the same service (e.g., physicians and nurse practitioners; or psychiatrists, psychologists, and clinical social workers).

Concerns about the effectiveness of psychological services may have emerged as an issue, in part, because of concerns about their cost-effectiveness. During the 103rd Congress, there were numerous policy discussions about the design of a health benefits package. At one meeting, the benefits manager of a large company stated that her company simply could not afford to pay for unlimited psychotherapy and repeated hospitalizations for adolescents with mental illness who do not show sufficient improvement in their condition to justify the cost. In response to several claims for more than $100,000 for what this company termed ''behavioral health care,'' it has greatly reduced its once generous fee-for-service mental health benefits and instituted a system of managed care to handle all mental health claims (O'Keeffe, personal communication, 1993).

Mental health benefits are not alone in being challenged, as ever-escalating health care costs have led insurance companies and self-insured employers to question the effectiveness, appropriateness, and cost-effectiveness of medical care as well. Increasingly, third-party payers are reluctant to pay for new or unproven treatments be they autologous bone marrow transplants for advanced breast cancer or cognitive rehabilitation for persons with traumatic brain injury. Even if new treatments are shown to be effective, third-party payers may understandably be unwilling to pay for them unless they cost less and achieve better outcomes than current effective alternatives. Payers also may be unwilling to reimburse psychologists at a higher rate than other mental health professionals without evidence that psychologists' services achieve better outcomes, that is, are more effective. Psychologists may believe that their more lengthy and rigorous training results in more effective and cost-effective services than those provided by master's-level psychologists or clinical social workers, but there is no extant research to support this view. IUPUI Conference discussions on work force issues raised similar concerns about the lack of documentation of relative cost-effectiveness and its consequences for reimbursement decisions.

Research on effectiveness and cost-effectiveness can also contribute to broader analyses for the purpose of informing policy decisions that have ramifications for clinical decision making. As the OTA report notes, the findings may be used to improve clinical decision making by practitioners, or to form part of the evidence base for more detailed analyses that incorporate information on costs and other important social considerations (OTA, 1994).

Cost-utility analysis (CUA) is a form of cost-effectiveness analyses in which quality-of-life outcomes are incorporated, for example, as "quality-adjusted life years," (Kaplan, 1996). This is a particularly useful method of analysis for policy makers because it allows comparisons of health care interventions that have different purposes (e.g., it can compare the cost utility of surgical vs. medical interventions or of psychotherapy vs. medication for the treatment of depression). It is also considered particularly useful because it includes both the quality and quantity of life in a single measure, without assigning a dollar value to that life (OTA, 1994). However, because the technique incorporates social preference factors into the analysis and assigns values to be placed on particular outcomes, this technique and other forms of cost-effectiveness analysis cannot address and may obscure crucial social policy concerns, for example, the need to redress social imbalances in access to health care (OTA, 1994). The OTA report (1994, p. 8) cautions that

> The quantitative calculations in CUA do not allow for the fact that society is not always indifferent to which groups benefit and which do not; an intervention that looks the most positive when measured by cost per QALY may in fact not always be the "best" allocation of social resources when these (other social policy concerns) are taken into account.

A type of cost-effectiveness research that is particularly relevant to psychological practice in health settings is cost-offset analyses. Cost-offset analysis attempts to determine if the provision of a particular service results in decreased use of other services. There have been several studies that support the view that providing greater insurance coverage for outpatient mental health services can reduce both medical and psychiatric inpatient stays, and total costs for the system (Bureau of National Affairs, 1994).

Overall Impact

A final component in the process of health technology assessment is an analysis of the overall impact of a specific intervention or class of interventions. In addition to assessing their effectiveness and cost, health interventions may also be assessed from a legal and ethical perspective. For example, as the result of a recent court ruling that a HMO was liable for millions of dollars in damages for denying coverage for autologous bone marrow transplantation to a women with advanced breast cancer, insurers may well decide to cover this procedure, even though there have been no randomized clinical trials supporting its effectiveness (Bureau of National Affairs, 1995).

Clinical Practice Guidelines

Clinical practice guidelines can be viewed as an extension of effectiveness research because they integrate existing research and use the educated opinions of specialists where research results are either lacking or controversial. However, they can also incorporate a consideration of many other factors (e.g., costs, and ethical and legal concerns). Their primary purpose is often to guide the formation of a clinical policy rather than insurance coverage policy (OTA, 1994). They are generally viewed as promising tools to promote cost-effective and appropriate care by a variety of practitioners (Eddy, 1990; Woolf, 1990).

Clinical practice guidelines are also viewed as a potential means to reduce the tremendous variability in practice patterns among physicians. Decades of research have documented the existence of this variation phenomenon in medical practice, wherein apparently similar patients are treated differently depending on the health care setting, a difference that often cannot be explained by confounding factors or undetected errors (Blumenthal, 1994). Geographic variations are particularly striking. For example, a study of inpatient care in New Haven, CT, and Boston, MA, found that per capita expenditures in Boston were approximately twice those in New Haven, and that about 80% of the higher use in Boston was attributable to higher hospital admission rates (Wennberg, Freeman, & Culp, 1987; Wennberg, Freeman, Shelton, & Bulboz, 1989). However, there was no evidence that the additional expenditures led to better outcomes. Other types of variation include differences in the frequency of laboratory tests, differences in surgery rates, and differences in referrals for diagnostic tests. In the latter case, research has shown that physicians who have a financial interest in the facility performing the diagnostic test refer patients for testing more often than physicians without an interest (Hillman et al., 1990). The variation phenomenon, which illustrates the lack of consensus among physicians about what constitutes appropriate health care, has undermined the claim by physicians that their unique scientific knowledge entitles them to special status in debates about health care organization and financing. Without this "scientific legitimacy," physicians become just one more interest group fighting to protect their economic interests (Blumenthal, 1994).

Analysis of Medicare data also indicates differences in practice patterns between physicians in the same geographic regions, with major implications for both quality and costs. It was partly due to concerns about this variation that the federal Agency for Health Care, Policy, and Research (AHCPR) was created in 1989. Its mandate is to further the evaluation of current clinical practice; to enhance the quality, appropriateness, and effectiveness of health care services; and to improve access to such services. These responsibilities are carried out, in part, through scientific research, assessment of health care technologies, the evaluation of current clinical practice, and the development of clinical practice guidelines, which, it is hoped, will reduce inappropriate variability in practice patterns.

There are approximately 1,500 clinical practice guidelines, issued by physicians' professional associations, health care insurers, and the federal government (Reichard & Vibbert, 1993). A major problem with these guidelines, which has compromised their potential effectiveness, is that they are inconsistent and not uniformly accepted as valid. This has caused confusion and undermined the basic credibility of the guidelines themselves. Some recent examples include contradictory recommendations for breast cancer screening (Kaplan, chapter 7, this volume), and controversial guidelines for the treatment of depression (AHCPR, 1993). The AHCPR depression guidelines were strongly criticized by the American Psychological Association (APA), because they state that pharmacological treatment is the treatment of choice for most depression, despite recent research suggesting that behavioral approaches in combination with pharmacological treatment are the most effective in preventing relapse (Sturm & Wells, 1995). As a result, it has been suggested that the APA should develop its own clinical practice guidelines for the treatment of depression.

If the APA guidelines are intended to improve the treatment of depression by psychologists and are targeted to this group, they may well accomplish their purpose. However, if the goal is to counter the AHCPR guidelines to influence insurance coverage, reimbursement policy, or managed care practices, they may or may not succeed, because, as noted previously, conflicting guidelines undermine the credibility of each. Additionally, if the guidelines are targeted to primary care physicians to educate them about the importance of psychotherapy in the treatment of depression, they also may not produce the desired outcome, because health care providers are more likely to ascribe credibility to information from sources they know and respect, such as organizations with which they are affiliated (OTA, 1994). Information provided by the American Medical Association or the Academy of General Practitioners would probably have more credibility for primary care physicians than that provided by the APA.

There are several factors that can influence health care providers to change their practice: financial incentives, such as favorable payment rates; administrative influences, such as utilization review; and the advice of acknowledged experts. Evidence to date indicates that the distribution of clinical practice guidelines alone will not be sufficient to change practices. Therefore, it is crucial that before practice guidelines are developed, there should be a clear articulation at the outset of the goals to be accomplished by the guidelines, followed by intensive and multipronged implementation strategies to achieve those goals (OTA, 1994).

RECOMMENDATIONS

Although the Clinton administration's attempt to comprehensively reform the health care system did not succeed, it created the impetus for examining and addressing important issues related to the practice of psychology, including the increasing demand for evidence of the cost-effectiveness of health and mental health interventions. Psychologists in a variety of mental health and health care settings have concerns about assuring access to comprehensive health care and the need to demonstrate the effectiveness and cost-effectiveness of their services. One of the purposes of the IUPUI Conference was to address these concerns, and the presentations and discussions on quality and outcomes indicators led to several recommendations for which there was a great deal of consensus.

1. *Increased research on the effectiveness, cost-effectiveness, and cost-utility of psychological and behavioral interventions, and on the effectiveness of integrated services.* At the conference, numerous examples of the interplay between psychological and physical factors were discussed, including the important influence of behavioral factors on treatment compliance, and the influence of psychosocial factors on morbidity and mortality rates (Blazer, 1982; McKinnon, Reynolds, Bowles, & Baum, 1989; Uchino, Kiecolt-Glaser, & Cacioppo, 1992). Given these relationships, conference

participants were in agreement that quality health care requires the integration of psychological services with traditional health and health-related services. Conference participants expressed major concerns that psychological services might be restricted to mental health domains through "carve-outs" for mental health services in the Medicaid program and in managed care health plans.

One way to encourage the integration of psychological and health services is to demonstrate the effectiveness of integrated services, their cost-effectiveness relative to alternative treatments, and their cost utility. The cost-utility of psychological and behavioral interventions could be shown through research that examines the effect of these services on an individual's quality of life (Kaplan, chapter 7, this volume). If, in addition, the provision of psychological services is found to reduce the length of hospital stays or the rate of rehospitalization, then these cost offsets will clearly show the cost-effectiveness of these services. For example, if parents caring for a child with a chronic medical condition, such as cystic fibrosis, are able to manage a home intravenous program as opposed to a hospital stay because of the provision of psychological services, this not only reduces costs but also increases that family's quality of life, and that child's social and academic functioning. Quantitative methods for conducting effectiveness, cost-effectiveness, and cost-utility research should be taught in graduate psychology programs, and this type of research should be incorporated into clinical research (Yates, 1994).

2. *Increased research to develop appropriate functional measures.* Conference participants strongly recommended more research to refine assessments of functional status both to determine the need for service and to measure the effectiveness and cost-effectiveness of services. The ability of a functional measure to assess the effectiveness of treatment for both physical and psychological disorders was deemed particularly beneficial. The use of a common measure may also be useful in supporting the integration of currently separate efforts to evaluate psychological services provided in traditional mental health and health care settings. Kaplan's quality-of-life measure was seen as an outstanding example of a functional indicator.

Although Kaplan's system was seen as an excellent starting point, several possibilities for expanding his measure were discussed. First, there was considerable agreement that functional measures should include both observable behaviors as well as more subjective indices of functioning (e.g., perceptions of stress and ratings of depression). At this point, additional research is needed to determine how and why objective and subjective ratings differ. The level of functioning of a person's family should also be considered when evaluating the effectiveness of psychological services, particularly when family members are in a caregiving role. Functional measures should also be developmentally appropriate for individuals in the later as well as the earlier stages of life.

Finally, conference participants recommended that functional measures should be developed by multidisciplinary groups to be maximally effective. Ideally, several professions would work collaboratively, including physicians, nurses, vocational counselors, and occupational and physical therapists.

3. *Development of clinical practice guidelines for psychological practice in health settings.* Conference participants viewed the development of clinical practice guidelines for psychologists working in health care settings as a top priority. Conference participants believed it was critical that psychologists working in health care settings develop practice guidelines that are relevant to the conditions they treat and the populations they serve. Guidelines should be developed for and disseminated to psychologists working in the areas of health psychology, neuropsychology, and rehabilitation psychology.

Three major issues related to the development of these guidelines were discussed: (a) There was consensus that, whenever possible, guidelines should be based on empirical evidence. There should be a systematic review of the literature to identify interventions that have been shown to be effective for particular health-related problems. For example, a substantial number of studies suggest that behavioral interventions aimed at preparing different subgroups (e.g., children) for various painful medical procedures have been highly effective not only in reducing the anxiety and psychological stress associated with these procedures, but also in facilitating the physician's goal of completing the procedure efficiently and successfully (Peterson, 1989). For health-related problems for which sufficient empirical evidence is not currently available, conference participants advocated the development of guidelines based on expert consensus. Ideally, areas where empirical evidence is lacking would be the focus of future empirical research.

(b) There was substantial agreement that practice guidelines must consider contextual factors, such as the individual characteristics of the patient, the developmental stage of the patient and family, the specific demands of the illness, and the availability of social support (e.g., family and community resources). Other important factors may also need to be considered, such as education, ethnicity, and gender. Consideration of these factors is likely to increase the value of these guidelines to both practitioners and consumers.

(c) Conference participants agreed on the need to develop practice guidelines that consider the positive aspects of functioning as well as the reduction of symptoms. Using this approach, guidelines could also be developed for psychological services aimed at maintaining health and preventing illness, particularly for individuals at high risk for becoming ill (e.g., individuals with human immunodeficiency virus infection and individuals with chronic diseases, such as multiple sclerosis, which are characterized by exacerbations and remissions). The importance of updating practice guidelines to reflect new research and to address issues that arise with their implementation in various settings was stressed. Consistent with the concerns raised about the application of clinical practice guidelines in the OTA report, there was agreement that considerable effort will be needed to educate practitioners and to encourage them to use the guidelines.

Recently, a template for developing and evaluating treatment guidelines for cognitive, emotional, and behavioral disorders and dysfunction was developed by an APA Board of Professional Affairs Task Force and approved by APA's Council of Representatives. One of the major purposes of the document (APA Task Force, 1995) is to provide guidance on how to develop sound guidelines for mental health services. APA's Division of Clinical Psychology (Division 12) is also working on developing criteria for evaluating treatment efficacy.

As psychologists undertake the development of practice guidelines, it is recommended that they review available analyses and critiques of guideline development so far, and that they be aware of guidelines being developed by other groups. The OTA report (1994) contains a comprehensive discussion of federal activities to develop practice guidelines, and the AHCPR has published a compendium of papers on the various methodological approaches used in developing clinical practice guidelines (AHCPR, 1995). A major focus of the AHCPR publication is to examine ways to analyze the diverse data used in formulating clinical practice guideline recommendations.

4. *Establishment of an APA task force of health care–oriented psychologists.* To facilitate implementation of the three previous

recommendations, conference participants advocated the establishment of a task force of health care–oriented psychologists under the auspices of the APA. The task force would include, for example, psychologists with expertise in health psychology, rehabilitation psychology, and pediatric psychology, and would have both a research and policy agenda. In the research area, the goals of the task force would include, but not be limited to, the development and dissemination of clinical practice guidelines, the development and evaluation of functional measures for individuals at different developmental stages, and the evaluation of the effectiveness and cost-effectiveness of psychological and behavioral prevention and intervention services, particularly in health settings.

In the policy area, the task force would work to encourage reimbursement for the full range of psychological services provided in traditional health care settings and for conditions that are not included in the DSM-IV codes, the provision of which can lead to improvements in both the quality of care and the quality of life.

In summary, the U.S. health care system will be undergoing many changes over the next decades. Clearly, the projected cost increases in the system are unsustainable, and continuing efforts will be made by third-party payers, both public and private, to contain costs. It is essential that such efforts not compromise the availability and effectiveness of care. Health services research, particularly in the area of effectiveness and cost-effectiveness, will play an increasingly important role in policy decisions. Thus, it is essential that research show both the efficacy of psychological services in the full range of health care settings and the cost-effectiveness of services delivered by psychologists relative to other providers.

REFERENCES

Agency for Health Care Policy and Research (AHCPR). (1993). *Depression in primary care: Vols. 1 & 2. Treatment of major depression* (Clinical Practice Guideline, No. 5). Rockville, MD: U.S. Department of Health and Human Services, Public Health Service, Agency for Health Care Policy Research.
Agency for Health Care Policy and Research (AHCPR). (1995). *Clinical practice guideline development: Methodology perspectives.* (AHCPR Publication No. 95-0009). Rockville, MD: U.S. Department of Health and Human Services, Public Health Service, Agency for Health Care Policy Research.

APA Task Force on Psychological Guidelines. (1995). *Template for developing guidelines: Interventions for mental disorders and psychosocial aspects of physical disorders*. Washington, DC: American Psychological Association.

Blazer, D. G. (1982). Social support and mortality in an elderly community population. *American Journal of Epidemiology, 115*, 684–694.

Blumenthal, D. (October 13, 1994). The variation phenomenon in 1994. *New England Journal of Medicine, 33*, 1017–1018.

Bowling, A. (1991). *Measuring health: A review of quality of life measurement scales*. Philadelphia: Open University Press.

Bureau of National Affairs. (1994, November 28). *Health Policy*, pp. 1976–1977.

Bureau of National Affairs. (1995, February 6). California Blue Shield announces pilot for disputed breast cancer treatments. *Health Policy*, pp. 216–217.

Eddy, D. M. (1990). Designing a practice policy—standards, guidelines, and options. *Journal of the American Medical Association, 263*, 3077–3084.

Eddy, D. M. (1992). Medicine, money and mathematics. *Bulletin of the American College of Surgeons, 77*, 36–49.

Hillman, B. J., Joseph, C. A., Mabry, M. R., Sunshine, J. H., Kennedy, S. D., & Noether, M. (1990). Frequency and costs of diagnostic imaging in office practice: A comparison of self-referring and radiologist-referring physicians. *New England Journal of Medicine, 323*, 1604–1608.

Kaplan, R. M. (1996). Measuring health outcome for resource allocation. In R. L. Glueckauf, R. G. Frank, G. R. Bond, & J. H. McGrew (Eds.), *Psychological practice in a changing health care system: Issues and new directions*. New York: Springer.

McDowell, I., & Newell, C. (1987). *Measuring health: A guide to rating scales and questionnaires*. New York: Oxford University Press.

McKinnon, W., Weisse, C. S., Reynolds, C. P., Bowles, C. A., & Baum, A. (1989). Chronic stress, leukocyte subpopulations, and humoral response to latent virus. *Health Psychology, 8*, 389–402.

Neuhauser, D. (1990). Ernest Avory Codman, MD, and end results of medical care. *International Journal of Technology Assessment in Health Care, 8*, 321–332.

Reichard, J., & Vibbert, S. (Eds.). (1993). *The medical outcomes and guidelines sourcebook*. Washington, DC: Faulkner & Grey.

Office of Technology Assessment. (1982). *Strategies for medical technology assessment* (Publication No. OTA-H-181). Washington, DC: U.S. Government Printing Office.

Office of Technology Assessment. (September, 1994). *Identifying health technologies that work: Searching for evidence* (Publication No. OTA-H-608). Washington, DC: U.S. Government Printing Office.

Peterson, L. (1989). Coping by children undergoing stressful medical procedures: Some conceptual, methodological, and therapeutic issues. *Journal of Consulting and Clinical Psychology, 57*, 380–387.

Sturm, R., & Wells, K. (1995). How can care for depression become more cost-effective? *Journal of the American Medical Association, 273*, 51–58.

Uchino, B. N., Kiecolt-Glaser, J., & Cacioppo, J. T. (1992). Age-related changes in cardiovascular response as a function of a chronic stressor and social support. *Journal of Personality and Social Psychology, 63*, 839–846.

Wennberg, J. E., Freeman, J. L., Shelton, R. M., & Bulboz, T. A. (1989). Hospital use and mortality among Medicare beneficiaries in Boston and New Haven. *New England Journal of Medicine, 321*, 1168–1173.

Wennberg, J. E., Freeman, J. L., & Culp, W. J. (1987, May 23). Are hospital services rationed in New Haven or over-utilised in Boston? *Lancet*, 1185–1189.

White, K. L. (1968). International comparisons of health services systems. *Milbank Memorial Fund Quarterly, 46*, 117–125.

Woolf, S. H. (1990). Practice guidelines: A new reality in medicine: 1. Recent developments. *Archives of Internal Medicine, 150*, 1811–1818.

Yates, B. (1994). Toward the incorporation of costs, cost-effectiveness analysis, and cost-benefit analysis into clinical research. *Journal of Consulting and Clinical Psychology, 62*, 729–736.

EDUCATION AND TRAINING ISSUES IN PSYCHOLOGY AND HEALTH CARE

Introduction

Paul D. Nelson

The two chapters that follow present thoughtful reflections on education and training issues for psychologists. DiCowden, Crosson, and McSweeny present a consensus report of participants at the national conference on which this book is based, a report that concludes with several recommendations for future initiatives. Dunivin's chapter is complementary to the preceding text, presenting a historical critique of professional education and training in psychology with suggestions for change if we are to be understood better by the public and to be valued by other professions as a disciplinary partner in our nation's health care system as it is being reconfigured.

Common to both chapters is a focus on the critical need for financial support of professional education and training in psychology. Dunivin's chapter offers a summary of the potential sources of such support. DiCowden, Crosson, and McSweeny recommend that psychology work for the establishment of a National Institute of Behavioral Health as one means to further education, training, and research in health care psychology. Admittedly, such recommendations come at a point in time during which Congress is seeking to downsize and eliminate federal programs of funding for education, research, and other public services. However, both chapters argue that psychologists should be a partner among the health care professions, and that public funding in support of education and training in all health care professions is an investment for the nation.

Present arguments for the inclusion of psychology among health care professions eligible for significant public funds in support of education and training rest largely on the principle of equity. These arguments are not persuasive, however. For psychology to receive a larger share of public funding, arguments based on the principles of supply and demand and efficacy of service will need to be articulated better than they have so far. The following chapters elucidate some of the reasons for which this has not been effectively accomplished to date. One of the major reasons has been the public's lack of understanding about what psychologists do and who they are. In fact, the authors remind us, we have not been clear among ourselves about our core identity. The authors observe the need for better articulation of the types of problems, settings, and roles with which psychologists are identified and the particular competencies that differentiate us from other health care professionals. In turn, these must be understood by our professional education and training programs and formally endorsed as goals.

This is no simple matter. The constancy of change requires that our professional education and training programs graduate psychologists who have sufficient breadth of training to be flexible in their practice modalities, who have the fundamental competencies expected of psychologists in health care systems, and who are prepared for a career of lifelong learning as psychologists. The importance of these competencies was realized by psychologists who served our nation during the World War II years (Fiske, 1946; Hunt, 1975), and their value has been the subject as well of recent reflections among scholars of our discipline (Kimble, 1989; Matarazzo, 1987).

The chapters in this section suggest that education and training models must focus much more on setting-specific training than they have in the past. Dunivin argues for much more training experience in multidisciplinary, comprehensive care, community-based settings associated with primary or secondary prevention in a public health model of health care. DiCowden, Crosson, and McSweeny make the case for more training to be conducted in major medical centers, tertiary care facilities in a public health model, for the opportunities that they afford graduate students in health care psychology to train for clinical and research competencies with other health care professionals in environments similar to those for which they are preparing to enter practice. Both viewpoints are valid. Psychologists are needed in primary, secondary, and tertiary health care service roles. They should be exposed broadly at the doctoral level of education and training to all three.

Although neither chapter devotes much attention to the accreditation process as a means of advancing quality in professional education and training, it is important to note that the APA's Committee on Accreditation has developed new guidelines by which doctoral programs will be accredited in the future. Central to those guidelines is the requirement that a program be clear about its purposes, education and training goals, objectives expressed in terms of foundational competencies, philosophy or model of training in preparing psychologists for practice, rationale for the didactic and field training components of its curriculum, and means of assessing its effectiveness in achieving these ends. Accredited programs also must show how they remain abreast of changes in the practice environment, as well as in the advancement of scientific psychology, reflecting on ways in which to advance the quality of training they offer students through such knowledge. In time, it will be possible to compare programs that prepare students for professional practice in health care systems, assessing the similarities and differences in their goals, approaches to training, and outcomes. Thus, by the time of the next national conference on psychological practice in health care systems, we should be even more informed about our education and training practices than we have been to date.

The current uncertainties about the future roles of psychology are both challenges and opportunities. This is as true for the future roles of psychologists in a changing health care system as it has been throughout our history as a discipline in other areas of societal concern.

REFERENCES

Fiske, D. W. (1946). Naval aviation psychology: 3. The Special Services Group. *American Psychologist, 1*, 544–548.

Hunt, W. A. (1975). Clinical psychology in 1944–45. *Journal of Clinical Psychology, 31*, 173–178.

Kimble, G. A. (1989). Psychology from the standpoint of a generalist. *American Psychologist, 44*, 491–499.

Matarazzo, J. D. (1987). There is only one psychology, no specialties, but many applications. *American Psychologist, 42*, 893–903.

Chapter 9

Graduate Education and Training: Current Status and Prospects for the Future

Debra Lina Dunivin

During its century-old life span, psychology has undergone a major transformation from a narrowly focused academic discipline to a broad, albeit ill-defined, field incorporating a science-based profession that provides, among other things, a wide range of health services. Several factors have limited full acceptance of professional psychology as a legitimate health care domain, including the lack of a consensual training model, confusion about the meaning of the PhD degree with respect to professional competence, and the narrow perception of the practice of psychology (Fox, 1994).

The significance of psychology as a health care profession (rather than a service primarily for persons with emotional difficulties) has become increasingly apparent. Yet most psychology PhD training programs have not acknowledged the profession's extended scope of practice. Neither have many programs considered current federal and state funding priorities in health professional education and the necessity of a focus on meeting societal need. One viable option for training psychologists for practice in health care settings is medicine's hospital-based training approach. Although there is considerable debate about the benefits of training health professionals in traditional hospital settings versus community-based ambulatory settings, psychologists may be better prepared for professional practice by programs that are interdisciplinary in nature and have strong associations with major medical health science centers or comprehensive community-based service delivery settings.

For more than a decade, several of psychology's key leaders, including Pat DeLeon, Ron Fox, Gary VandenBos, and Jack Wiggins, have called attention to several substantial impediments to the healthy growth and development of the field. These leaders, all members of the executive board of the APA, have underscored the significance of establishing a representative and coherent definition of professional psychology that embraces the diversity of the field and highlights its relevance to meeting societal needs (DeLeon, 1983; DeLeon, VandenBos, & Kraut, 1986; Fox, 1980, 1982, 1994; Shapiro & Wiggins, 1994; VandenBos, 1993; VandenBos, DeLeon, & Belar, 1991). These individuals, some of psychology's visionaries, have emphasized the importance of developing comprehensive psychological service centers as training sites and the value of an interdisciplinary component in professional education. These concepts strikingly parallel federal priorities.

Resolution of the underlying conceptual problems would eliminate some of the unintended consequences and statutory confusion from policy makers' use of such terms as *clinical psychology* and *mental health practice*. Policy makers often use such designations when their intended reference is to practicing psychologists. Definitional clarity could help prevent, for example, situations in which professional psychologists and graduate psychology programs are excluded from various federal programs on the basis that they hold or offer degrees in health, medical, or counseling psychology rather than in clinical psychology. Conceptual and definitional clarity would thus enhance psychology's access to federal employment and reimbursement, and to federal funding for graduate education.

Psychology has been shaped significantly during its first century of development by federal funding for graduate education (Dunivin, 1994). Federal support was provided on recognition of psychology's unique contribution to meeting a particular societal need, that is, the assessment and treatment of veterans with neuropsychiatric disorders and research into their conditions. In this chapter, the current status of federal support for health professions education is addressed. Future opportunities for psychology are discussed within the context of a changing health care delivery system in a country where the major health risks are primarily behaviorally based.

NARROW AND AMORPHOUS PERCEPTION OF PSYCHOLOGY: CONTRIBUTING FACTORS

Full recognition of psychology, by individuals both within and outside the field, is inhibited by several factors related to the definition and conceptualization of professional psychology. More than 35 years ago, the difficulty defining a psychologist was described in a discussion of "manpower" trends in mental health professions. This difficulty was attributed to psychology's being a "broader and more loosely defined field [than psychiatry] in which are employed people with various amounts of formal training" (Albee & Dickey, 1957, p. 64). More recently, we have been cautioned about the limitations resulting from confusion of the profession of psychology with a subdomain of psychological practice (e.g., clinical, counseling, and school), with specific techniques (most often psychotherapy), and with limited problem areas (as frequently occurs with mental health) (Fox, 1994). Three particular conceptual impediments demand attention in a changing national health care delivery system: (a) the lack of a consensual training model, (b) the PhD degree and the postdoctoral licensure requirement, and (c) the discrepancy between prevailing views about professional psychology services and its actual scope of practice (Fox, 1994).

Lack of a Consensual Training Model

Over the past 50 years, various distinct training models have emerged, with some overlap of core competency areas identified as basic to professional psychology but with little consensus between models. Core training areas for psychology were delineated in the 1940s (Shakow, 1947): general psychology (e.g., developmental, social, comparative, and physiological psychology), psychodynamics of behavior, diagnostic methods, research methods, related disciplines (e.g., neuroanatomy and endocrinology), and psychotherapy. The similarity of these competency areas to those identified at conferences during the next four decades enabled Fox and Barclay (1989) to argue convincingly that "there is a de facto common core of knowledge that has generally characterized professional programs since the time of the well-known and oft-quoted Shakow (1947) report" (Fox, 1994, p. 203). Fox (1994) draws a distinction between principles and values inherent in graduate education (e.g., resistance to restrict freedom of inquiry and right of the faculty to design program requirements) and those inherent in professional education (e.g., standardized education criteria to ensure students' licensure and competence to practice). This distinction is helpful in explaining the manifest, although not necessarily antithetical, differences in recommendations emerging from various conferences. For example, the Utah Conference on Graduate Education and Psychology, comprised largely of graduate educators, avoided endorsement of a prescriptive core (Resolutions Approved, 1987), whereas the Mission Bay Conference on Education and Training, comprised mostly of professional school faculty, agreed on six identifiable areas of competency (Bourg, Bent, McHolland, & Stricker, 1989).

The lack of a common core curriculum and standardized training models is a major factor limiting recognition of the wide range of competencies of professional psychology. The failure to differentiate clearly between professional and academic education has led to significant confusion about the nature of doctoral training and the specific competencies of psychologists for both the lay public and the profession. Uniform professional education is necessary for the healthy growth of the profession and essential for the development of reliable expectations by prospective practitioners and the public about the scope of professional competence (Fox, 1982, 1994; Weitz, 1992).

The PhD and Postdoctoral Licensure Requirements

The PhD degree clearly communicates scholarly, scientific expertise but does not necessarily communicate professional competence. Medicine, the prototypical science-based profession, distinguishes between its researchers and practitioners via an MD degree for practitioners of the medical arts and a PhD degree for researchers in the biomedical sciences. Medical scientist-practitioners generally hold both degrees. Shapiro and Wiggins (1994) have called for "truth in labeling" by using the PsyD degree to designate psychologist practitioners and offer a mechanism for implementation of such a plan. They have joined the ranks of earlier proponents who argued for a clear differentiation of practitioner training from other forms of psychology education via the mechanism of the PsyD degree (e.g., Fox, 1980; Fox, Kovacs, & Graham, 1985; Peterson, 1976). Graduate students also have been given conflicting messages about the professional nature of PhD versus PsyD training programs. Often program descriptions do not accurately reflect specific professional training opportunities. As a consequence, aspiring practitioners are often steered away from PhD programs that would actually prepare them for the kind of career they seek.

The earliest argument favoring a PsyD degree for professional psychologists appeared almost three-quarters of a century ago (Crane, 1925; referred to a PsD degree). About the same time, several great idealogues argued that the discipline of medicine provided an insufficient base for a profession dealing with psychological conditions. Sigmund Freud maintained that the practice of psychoanalysis should rest within the discipline of psychology, and Karl Menniger proposed that a field combining psychological, social, and biological content was the necessary foundation for a profession that dealt with the full range of human problems (Peterson, 1992).

The message of opportunity was largely unheeded by the infant profession of psychology, which embarked on a phase of scientist-practitioner identity in its adolescent development. Almost 40 years after the initial call for a PsyD degree, APA recommended a two-track educational system—leading to a PhD degree for students preparing for a career in psychology research and to a PsyD for students preparing for professional practice (APA, 1967). During the next quarter-century, PsyD programs emerged. In a recent survey, Peterson (1992) cited 17 independent professional schools in 10 states that award the PsyD degree.

A significant conceptual obstacle inherent in both the PhD and PsyD degrees is the year of supervised postdoctoral experience required for licensure in most states. One implication of this requirement is that neither type of training program adequately prepares their graduates for independent, entry-level professional functioning. An inadvertent consequence is that graduate schools are not held accountable for the quality and competence of their graduates (Fox & Barclay, 1989; Fox, Kovacs, & Graham, 1985). This implication is one not missed by policy makers and regulatory agencies in discussions of reimbursement for psychological services rendered during the postdoctoral, prelicensure year.

Perception of Psychology Narrower than the Practice

Psychology's difficulty in defining itself or, perhaps more accurately, difficulty in updating its definition to conform with changes in identity and practice, necessarily contributes to misperceptions and a lack of recognition from both within and outside the field; this has tremendous implications for psychology's role vis-à-vis public policy making. As the range of psychology's knowledge base has expanded through basic and applied research, so has its practical application (VandenBos, DeLeon, & Belar, 1991). Illustrative of this expansion is the area of health psychology, which encompasses the promotion of physical health and prevention of biological illness, as well as the psychological aspects of physical illness, sometimes characterized as the mind-body interface. Likewise, the explosive growth of the neuropsychologist's database has provided a multitude of rehabilitative applications.

VandenBos (1993) divides psychological care into four types of services or interventions: (a) preventive care (primary, secondary, and tertiary preventive approaches), screening, and diagnostic assessment; (b) short-term acute care (brief and crisis-oriented psychotherapy); (c) rehabilitation services and restorative psychotherapy (helping individuals to cope more effectively with long-term effects of disease and physical trauma); and (d) long-term care (psychological assistance to those coping with chronic disease and emotional conditions). Only one of these four types of psychological services (i.e., acute care psychotherapy) is typically included in most insurance plans, public and private; it is also the one most closely identified with mental health care. Diagnostic assessment, rehabilitation therapy, and long-term treatment are covered in varying degrees, whereas preventive services have been almost completely neglected.

Interestingly, this focus on acute care within psychology parallels the national health policy focus on hospital-based, acute care services. Such a focus on acute care of emergent conditions at the expense of preventive services, outpatient delivery, and chronic care contributes to the excessive costs of our health care delivery system and is doomed to failure (Kiesler, 1992). Unfortunately, this type of intervention (i.e., brief psychotherapy) is the one most commonly identified with psychology.

> At a time when society needs a broad-gauged profession able to take on its most pressing health needs (which are behavioral in nature), psychology has become a narrow field with an arcane and invisible delivery system. We've defined ourselves and are seen by others as merely a mental health specialty. (Fox, 1982, p. 1052)

Included in the practice domains of psychology are clinical, counseling, and school psychology, as well as health psychology, community psychology, rehabilitation psychology, and applied developmental psychology (Fox, 1994). Industrial/organizational, engineering, and applied experimental psychology might be included as well. Psychologists have developed management protocol and intervention strategies to deal with a wide range of health conditions not usually related to mental health (Eisenberg, Glueckauf, & Zaretsky, 1994; Millon, Green, & Meagher, 1982). Never has it been more important for psychology to articulate this in conversations with policy makers. At this time in history, when the nation's major health risk factors are behavioral in origin (i.e., diet, alcohol and tobacco use, violence, unsafe sex, and unintentional injury), psychology must define itself more accurately as the health profession most interested in and knowledgeable about health promotion and lifestyle change.

FEDERAL FUNDING OF HEALTH PROFESSIONAL EDUCATION: AN UNTAPPED RESOURCE

Health professions education is financed through a variety of mechanisms. The federal government has been described as both a patron and a proprietor of education for the health professions, and has shaped the growth and development of various health professions, including medicine and psychology, through financing graduate education. The provisions for funding education and training of health professionals include both direct and indirect means (Dunivin, 1994).

Currently, patient care revenue is the major source of financial support for graduate medical education (GME) (Institute of Medicine, 1994); however, this has not always been the case. Historically, federal funds for biomedical research were the largest single source of medical school revenues. Other sources for GME include the Veterans Administration (VA), the Department of Defense, grants and loans through Title VII of the Public Health Service (PHS) Act, and states and nonfederal third-party payers, to a varying extent.

Psychology, too, has been supported by federal funds—the profession has been shaped by its relationship to the federal government (Dunivin, 1994). Graduate psychology and psychological research received federal funding because they provided unique services that met a national need during and following the world wars. Some federal psychology education programs are still viable means of support, although they are in jeopardy of being eliminated (e.g., the VA Psychology Training Program). Others have dwindled to such an extent that they have become almost inconsequential (e.g., National Institute of Mental Health [NIMH] predoctoral clinical psychology training grants, often referred to as "clinical training" and now provided through the Center for Mental Health Services [CMHS]). Psychology must come to terms with the fact that federal support is not an entitlement. We would do well to seek other avenues of currently available funding for health professional education (e.g., Title VII and GME), and, at the same time, to ask ourselves why we are no longer perceived by federal authorities and policy makers, among others, as contributing substantially to solving societal ills.

Veterans Administration (VA)

The VA conducts the largest coordinated health professional education and training effort in the nation. Approximately 100,000 individuals, in a wide range of disciplines and academic training levels, receive clinical training in VA facilities each year. During the last 50 years, the VA has played a significant role in the education of both physicians and psychologists through affiliation with accredited schools of medicine and departments of psychology. Attention to VA activities is important not only from a historical perspective but from what it can tell us about future directions.

Following World War I, the Veteran's Bureau (predecessor of the VA) implemented a specialized training program in neuropsychiatry for physicians to address the shortage of doctors able to treat veterans with psychological problems (U.S. Veterans Bureau, 1922, 1929). Returning World War II veterans exacerbated the shortage of available health professionals. Affiliations between veterans' hospitals and medical schools were established based on a model used during the world wars by the U.S. Army medical units. The VA-university affiliation continued through the next five decades and is still in operation.

Currently, 127 VA medical facilities are affiliated with 104 of the nation's 125 medical schools. More than 30,000 medical residents are expected to rotate through 8,826 positions in VA facilities during 1995. Total funding for residents' salaries and fringe benefits is anticipated to be more than $360 million (Department of Veterans Affairs, 1994). The Institute of Medicine (1989) reported that the VA subsidized 12% of U.S. residency positions in 1988; current support is probably similar. Recent plans for VA physician training include an expansion in primary care.

A training program for psychologists was implemented by the VA in the mid-1940s to address the continuing shortage of professionals capable of treating veterans with neuropsychiatric disorders and of performing research on these conditions. A training program was developed by the Chief of the Clinical Psychology Division in conjunction with the APA and university psychology departments. Guidelines for didactic and experiential training in the practice of clinical psychology were cooperatively established (Ash, 1968; Miller, 1946; Moore, 1992).

Sixteen hundred psychologists are employed in the VA's 171 health care facilities; training for psychology students is provided in most of the 151 independent Psychology Services within these facilities. Each year, more than 1,000 psychology students at various levels of education receive some form of clinical psychology training at VA facilities. Postdoctoral fellowships are offered in geropsychology, substance abuse, and posttraumatic stress disorder. The VA Psychology Training Program has expanded from 200 training positions in 1946 to an expected size of 586 in 1995; compensation to psychology interns is expected to be more than $8 million annually (Department of Veterans Affairs, 1994).

Clinical Training

About the same time that the VA implemented its Psychology Training Program and the VA–medical school affiliations, Congress established funding for clinical training. As previously noted, the need for specialized assessment, diagnosis, and treatment of veterans with serious emotional disturbances led to the development of specialized education and training programs. The growth of graduate programs throughout the nation was "closely paralleled by Congressional support for Clinical training funds provided through the NIMH" (Strickland & Calkins, 1987, p. 32). Indeed, their growth was greatly facilitated by this federal support.

Initial funding for clinical training in fiscal year 1948 was $1.1 million; it gradually increased to a peak of $111 million in fiscal year 1974 and has been declining steadily ever since (NIMH, 1990). For the past decade, federal administrations have zero-funded such clinical training; the program has survived only through congressional intervention (Dunivin, 1994). These funds have been administered through the CMHS since the Alcohol Drug Abuse and Mental Health Administration reorganization. Strickland and Calkins (1987) described this particular public policy initiative as having had "perhaps, the most dramatic impact on clinical psychology and clinical psychologists" (p. 31) because of the sheer numbers of individuals and programs assisted through this funding mechanism for several decades. They emphasized the need to address the underrepresentation of minorities in psychology and the geographic maldistribution of mental health professionals.

Title VII

The hallmark of the federal provision of direct health professional education since the mid-1960s has been Title VII of the Public Health Service Act (Dunivin, 1994). The original goals included increasing enrollment in schools of medicine, osteopathy, and dentistry, and ensuring their financial viability through student loans and matching grants to schools for construction and improvement of facilities. Successful in meeting these goals, the Title VII programs have been expanded to include support for students in many additional health professions—veterinary medicine, optometry, podiatry, and pharmacy, as well as public health and graduate programs in health administration. Support for nursing education is provided through Title VIII.

Title VII legislation has been amended and expanded almost every year since its enactment, as have other provisions within the PHS Act. In the years following its initial implementation, appropriations were expanded and programs were added, including scholarships for students with extreme financial need, loan forgiveness for students beginning practice in designated health professional shortage areas, and educational improvement grants. In the mid-1970s, when increasing the number of physicians in the nation was no longer an issue, the focus of Title VII amendments shifted to redistribution of health professionals across geographic and specialty areas (Franco & Klebe, 1991; Klebe, 1992).

Currently, Title VII assistance is provided in the form of scholarships, loans, and loan guarantees to certain health professions students, and in the form of grants and contracts to health professions schools for special training programs. Title VII programs are administered by the Health Resources and Services Administration (HRSA), a federal agency within the Department of Health and Human Services. HRSA is responsible for the determination and projection of the national need for health professionals.

Students of psychology and institutions and departments of psychology are eligible for about half of the Title VII programs; eligibility has been won program by program. A thorough discussion of Title VII legislation specific to psychology is provided in a recent publication (Dunivin, 1994); two points made therein are particularly relevant to this discussion. First, the existing psychology-specific health professions education legislation is largely attributable to the efforts of a single individual, Patrick H. DeLeon, administrative assistant to Senator Daniel K. Inouye. Second, psychology often does not apply to those programs for which it is eligible. Although $309 million dollars were available to psychology in fiscal year 1994, there was no coordinated effort to use these Title VII funds.

GME

The largest single funding mechanism for health professional education (primarily for physicians, but also for physician assistants and nurses who receive training in teaching hospitals) is Medicare's GME. The legislation that established the Medicare program (i.e., the Social Security Amendments of 1965) greatly enhanced the federal government's role in shaping the physician work force in this country (Dunivin, 1994). Over and above the reimbursements provided for services to beneficiaries (the elderly and certain disabled populations), Medicare makes additional payments to certain facilities (i.e., teaching hospitals) to offset the costs of medical education programs.

GME costs are currently offset through two mechanisms under the prospective payment system: an indirect medical (IME) adjustment (to per-case payments) and a direct medical education (DME) payment (for salaries of faculty and residents, administrative expenses, and institutional overhead). Total GME payments expected for fiscal year 1994 are $5.526 billion—$1.928 billion for DME and $3.98 billion for IME. These GME payments to hospitals are in addition to the payments made through Part B for services rendered to Medicare beneficiaries by teaching physicians.

MEDICINE'S HOSPITAL-BASED TRAINING: WHAT CAN WE LEARN?

The large role of the federal government in shaping the discipline of medicine through funding of professional education (e.g., VA medical-school affiliations and Title VII) and reimbursement for services (e.g., Medicare GME) is apparent on review of the programs (Dunivin, 1994). Another significant factor shaping the practice of medicine and the training of physicians has been the federal government's financing of hospital construction. In addition to meeting their stated goal of increasing the physician work force, these federal policies have had the inadvertent consequence of perpetuating the acute care, hospital-based emphasis of our nation's health care delivery system. Current efforts to reform this aspect of our system reveal the significant power and political savvy of the teaching hospitals.

Training Model: Reimbursement for Services

The practice of medicine and the training of physicians are both closely tied to hospitals. Service delivery within the hospital setting is based in acute care, advanced technology; as such, it is a highly profitable enterprise. The nation's hospital delivery system is characterized by pluralism and volunteerism. Although there are many major medical centers throughout the country, there are also a multitude of small hospitals representing community values; serving diverse ethnic, racial, and religious groups; and, in essence, reflecting the pluralism of our society. Our nation's hospital delivery system is also characterized by social stratification with hospitals originally serving either the wealthy or the poor; this dichotomy permitted the poor to become ''teaching material'' for American medical schools.

Interestingly, the elderly and certain disabled populations have joined the ranks of ''teaching material'' for American physicians-in-training through the mechanisms of Medicare's GME. Of the three federal programs funding health professions education (i.e., Clinical Training, Title VII, and GME), almost 95% or $5.5 billion of these federal dollars (in 1994 expected outlays or appropriations) is expected to be spent for

Medicare GME (Dunivin, 1994). In creating this funding mechanism for teaching hospitals, the federal government encouraged the shift from reliance by institutions of medical education on biomedical research (36% in 1963–64) to provision of clinical services (47% in 1991–92) for most financing of their educational enterprise (Dunivin, 1994). In effect, the GME provision within the federal entitlement program has inextricably tied graduate medical education to the provision of services to Medicare beneficiaries in hospitals.

Unintended Consequences of Specialization

Hospital medicine emphasizes specialization, as do the technological advances in diagnosis and treatment of disease, which emanated from post–World War II biomedical research. Paradoxically, the federal government has continued to encourage urban medical specialization for at least two decades beyond the recognition that a redistribution across geographic and specialty areas was warranted.

Correcting the imbalance of medical specialists to general practitioners and the geographic maldistribution of health professionals has been subject to congressional debate and inquiry for 20 years and has been repeatedly linked to the escalating costs of health care in this country. The complexity of health work force planning and presence of significant forces to maintain the status quo have resulted in limited modification of the existing system despite generally consistent recommendations to remedy these problems from the congressionally established advisory bodies (i.e., the Graduate Medical Education National Advisory Committee and the Council on Graduate Medical Education [COGME]) (Dunivin, 1994).

The Dollars Are Big: Even From a Rockefeller Perspective

A significant factor is that the $5.5 billion in federal expenditures through Medicare GME to teaching hospitals is entitlement money. That is, it does not go through the federal budgetary process. It is paid via a prospective payment system, providing adjustments (i.e., higher reimbursement for the same services provided in other settings) to offset the costs of the institutions' medical education program. These are not discretionary funds that must go through the annual authorization and appropriations process, as must programs such as the CMHS Clinical Training and PHS Act Title VII programs. GME offsets are almost like "invisible money" (until it is spent), and $5.5 billion seems to be a gross underestimate of the actual dollars involved. Extra costs to teaching hospitals in a single state (i.e.,

New York, which has the largest number of teaching hospitals in the country) have been estimated by the Greater New York Hospital Association to be $5 billion (Kosterlitz, 1994). In the words of Senator John Rockefeller:

> this is an enormous amount of money, and it has everything to do with the future of health care. . . . One could pass reform, and if we did not deal with [reshaping the medical] work force, we're going to have done precious little. (Kosterlitz, 1994, p. 1970)

Unfortunately, Senator Rockefeller is one of only a few elected officials who truly appreciates that significant reform of the nation's medical/ health professional work force and the training of health professionals is essential to coping with our nation's health care crisis.

HEALTH PROFESSIONS TRAINING IN COMMUNITY-BASED SETTINGS: A FUTURE HORIZON

The fact that most health care is currently delivered in ambulatory settings, while most medical training occurs in inpatient hospitals, is a paradox. Few in the health policy, delivery, or training sectors question the need for health professionals to acquire more clinical experience in outpatient settings. Indeed, the demand for practitioners with ambulatory care experience is great from managed care organizations providing primary care services in outpatient settings, as well as from community-based providers (e.g., rural clinics, community and migrant health centers, school based clinics) offering preventive and primary care. Yet changes in training have not occurred.

"Encased in specialty- and research-based medicine, the inpatient hospital training model is one of the hardest nuts for policymakers to crack" (National Health Policy Forum, 1994, p. 2). The significant financial rewards reaped by teaching hospitals for research, clinical education and supervision is only one of several factors maintaining the present system. Essential community needs are met by provision of services to poor and indigent patients by teaching hospitals. Community employment and pride in the facility, as well as public and private grants, are stimulated by the combination of education, research, and service provided by teaching hospitals. Thus, the resistance to shift most training out of hospitals into outpatient settings is formidable and multidimensional—financial, structural, cultural, and political.

It has been asserted that, of the many barriers to implementing training programs in ambulatory settings, "financing . . . is at the core of the problem that must be solved first [and when] solved, ancillary issues . . . can be overcome" (Bentley, Knapp, & Petersdorf, 1989, p. 1534). Creative solutions to financing impediments have been discussed, and innovative programs have been implemented in various parts of the country. For example, linkages among community, migrant, and family health centers have been established, and close working alliances between internal medical group practices and health professional education programs have been developed (Brush & Moore, 1994; Colwill, 1992; Curley, Orloff, & Tymann, 1994; Eisenberg, 1989; Gordon & Hale, 1993; Greer, Schneeweiss, & Baldwin, 1993; Verdon, 1993; Wartman, O'Sullivan, & Cyr, 1992). These efforts by our medical colleagues have particular relevance for the future of psychology education.

Expansion of Reimbursable Settings, Providers, and Services

Transition to a training format that would provide future practitioners with learning experiences in ambulatory settings is reasonable, and is generally supported by policy makers as well as those involved in medical education and service delivery. Such a format would provide the most suitable training to help providers meet the demands of both current and future patients. Indeed, much reform legislation proposed during the 103rd Congress incorporated provisions for expanding GME adjustments to reimbursements for services provided to beneficiaries in various other settings. Such settings included hospital-owned community health centers, rural federally qualified health centers and medical assistance facilities, non–hospital ambulatory sites and non–hospital-owned facilities (Dunivin, 1994). Interestingly, it was almost a decade ago when Congress first provided directives for including into the adjustment formula the time spent by residents in outpatient settings. However, the control and the funds remained with the teaching hospitals because of a requirement that "all or substantially all" of the cost of the training was incurred by the hospital. It has had little effect in shifting the hospital-based medical training model.

Given the widespread acknowledgment of the specialty and geographic imbalance hindering access to care by significant portions of the population, incentives are needed to shift the ratio of primary care physicians to specialists and relocation to underserved areas. It is also necessary to include training dollars for those health professionals whose education focuses on integration of services, interdisciplinary team development, and emphasizes the provision of preventive, primary care, and continuity of services. Some reform proposals during the 103rd Congress addressed the ratio of primary care to specialist physicians by providing disincentives to schools producing lower numbers of primary care physicians relative to specialists and offering incentives for those medical students entering primary care training. Few bills introduced during the 103rd Congress expanded training to include health professionals other than physicians, with the exception of nurses and allied health professionals whose training was considered coincidental to resident training and are already figured into the formula. President Clinton's plan was a notable exception in that it would have provided funding for graduate nursing education through the all-payer pool.

The 1994 Reform Debate: GME Evolution or Enhancement?

As the health care reform debate continued through the 103rd Congress, it became increasingly clear that providing universal coverage or increasing the number of primary care physicians, although a significant step forward, would not automatically improve access to health care services for many of the currently underserved populations. Developing delivery systems to provide access to a full range of services for all is the essential challenge facing the nation, and it is intrinsically linked to the recruitment and retention of health professionals in medically underserved areas throughout the country.

The hospital-based tertiary care teaching model is different from the ambulatory community-based teaching model; it produces different products and different results. Training in outpatient, community-based settings socializes health professionals toward continued primary care and preventive work in such settings. Education in the typical academic medical center, with its tertiary care teaching hospital, produces a major socializing force toward specialization (Colwill, 1992) and consequently toward practice location in areas that are relatively well served by health professionals.

In the face of such considerations, the events that transpired during the evolving reform debates are even more amazing. The original Clinton proposal included about $9.6 billion per year in trust funds for teaching hospitals; a Kennedy amendment would have expanded that amount to about $17 billion per year; the Moynihan plan included a similar amount (Kosterlitz, 1994). Soon other trust funds were added—for dental schools and schools of public health, one referred to as "the deans' fund" (reputedly a slush fund) and one for the National Institutes of Health; the original Clinton proposal for nursing education was maintained (Kosterlitz, 1994). Eventually the trust funds included in the reform proposals . . . working their way through the Senate included nearly $70 billion in tax revenues over five years, primarily to support the operations of teaching hospitals across the nation. About half of these revenues would be new, raised through a surtax on private health care plans. Health Care legislation pending the House had similar provisions. (Kosterlitz, 1994, p. 1970)

The effectiveness of the lobbying efforts by the medical schools and teaching hospitals is certainly a factor in their successful maneuvering through the reform process. The specifics of their efforts and the players involved have been outlined in an article worthy of review (Kosterlitz, 1994). However, many of the other factors alluded to earlier—for example, the pride, prestige, and jobs brought to the local communities of the teaching hospitals as well as the "medical miracles"—carry their own, unpurchasable, political clout.

The Message for Psychology

During the last 50 years, federal funding has significantly influenced psychology's growth and development, both as an academic research discipline and as a health profession. This federal support was tied to recognition of psychology's ability to meet societal need, that is, the ability of psychology to provide treatment to veterans suffering from psychological (neuropsychiatric) disorders and to conduct research into these conditions.

Most of the greatest health risks facing the nation today are behavioral in origin. Addressing these health risks is a poignant societal need—both now and for the 21st century. Psychologists have developed various techniques and management programs that provide solutions to many of these problems. Yet this has not been made clear to federal funding authorities nor, arguably, to society at large. Psychology must come forward and demonstrate it in a very public way or lose federal support.

Reformation of the current health care delivery system has been necessitated by the unfeasibility of its focus on hospital-based, high-technology, acute care at the expense of preventive primary care rendered in outpatient settings and long-term community-based care for chronic conditions. Health profession education and training models will shift along with health care delivery systems—from a focus on clinical experience gained in teaching hospitals and traditional academic medical centers to clinical experience gained in community-based ambulatory settings.

The "model training centers" of the 21st century are likely to be comprehensive centers of excellence incorporating service delivery—

focusing on preventive and primary care, and research into treatment and program effectiveness. Despite the multidimensional powerful forces inhibiting physician training in ambulatory settings, several innovative training models have been implemented by forward-thinking medical schools. Psychology would benefit from examination of these programs, as well as those created by other disciplines.

Psychology must bring to resolution the conceptual conflicts inhibiting its recognition as a broad-based health profession. By parallelling federal priorities, psychology can maximize financial support for the profession, while meeting its societal obligation of promoting human welfare. Without coming forward to meet such challenges, psychology may fail to realize its full potential as a health care discipline.

REFERENCES

Albee, G. W., & Dickey, M. (1957). Manpower trends in three mental health professions. *American Psychologist, 12,* 57–70.

American Psychological Association (Committee on Scientific and Professional Aims of Psychology). (1967). The scientific and professional aims of psychology. *American Psychologist, 22,* 49–76.

Ash, E. (1968). Issues faced by the VA Psychology Training Program in its early development. *Clinical Psychologist, 21,* 121–123.

Bentley, J. D., Knapp, R. M., & Petersdorf, R. G. (1989). Education in ambulatory care: Financing is one piece of the puzzle. *The New England Journal of Medicine, 320,* 1531–1534.

Bourg, E. F., Bent, R. J., McHolland, J., & Stricker, G. (1989). Standards and evaluation in the education and training of professional psychologists: The National council of Schools of Professional Psychology Mission Bay Conference. *American Psychologist, 44,* 66–72.

Brush, A. D., & Moore, G. T. (1994). Assigning patients according to curriculum: A strategy for improving ambulatory care residency training. *Academic Medicine, 69,* 717–719.

Colwill, J. M. (1992). Where have all the primary care applicants gone? *The New England Journal of Medicine, 326,* 376–393.

Crane, L. (1925). A plea for the training of professional psychologists. *Journal of Abnormal and Social Psychology, 20,* 228–233.

Curley, T., Orloff, T. M., & Tymann, B. (1994). *Health professions education linkages: Community-based primary care training.* Washington, DC: National Governors' Association.

DeLeon, P. H. (1983). The changing and creating of legislation. In B. D. Sales (Ed.), *The professional psychologist's handbook* (pp. 601–620). New York: Plenum.

DeLeon, P. H., VandenBos, G. R., & Kraut, A. G. (1986). Federal recognition of psychology as a profession. In H. Doreen & Associates (Eds.), *Professional psychology in transition: Meeting today's challenges* (pp. 99–117). San Francisco: Jossey-Bass.

Department of Veterans Affairs. (1994). *Financial support for trainees in the health professions with specific data for medicine and psychology.* Unpublished manuscript.

Dunivin, D. L. (1994). Health professions education: The shaping of a discipline through federal funding. *American Psychologist, 49,* 868–878.

Eisenberg, J. M. (1989). How can we pay for graduate medical education in ambulatory care? *The New England Journal of Medicine, 320,* 1525–1531.

Eisenberg, M. G., Glueckauf, R. L., & Zaretsky, H. H. (Eds.). (1994). *Medical aspects of disability: A handbook for the rehabilitation professional.* New York: Springer.

Fox, R. E. (1980). On reasoning from predicates: The PhD is not a professional degree. *Professional Psychology, 11,* 887–891.

Fox, R. E. (1982). The need for a reorientation of clinical psychology. *American Psychologist, 37,* 1051–1057.

Fox, R. E. (1994). Training professional psychologists for the twenty-first century. *American Psychologist, 49,* 200–206.

Fox, R. E., & Barclay, A. (1989). Let a thousand flowers bloom: Or, weed the garden? *American Psychologist, 44,* 55–59.

Fox, R. E., Barclay, A., & Rodgers, D. A. (1982). The foundations of professional psychology. *American Psychologist, 37,* 306–312.

Fox, R. E., Kovacs, A. L., & Graham, S. R. (1985). Proposals for a revolution in the preparation and regulation of professional psychologists. *American Psychologist, 40,* 1042–1050.

Franco, C., & Klebe, E. (1991). *Health professions education and nurse training: Titles VII and VIII of the Public Health Service Act* (Report No. B188055). Washington, DC: Congressional Research Service.

Gordon, P. R., & Hale, F. (1993). The service-education linkage: Implications for family practice residency programs and community and migrant health centers. *Family Medicine, 25,* 316–321.

Greer, T., Schneeweiss, R., & Baldwin, L. M. (1993). A comparison of student clerkship experiences in community practices and residency-based clinics. *Family Medicine, 25,* 322–326.

Institute of Medicine. (1989). *Primary care physicians: Financing their graduate medical education in ambulatory settings.* Washington, DC: National Academy Press.

Kiesler, C. A. (1992). U.S. mental health policy: Doomed to fail. *American Psychologist, 47*, 1077–1082.

Klebe, E. (1992). *The U.S. Public Health Service: Health care services and resources* (Report No. 92–825 EPW). Washington, DC: Congressional Research Service.

Kosterlitz, J. (1994, August 20). The spoils of reform. *National Journal*, pp. 1970–1974.

Miller, J. G. (1946). Clinical psychology in the Veterans Administration. *American Psychologist, 1*, 181–189.

Millon, T., Green, C., & Meagher, R. (Eds.). (1982). *Handbook of clinical health psychology*. New York: Plenum.

Moore, D. L. (1992). The Veterans Administration and the training program in psychology. In D. K. Freedheim (Ed.), *History of psychotherapy: A century of change* (pp. 776–800). Washington, DC: American Psychological Association.

National Health Policy Forum. (1994). *Health professions training in ambulatory settings: Turning talk into action* (Issue Brief No. 658). Washington, DC: George Washington University.

National Institute of Mental Health. (1990). *Appropriation history table*. Unpublished manuscript.

Peterson, D. R. (1976). Need for the doctor of psychology degree in professional psychology. *American Psychologist, 31*, 792–798.

Peterson, D. R. (1992). The doctor of psychology degree. In D. K. Freedheim (Ed.), *History of psychotherapy: A century of change* (pp. 829–849). Washington, DC: American Psychological Association.

Resolutions approved by the national conference on graduate education in psychology. (1987). *American Psychologist, 42*, 1070–1084.

Shakow, D. (1947). Recommended graduate training programs in clinical psychology. *American Psychologist, 2*, 539–558.

Shapiro, A. E., & Wiggins, J. G. (1994). A PsyD degree for every practitioner: Truth in labeling. *American Psychologist, 49*, 207–210.

Social Security Amendments of 1965. Pub. L. No. 89–97, 79 Stat. 286.

Strickland, B. R., & Calkins, B. J. (1987). Public policy and clinical training. *The Clinical Psychologist, 40*, 31–34.

U.S. Veterans' Bureau. (1922). Annual report of the director, United States Veterans' Bureau for the fiscal year ended June 30, 1922. Washington, DC: U.S. Government Printing Office.

U.S. Veterans' Bureau. (1929). Annual report of the director, United States Veterans' Bureau for the fiscal year ended June 30, 1929. Washington, DC: U.S. Government Printing Office.

VandenBos, G. R. (1993). U.S. mental health policy: Proactive evolution in the midst of health care reform. *American Psychologist, 48*, 283–290.

VandenBos, G. R., DeLeon, P. H., & Belar, C. D. (1991). How many psychological practitioners are need? It's too early to know! *Professional Psychology: Research and Practice, 22,* 441–448.

Verdon, M. E. (1993). Establishing a linkage between a family practice residency and a local health department. *Family Medicine, 25,* 312–315.

Wartman, S. A., O'Sullivan, P. S., & Cyr, M. G. (1992). Ambulatory-based residency education: Improving the congruence of teaching, learning, and patient care. *American College of Physicians, 116,* 1071–1075.

Weitz, R. D. (1992). A half-century of psychological practice. *Professional Psychology: Research and Practice, 23,* 448–452.

Education and Training

Marie A. DiCowden, Bruce A. Crosson, and A. John McSweeny

OVERVIEW

The education and training of psychologists providing services in health care settings require a new perspective. A key feature of this perspective is the conceptualization of psychologists as health care providers. Current membership in health care divisions of the APA reflects this concept. APA statistics indicate that in 1993, Division 40 (Neuropsychology), 38 (Health Psychology), and 22 (Rehabilitation Psychology) were the 6th, 8th, and 23rd largest divisions in the national association (Office of Demographics, Employment, Education and Research, 1995). The continued growth in the number of neuropsychologists, rehabilitation psychologists, and other health care psychologists also underscores this trend.

A review of the growth in these divisions compared with overall growth in APA over the last 10 years provides the evidence. Since 1985, APA membership has increased from 50,131 to 76,008. Growth in membership in Division 22 grew from 974 to 1,347; Division 38, from 2,507 to 3,160; and Division 40, from 1,785 to 3,605. This reflects an overall growth in APA membership of 26%. The growth in Divisions 22, 38, and 40 were 38%, 26%, and 102%, respectively (APA Directory, 1985; APA Registry, 1994).

These developments represent a significant departure from the past, in which clinical psychologists were considered primarily or perhaps even exclusively mental health practitioners. These changes not only redefine the practice of psychology but also call into question the specific competencies psychologists in health care settings require, the most effective methods for providing predoctoral and postdoctoral training, and funding alternatives for health-oriented training programs. Accordingly, this consensus report focuses on three primary issues: (a) core competencies for health care psychologists, (b) training models, and (c) funding of education and training.

The issue of core competencies involves defining the basic skills that a health care psychologist would need to be an effective practitioner, especially as psychologists are less and less limited to office settings. In general, core competencies refer to the basic repertoire of assessment, consultative, and intervention skills and knowledge of psychologists who practice in hospital and community health care settings. However, a formal statement of these competencies currently does not exist. Articulation of such competencies by a consensus board of health care psychologists would potentially benefit both the profession and the individuals it serves.

The development of training models is closely related to the issue of core competencies. The competencies that are required of health care psychologists will determine, to some extent, how they should be trained. These competencies can most easily develop in settings, such as medical schools, university health science centers, and other health care agencies, that can incorporate both academic and applied experience. In addition, the training models and their curricula should be appropriate to the type of health care psychologists who will be needed in the future. Doctoral program practica, internships, and postdoctoral residencies need to be developed in these settings to train health care psychologists in core competencies that go beyond generic psychological assessment and intervention. These competencies might include training in areas, such as medical vocabulary, exposure to basic medical procedures and tests, acute versus postacute psychological assessment and intervention in health care crises, and health care promotion. Thus, it is important to survey the various types of services that psychologists are called on to provide in health care settings.

Although applied training in health care psychology at the master's level is common in the United Kingdom and exists in selected locations in the United States (e.g., West Virginia), the major commitment in this country has been training at the doctoral level. Nevertheless, health care psychology should examine the roles that nondoctoral personnel should perform, determine the core competencies required for these roles, and develop appropriate master's-level training models. We should be cognizant also that the issues of education and training apply not only to students, but also to other professionals and consumers. Accordingly, we must develop methods for educating these groups about our services and training models as well.

Funding of training and education in health care psychology represents a significant challenge. Federal support for the training of psychologists in health care settings has not been extensive. The Department of Veterans Affairs has been the largest source of training monies for psychologists since World War II. Other federal funding programs have been available to psychology graduate students, such as Health Education Assistance Loans, but generally have been underused, perhaps because of ignorance on the part of training directors. Health care psychologists need to understand the federal system and develop ways of gaining access to appropriate funding mechanisms.

This report on education and training concludes with a recommendation for APA to establish a national task force with mandates to address: (a) core competencies, (b) training models and sites, (c) funding, (d) a National Institute of Behavioral Health, and (e) state certification.

SUMMARY OF KEY ISSUES AND CONCLUSIONS

Core Competencies

For a long time, professional psychology has struggled with the definition of the fundamental skills that a professional psychologist must have to practice competently. Some have suggested that a common curriculum across programs should be established and met by all accredited programs. However, it has been virtually impossible to establish a consensus regarding a basic curriculum. Others have suggested that the core competencies necessary to practice psychology should be specified, but the methods for achieving these competencies should be left to the various doctoral programs accredited to train psychologists.

Though a greater consensus exists, at least conceptually, regarding the specification of core competencies, the profession has failed to achieve agreement on this issue. There is constant pressure in emphasis that continually shifts between the scientist and practitioner aspects of training. The impact of this failure is felt both within and outside the profession. Within professional psychology, we lack agreement regarding the end product of our training programs. The ambiguity results in variability in the skills and proficiencies attained by our graduates. Given this circumstance, it is only natural that the public is confused regarding what to expect from a psychologist. We have inadvertently created an identity crisis: We are not able to articulate who we are, and our potential clientele often is not able to formulate a clear idea regarding what to expect from our services.

This identity crisis exists not only within the broader context of professional psychology, but is also apparent for psychologists practicing in health care settings. There has been no set of core competencies specified for psychologists who practice in hospitals, rehabilitation centers, or other health settings (Glueckauf, in press). Clearly, these competencies must extend beyond basic clinical skills and be specifically tailored to health promotion, adjustment to illness, prevention or mitigation of illness, and rehabilitation. The specification of core competencies for psychologists practicing in different health care settings would facilitate the development of a positive identity for these professionals and recognition of the potential benefits of their services by the general public and prospective clients.

In specifying core competencies, it must be recognized that multiple psychological specialties practice in health care settings. For example, health psychology, rehabilitation psychology, and clinical neuropsychology have all developed strong identities, as evidenced by divisions for each within the APA. Further evidence of their strong identities is the fact that all these specialties have either established, or are in the process of establishing, a board under the auspices of the American Board of Professional Psychology for granting the status of diplomate within the specialty. Yet, there are common skills that all these specialties possess. Although there may be some resistance to establishing common competencies among the specialties practicing in health settings, this goal will not only benefit the training of our doctoral students, it will also foster collaboration among the specialties.

Training Settings

Psychologists practice in diverse settings. Although many psychologists perform diagnostic and treatment services within mental health settings, a significant portion of the profession practices in health care settings, such as hospitals, rehabilitation centers, or private clinics, which emphasize aspects of physical health, physical disease, or cognitive or physical disability. Further, practice in such settings is not merely the application of traditional mental health services within a different setting. To deliver psychological services successfully within health settings, specific knowledge and skills regarding the interaction of biological, psychological, and social factors are required. For example, prospective providers within these settings must learn the impact of psychological reactions on physical status; the nature and results of various diseases on cognitive, behavioral, and emotional functioning; and the emotional impact of various acute and chronic diseases and disabilities. Assessment and treatment strategies adapted for use with such problems differ significantly from those of traditional mental health, and require training beyond traditional mental health skills to attain basic competency.

Thus, it is imperative that psychologists who intend to practice in health settings (e.g., health and rehabilitation psychologists and clinical neuropsychologists) be trained in health care settings to acquire the unique competencies needed there. Significant progress has been made in establishing internship and postdoctoral programs in these settings. The 1994 Association of Postdoctoral Psychology Internship Centers directory lists more than 500 psychology internships, with 45% indicating major rotations in clinical neuropsychology, medical psychology, or both (Krieshok & Cantrell, 1994).

However, it has been more difficult to establish doctoral academic programs in health care settings. The number of professional psychology doctoral training programs located in academic health and rehabilitation settings is relatively small. However, a few such programs do exist and should be used as models to extend predoctoral programs in these settings. For example, the Indiana University-Purdue University at Indianapolis (IUPUI) provides a PhD training program in clinical rehabilitation psychology. The University of Alabama at Birmingham trains PhD students in clinical medical psychology. In Florida, the University of Florida provides a clinical psychology internship in an independent, free-standing clinical psychology department of a major health science center, with tracks in clinical neuropsychology, medical psychology, and clinical child psychology. Biscayne Rehabilitation Institute, Inc., a free-standing, private health care institution in Miami, Florida, in conjunction with the University of Miami School of Medicine, trains postdoctoral fellows in a 2-year program, with tracks in adult clinical neuropsychology, pediatric clinical neuropsychology, and rehabilitation psychology. It also provides predoctoral training to clinical psychology students in conjunction with Nova University, with emphasis in these specialty areas as well. The Medical College of Ohio is also initiating a postdoctoral training program for students in medical psychology, rehabilitation psychology, and neuropsychology. This program integrates applied experience and supervision with the neuroscience sequence at the medical school that is given to medical students.

The advantages of predoctoral internships and postdoctoral training in health care settings are many. Trainees from these programs not only learn specific assessment and intervention skills needed to address a health care population but also have the opportunity to interact within an interdisciplinary health care framework. They learn a health care vocabulary as well as a psychological vocabulary and gain experience in providing psychological consultation that is directly meaningful in a health care context to both the patients and the health care team (e.g., physicians, nurses, physical, and occupational and speech therapists). Academic health science centers offer an ideal environment for training psychologists who will practice in health settings, and efforts should be made to establish more predoctoral and postdoctoral training programs in such centers.

Nondoctoral Personnel

Professional psychology has established the doctoral degree (PhD, PsyD, and EdD) as the entry-level credential for independent practice. In other words, the term *psychologist* has been reserved by the APA for persons holding a doctoral degree in psychology, and the responsibility for the practice of psychology is ultimately in the hands of such persons. Nonetheless, nondoctoral personnel play important roles in psychological service delivery. In particular, persons trained at the bachelor's or master's-level can extend the practice of doctoral personnel and improve the cost-effectiveness of service delivery. At present, there is only one state that certifies master's-level personnel for independent practice (West Virginia), and this is a result of "grandfathering" practitioners in the state (Association of State and Provincial Psychological Boards, 1995). However, Illinois has recently passed legislation that would allow a master's-level clinician with 2 years of supervision to practice independently. Frequently, tasks, such as relaxation or biofeedback training, administration of psychological tests, or cognitive rehabilitation, can be performed at lower cost by nondoctoral personnel. Until recently, the profession has ignored the participation of nondoctoral personnel in psychological practice for health settings. What types of tasks should these practitioners perform? What kind and what level of training will be necessary to accomplish these tasks?

There are models for the use of nondoctoral personnel in health settings. In clinical neuropsychology, technicians are frequently used and their role has been acknowledged as important in facilitating the delivery of neuropsychological services by providing trained personnel to administer time-consuming testing procedures. Their role, however, is clearly limited to administration and scoring of tests. It has been stated that "the selection of tests, interpretation of those tests, clinical interviewing of patients or family members, and communication of test results and their implications is the sole responsibility of the licensed (neuro)psychologist" (Division 40 Task Force on Education, Accreditation, and Credentialing, 1989,

p. 24). The minimum level of education for neuropsychology technicians has not been specified, though they are frequently bachelor's level personnel. In such instances, the psychologist maintains the responsibility for determining the necessity and modality of treatment.

Certainly, no clear statements regarding master's-level personnel in health settings have been formulated. The employment of master's-level personnel as independent practitioners of rehabilitation counseling in the public and private arena has been commonly accepted, even though few states allow the independent practice of master's-level personnel as psychologists. But can master's level personnel be valuable in the practice of psychology in health care settings? The use of physicians' assistants and nurse practitioners to extend the practice of physicians is another model that is worth exploring. Yet some cautions have been provided about the use of such personnel (Schwartz et al., 1993).

Thus, the first step in addressing roles for nondoctoral personnel in health settings is to define what roles they might play. Existing models might provide some guidance in determining these roles. Once the roles for nondoctoral personnel are defined, then the skills necessary to function in these roles can be articulated. Only then can the level or type of training to obtain these skills be defined.

Models of External Education

It is necessary not only to address internal training issues for psychology in health care settings but also to confront external education issues. Not only the general public but also other professions as potential consumers of services must be educated about the unique contributions that psychologists can make to patient care in various health care settings. In large part, these contributions complement activities of physicians. Physicians need to be educated as to how psychologists can contribute to health care of patients via the mind-body connection. Insurance adjustors and managed care administrators need to become aware as to how timely assessment and intervention by a health care psychologist can decrease health care costs.

The psychologist's role as an independent health provider must be emphasized. These consumers must be educated that psychology in general, and, more specifically, the various specialties practicing in health care settings have a long history of empirical investigation. In many instances, significant research findings can be used to support the efficacy of psychology's contributions to health care. Thus, the scientific basis of various assessments and treatments can be underscored.

Funding

Funding for education and training in health care psychology presents several challenges. The situation is both difficult and fluid. Federal clinical training dollars for psychology, once provided by primarily the NIMH, have slowed to a mere trickle in the 1980s and 1990s. In addition, many of these funds are tied to training in mental health rather than health care psychology.

In recent years, money delivered from fees for services have been increasingly used to support clinical training, particularly in neuropsychology, rehabilitation psychology, and related areas of health care psychology. The changing scene in health care reimbursement has had an impact here as well. Some managed care programs, both private and public, refuse to reimburse services provided by psychology trainees, especially at the predoctoral level, even though the trainees are supervised by a licensed psychologist. Also, the trend is toward more modest reimbursement for psychological services, meaning that there are fewer funds available in many clinical centers that can be used to support graduate training. Consequently, we must look anew at the issue of funding and determine what alternatives we can pursue to provide a sound financial basis for education and training in health care psychology.

There are several federal agencies and programs that support training in the health care professions. A review of these programs quickly reveals that most federal training dollars go toward the training of physicians and that most programs are either not available to or have not been used by psychologists. One exception to this pattern is the Department of Veterans Affairs and its predecessors: the VA and the Veterans Bureau. Although the picture in other federal programs in relation to psychology has been less bright, a brief review of federal funding for the training of health care providers is in order. In addition, readers should consult the chapter by Dunivin in this volume, as well as other sources (Carr, 1987; Dunivin, 1994) for more detail.

First, it should be noted that there are two general types of federal programs: discretionary and entitlement. Discretionary funds are those that are appropriated on a yearly basis. Entitlement funds, such as Medicare, are appropriated as part of an ongoing program. In addition, federal training support in the health professions may be direct or indirect. Indirect support for training is often available in the form of postdoctoral fellowships included in research support funds (grants), such as those provided by the National Institutes of Health and related programs. Indeed, several of the National Institutes of Health, most notably the National Cancer Institute, the National Heart Lung and Blood Institute, and the National Institute of Child Health and Human Development, include mission statements that encompass developing expertise in the behavioral sciences. Typically, however, they do not explicitly mention psychology and are primarily concerned with the development of research programs. Thus, they provide a minority of health care training funds. The VA, Title VII of the Public Heath Service Act, and Medicare constitute the major forms of direct federal support training in the health care professions (Dunivin, 1994).

The Department of Veterans Affairs represents the major program for federal support of training in psychology currently. Although most Department of Veterans Affairs training funds have been used for physician training, the Department of Veterans Affairs has a tradition of supporting training in psychology that stretches back to the post–World War II period (Moore, 1992). Internships and postdoctoral fellowships at the Department of Veterans Affairs are well known in the fields of health care psychology, as well as clinical psychology in general. In 1995, it is expected that nearly 600 psychology students at different levels will receive training stipends from the Department of Veterans Affairs (Dunivin, 1994).

Title VII funds, which are administered by the HRSA, provides a major discretionary program for the training of physicians. Two types of Title VII programs are available: (a) grants and contracts to training institutions; and (b) financial assistance in the form of scholarships and loan programs to students (Dunivin, 1994). Originally, the programs were available only for the training of physicians, osteopaths, and dentists. Later, the program was expanded to include other health care professions, such as veterinarians, optometrists, and dentists. In theory, approximately one half of the programs in Title VII are potentially available for psychology training, but most are not made available by the agency and are not well known to psychology training directors. Thus, few apply for such funding.

The Health Education Assistance Loan program is one that is available to psychology trainees and has been used. According to Dunivin (1994), 807 psychology students constituted 2.6% of the total borrowers in fiscal year 1993 and the loans to these students amounted to $6.9 million. The Health Careers Opportunities Program provided three grants to psychology training programs last year, and a fourth program received an award for training minority and disadvantaged students. Other programs, such as the Faculty Loan Repayment Program, may be available to psychology trainees but have not been used, perhaps because psychologists are not aware of them. Finally, several important Title VII programs, such as the Health Professions Student Loan Program are not available to psychology training.

One aspect of Title VII that needs to be examined in relation to health care psychology is the fact that psychology training programs are considered to be graduate programs in mental health practice along with training programs in social work and marriage and family counseling. This reinforces the notion of psychology as a mental health rather than a health profession, and we should strive to change this conception.

The major entitlement program that funds health professional training is Medicare. Although the total funding provided by Title VII and related programs amounted to more than $300 million in fiscal year 1994, Medicare provided over $5 billion (Dunivin, 1994). Medicare funding mechanisms involve payments to teaching hospitals known as IME and DME costs. DME funds are provided to hospitals to support the salaries of residents and faculty, whereas IME funds are used to adjust per-case payments for purposes of education support. Dunivin (1994) notes that although one fourth of DME funds are used to support the training of nurses and physician's assistants, almost all the rest goes toward training physicians.

Additionally, psychology is not well represented in the advisory panels in the different federal programs that oversee the distribution of funds. This is a problem that should be addressed further. Legislative mandates are needed for the inclusion of health care psychology, in practice as well as theory, in federal programs, such as Title VII and Medicare. Appointment to the advisory panels that make recommendations for the implementation of funding programs is imperative to facilitate the process of making psychology trainees and psychology training programs eligible for federal health monies.

Further, there is a compelling case for the need to train psychologists with special expertise in health care, particularly with underserved populations. Traditional clinical psychology is not seen as underpopulated, and we are not likely to witness growth in federal funding for training in the discipline of psychology in general. However, professional psychology needs to avoid the impression that it is in competition with its sister health care professions, including medicine and nursing.

Finally, the psychology profession should develop models of funding that are also based on local and state support. Although federal funding will continue to be an important source of support for training in the health care professions and, it is hoped, health care psychology, we cannot depend on federal funding exclusively. Rather, funding of education and training in health care psychology is likely to be composed of monies from several sources at the local, state, and national level.

CONCLUSION

There was consensus among conference participants that changes in psychology's approach to health education and training should be instigated at the national level. APA should appoint a national task force that has the power to develop policies for education and training in health care psychology and then act on those policies.

The APA Task Force for Education and Training in Health Care Delivery would consist of five subcommittees. The head of each subcommittee would then make up the main committee. Issues to be addressed by each of the five subcommittees would be the following:

1. *Core competencies.* The development of a set of core competencies or a core curriculum for training health care psychologists.
2. *Training models and sites.* The establishment of doctoral programs and other training opportunities within academic health science centers.
3. *Funding.* Funding from all levels (local, state, and federal) for training health care psychologists.
4. *National Institute of Behavioral Health.* The development of a National Institute of Behavioral Health to further education, training, and research in health care psychology.
5. *State certification.* Pursuit of state certification for health care psychologists.

The core competencies subcommittee would develop a basic set of proficiencies that would be necessary to be considered a health care psychologist. Subspecialties within health care psychology (rehabilitation, neuropsychology, health psychology, etc.) would continue to be addressed by the particular APA Divisions relevant to the subspecialty and the diplomate boards of such subspecialties. However, the need to emphasize core competencies and similarities in the delivery of health care psychology services is paramount in the current health care reform climate. In addition, the subcommittee would address the roles of master's-level psychology professionals in the health market and define the requisite competencies for practice.

The subcommittee on training models and sites would address the need for adequate training in multidisciplinary settings providing health care. Although this training model is available at some sites for internship and postdoctoral fellows, there is a dearth of training opportunities in these settings for predoctoral graduate training. Expansion and development of training at all levels, however, are needed. This subcommittee may well want to survey existing training sites located in academic health, hospital, and rehabilitation centers to assist in networking and facilitating the growth of new training sites. This subcommittee would provide a vital link between the core competencies subcommittee and the funding subcommittee. Liaison work with both subcommittees could then be used productively to enhance training models and opportunities.

The funding subcommittee would address two vital components: (a) dissemination of information about current funding sources available for research; (b) development of funding available for training that is currently underused or not used at all by psychology. Greater awareness and promotion of the active use of information available on Internet from the APA Science Directorate for grant opportunities in health care research need to be pursued. Additionally, a major effort toward getting qualified psychologists appointed to panels concerned with the distribution of funds for training of health care providers must be made. Representation on boards distributing Title VII funds needs to be pursued. Entitlements paid through Medicare to teaching hospitals need reform and legislation requiring support of training for health care psychologists is also needed.

A fourth subcommittee should be developed with the mandate to address the concept of a National Institute of Behavioral Health. This subcommittee can (a) gather information showing the lack of follow-through in behavioral health research and training at nationally funded organizations despite legislative mandates over the years to do so, and (b) study the already existing model for the development of the National Center for Nursing. The primary goal would be to show the need for and the establishment of a national center to further behavioral health research and training. Such a program modeled after the National Center for Nursing may well be looked on favorably in Washington given the successful precedent set by nursing. A National Institute of Behavioral Health established and run by health care psychology could have a major impact on the advancement of our profession in the health care field.

The state certification subcommittee would work with the state psychological associations to pursue the feasibility of establishing state standards for health care certification—in addition to licensing—such as already exists in several states. Again, the development of policy at a nationally sanctioned level of APA would be invaluable in encouraging state standards for qualified practitioners. Additionally, guidelines emerging at that level would help to ensure that an arbitrary patchwork system of certification does not develop across states.

Development of an APA task force for Education and Training in Health Care Delivery must emphasize the identity of health care psychology as complementary, not competitive, with other health care colleagues (e.g., physicians and nurses). If professional psychology is seen as being a competitor, it may not be well received by legislators and certainly will not receive the support, or at least acquiescence, of other professional groups. Although some of the initiatives to be enacted by this task force and APA may be initially controversial with other disciplines, it is the role of the health care psychologist in practice to enhance the integrated and holistic care provided by the treatment team in medical settings. Where such an interdisciplinary approach occurs, health care psychologists are more often than not eventually welcomed as much needed colleagues. Enhancing professional psychology's identity as a major health care provider is essential for psychology as a profession and for the consumers of such services, including other professional colleagues, as well as the legislators and the public in general. Our future as a profession—as well as the goal of providing integrated health care that addresses the whole person—depends on developing this identity.

REFERENCES

Association of State and Provincial Psychology Boards. (1995). *The handbook of licensing and certification requirements*. Montgomery, AL: Author.

Carr, J. E. (1987). Federal impact of psychology in medical schools. *American Psychologist, 21*, 121–123.

Division 40 Task Force on Education, Accreditation, and Credentialing. (1989). Guidelines regarding the use of nondoctoral personnel in clinical neuropsychological assessment. *Clinical Neuropsychologist, 3*, 23–24.

Dunivin, D. L. (1994). Health professions education: The shaping of a discipline through federal funding. *American Psychologist, 49*, 868–878.

Glueckauf, R. L. (1995). Boundaries among health care psychology specialties: A call for experimentation and unification. *Professional Psychology: Research and Practice, 26*, 341–365.

Krieshok, T. S., & Cantrell, P. J. (Eds.). (1994). *Association of Psychology Postdoctoral and Internship Centers Directory, 1994–1995: Internship and postdoctoral programs in professional psychology*. Washington, DC: Association of Psychology Postdoctoral and Internship Centers.

Moore, D. L. (1992). The Veterans Administration and the training program in psychology. In D. K. Freedheim (Ed.), *History of psychotherapy: A century of change* (pp. 776–800). Washington, DC: American Psychological Association.

Office of Demographics, Employment, Education and Research, American Psychological Association Education Directorate. (1985). *APA directory*. Washington, DC: American Psychological Association.

Office of Demographics, Employment, Education and Research, American Psychological Association Education Directorate. (1994). *APA registry*. Washington, DC: American Psychological Association.

Office of Demographics, Employment, Education and Research, American Psychological Association Education Directorate. (1995). *Profile of all APA members, 1993*. Washington, DC: American Psychological Association.

SUMMARY AND CONCLUSIONS

Chapter 11

Integrative Summary and Future Directions

Robert G. Frank, Robert L. Glueckauf,
Gary R. Bond, and John H. McGrew

Since the Indianapolis conference was conceived, the great wave of health reform has surged only to fade amidst the tide of conservative "governmental reductionism." Despite the change in philosophy regarding the role of government, the health sector of our economy continues to grow, almost 50% faster than overall consumer prices (Medical Care Costs, 1995). Between 1980 and 1993, the share of the population covered by private health insurance has declined from 73% to 65% (Prospective Payment Assessment Commission [ProPAC], 1994). Forced from the rolls of private insurers, Americans have increasingly turned to the federal government for health services. Medicare has an annual enrollment increase of about 2%. By the end of 1993, there were 37 million Medicare enrollees, 11% of whom were eligible because of disability or end-stage renal disease. The Medicaid Program is growing even more quickly. In the 8 years between 1985 and 1993, Medicaid costs tripled and enrollees increased by 50% (Medicaid, 1995).

Escalating costs and lack of access to health services assures that debate on reform of the health care system will return to the national forum. Indeed, since 1935, the United States has revisited health reform every 10 to 15 years (Frank & VandenBos, 1994). When Congress failed to pass legislation reforming the health care system, efforts to limit health spending moved to the private sector. Almost 60% of the U.S. population receives health coverage through their employer (ProPAC, 1994). An increasing number of employers offer managed care plans to their employees (ProPAC, 1994). Managed care plans span a wide array of service delivery models from HMOs to PPOs. Regardless of the type of plan they offer, employers are paying less of the premium. For HMOs and PPOs, in the 6-year period between 1988 and 1993, employer contributions to plan costs dropped roughly 14%. In addition, in most PPO plans, employees are paying higher deductibles (the amount paid before benefits apply). Employers are also opting to self-insured health plans (Frank, Sullivan, & DeLeon, 1994). First, established in 1974, self-insurance was used by 44% of the private-sector employers by 1992 (ProPAC, 1994).

Rapid changes in the health delivery system have created concerns regarding the quality of care. Quality is measured by voluntary and mandatory methods. Quality of health care is correlated with many factors governing access to health services, including provider availability, health insurance coverage, and use of services (see Hofschire & Foote; Frank & Johnstone in this volume). There are no uniform, national standards of quality that apply to all payers, providers, and facilities. The emergence of new service delivery models increases concerns regarding the quality of care delivered.

External reviews are provided by national accrediting bodies, such as the Joint Commission on the Accreditation of Healthcare Organizations and the Commission on the Accreditation of Rehabilitation Facilities. Medicare certifies many facilities and uses the Peer Review Organization program to monitor hospital programs. Similarly, as the private sector has increased its effort to control health costs, there has emerged a parallel concern regarding quality. For example, the HMO Employer Data and Information Set (HEDIS I and II) developed by the National Committee for Quality assurance have been sponsored by private payers (ProPAC, 1994). In addition, monitoring of individual clinicians through practice profiling has become more common.

In 1992, 39% of physicians were subject to clinical profiling, 22% to economic profiling (examining expenditure and cost patterns), and 45% to either (ProPAC, 1994). Quality assessment will focus practitioners on the importance of assuring good service and good outcomes. The increased attention to quality is one tangible reminder of the degree of change in the health system. Changes in the financing of the health system will further alter the practice of psychological services.

This book has focused on the long-term trends of changes in the health care system and the implication of the changing system for the delivery of psychological services. The themes of the conference, reflected in this volume, focused on four key issues. Each theme will be examined in turn.

WORK FORCE

The rapid growth of psychology has led to significant increases in the number of psychologists. Similar growth has been apparent in other health professions, including those that provide mental health services. Although the growth among these professions is apparent, the implications of the increase in mental health oriented professions is less clear. The overlap in skills among these professions further complicates projections of work force adequacy to meet health care needs (Frank & Ross, 1995). Although health psychologists have developed unique skills, allowing them to encounter less competition, the increase in the number of psychologists, as well as displacement of physicians from other practice areas, may alter the level of market competition health psychologists experience.

Currently, organized psychology has no method of determining the number of practicing psychologists, geographic distribution of psychologists, or skills of competing health professionals. Even within psychology, there are no consensual guidelines regarding credentials needed to practice in health as opposed to mental health settings. Nor is it clear the level of training needed to provide services. These problems also plague other professions in the mental health arena. Clearly, there is need for information on each of these issues. Development of programs to map the skills of different health professions and determine skills unique to the differing training models would be beneficial. Because organized psychology lacks information on the supply and distribution of psychologists, public policy makers also lack information. The dearth of information on the supply, skills, and distribution of psychologists stands in contrast to the information available on the physician work force. COGME provides extensive information on the physician work force (Frank & Ross, 1995). As competition among health providers increases, public policy will tend to be guided by the information available to policy makers. Professions that are poorly understood will likely encounter lower levels of federal support.

Organized psychology should support any federal effort to systematically assess the status of the psychology work force. Ideally, psychologists should be included under COGME (Frank & Ross, 1995), but the critical issue is that psychology be viewed as a profession that is essential to the nation's health system as demonstrated by a federal mandate to assess the status of the profession routinely. To attain this outcome, the APA should emphasize the importance of comprehensively assessing the number and skills of psychologists. In addition, the APA should address the issue of master's-level practice. The success of master's-level clinicians in managed care settings clearly indicates the importance of this category of provider. Rather than ignoring the issue, the APA should forthrightly examine the skills, distribution, and future need of master's-level clinicians. The readiness of managed care organizations to use master's-level providers indicates the importance of this level of provider. Psychology as a profession should respond by developing a clear continuum of care that specifies the level of provider needed for differing services.

ACCESS

Access to psychological services is critical to organized delivery systems, consumers, and psychologists. Services provided to managed health systems will emphasize economy and quality. When confronted with these principles, many psychologists respond that services to their patients should not be limited, regardless of their progress in treatment. Instead of recognizing that psychologists are well prepared to show treatment outcomes, psychologists have veiled themselves in the cloth of patient protectionism. Aided by the move to cost control, payers have insisted on lower cost services, often necessitating the use of clinicians with lower levels of training.

As managed care systems have become more sophisticated, delivery systems have become more efficient. This efficiency has been created by integrating services, limiting use, and reducing payment to providers. These new systems are often referred to as integrated delivery systems. The integration of delivery systems services has spanned new methods of practice and opportunities to acquire new roles. Psychologists have created many new roles in the health care system, especially in health care settings. Often these roles have developed informally to meet the demands of the treatment program. The reshaping of the delivery system under the pressure of managed care offers psychologists opportunities to consolidate these roles. One frequently cited example is leadership of interdisciplinary teams designed to delivery primary care. In this model, psychologists serve as the manager of teams composed of nondoctoral-level providers. These teams are economical, flexible, and capable of providing quality care.

The formation of integrated delivery systems also poses real challenges to psychologists. Historically, psychologists have functioned as small "cottage industries," with most psychologists working individually or in small groups of financially independent practitioners. Unlike physicians who have tended to be associated with hospitals even when practicing alone, most psychologists have few formal connections to the medical community. Because of this practice style, as integrated delivery systems have formed, psychologists have often been excluded. Exclusion from integrated delivery systems, because of either practice style, higher cost, or other factors, is a major threat to psychology and access to psychological services.

Access to psychological services may be determined by the profession's ability to blend into integrated delivery systems. In the near future, publicly funded integrated delivery systems will be critical to psychology's ability to remain viable in the health market. The demise of the health reform legislation debate has pressured state governments to seek Medicaid waivers. State governments have taken the role of innovators in the health delivery system (Frank, Sullivan, & DeLeon, 1994; Sullivan, 1995). Huge public health purchasing systems created by Medicaid waivers offer important opportunities for psychologists to seek inclusion as approved providers to show the value of psychological services. The usefulness of psychological services in reducing overall health costs and reducing distress has been clearly shown for Medicaid populations (Cummings, Pallak, Dorken, & Henke, 1993). The creation of large, integrated delivery systems vying for opportunities to provide coverage offers psychologists the opportunity to practice in areas previously denied. Currently, only 22 states allow psychologists to be reimbursed under Medicaid (Frank, Sullivan, & DeLeon, 1994). The proliferation of Medicaid waivers creates the opportunity for psychologists to gain inclusion in Medicaid and assure that psychologists play a critical role in the provision of services to the indigent (Frank, Sullivan, & DeLeon, 1994).

EDUCATION AND TRAINING

The education and training of psychologists during this era of change in the health care system presents enormous challenges. The rapid growth of the practice component of psychology has moved training toward a professional school model. This shift has been exacerbated by the move toward subspecialization (Johnstone et al., 1995). Both of these trends may serve to undermine the profession in the future.

As competition for psychological services increases, the value of doctoral providers remains undemonstrated. The increase in professional schools has increased the number of doctoral psychologists (Shapiro & Wiggins, 1994), and the number of mental health providers has increased markedly (Frank & Ross, 1995). The looming oversupply of psychologists and reduction of demand for providers in the health sector (Frank & Johnstone, chapter 3, this volume; Frank & Ross, 1995) will profoundly alter skills required of future psychologists. It seems likely that the skills emphasized in training the "scientist-practitioner" model are more likely to be in demand than clinical skills engendered in the "professional school" model. Analytic and management skills emphasized in the "scientist-practitioner" training model will be useful to future psychologists who will lead teams and provide less clinical service.

At the same time that other health professions move toward "generalist" training models, some psychologists are arguing that subspecialties are preferable within psychology (Colwill, 1992). If psychologists have any leverage on the claim of a primary care role, the wholesale movement of the profession toward subspecialization threatens that assertion. Despite the clear trends among most health professions, educational programs in psychology have not established a clear core curriculum, or set of essential skills required of the generalist psychologist. In response to this trend, participants at the Indianapolis conference recommended the convergence of health psychology under one large division or an academy APA. This division could be modeled after Division 12 of the APA, Clinical Psychology. Because health psychology (broadly defined to include psychologists working in health care settings or with medical patients) includes a substantial proportion of all psychologists, merging the health divisions in APA into one large division with sections representing areas of unique practice, such as rehabilitation, health, or pediatrics seems desirable. This large division, which might be labeled "Health Care Psychologists," would have significant political leverage and would focus attention on the importance of training psychologists in "generalist" skills (see Johnstone et al., 1995, pp. 352–354).

The 104th Congress, elected in November 1994, focused on dismantling many federal programs (Inglehart, 1995). The programs contained in Title VII of the U.S. Public Health Act were a target of congressional budget reductions. These programs provide little support for psychology training, yet the existence of these programs offered an opportunity for greater funding (Dunivin, 1994; Dunivin, 1996). Although it is possible that psychology may find opportunities in the reduced spending environment, it is unlikely. The importance of these programs and the potential opportunities associated with them have been only poorly understood by psychologists.

The National Institute Health (NIH) may weather the 104th Congress with relatively less scrutiny of the size of its budget. However, pressure on budgets for behavioral research has increased (Behavioral Research Under Attack, 1995) during recent years, especially during the 104th Congress. Despite frequent rhetoric about the importance of behavioral factors, funding for behavioral health research is severely challenged. One response to this problem, supported by the participants at the Indianapolis conference, was the creation of a National Center for Behavioral Research at the NIH. This institute could be created in the same manner as the National Institute Center for Nursing Research (DeLeon, Kjervik, Kruat, & VandenBos, 1985; NIH, 1984).

QUALITY AND OUTCOME

As has been shown by Kaplan and his colleagues (Kaplan, 1994; Kaplan, 1996), psychologists have much to contribute to the measurement of health outcome. Behavioral outcome measures may be among the more effective health outcome measures (Kaplan, 1994). Using behavioral outcome measures is one method of enhancing recognition of the value and importance of behavioral interventions in the treatment of health conditions.

Kaplan (1994; chapter 7, this volume) argued that behaviorally derived, health outcome measures provide one of the most effective measures of health interventions. The application of this method to the measurement of health status provides an example of the flexibility of psychological applications. Application of Kaplan's methodology to mental health outcomes would substantially enhance demonstrations of efficacy in that arena.

Measurement of quality and outcomes has become a fundamental principle of the market-driven changes currently occurring in the health care system (Frank & VandenBos, 1994). The managed care industry has joined together to support the development of outcome measures (ProPAC, 1994). The most popular outcome measures, HEDIS II (ProPAC, 1994), focus on simple, relatively crude scales that could be augmented by behavioral and psychological measures to improve the sensitivity of the measures.

Practice guidelines provide one method to enhance quality control. They have become increasingly important to professional societies (DeLeon, Frank, & Wedding, 1995). Guidelines provide a method of determining the most effective treatment of a disorder and establish accepted treatment approaches and duration of treatment modalities. Guidelines also are critical to acceptance of psychological interventions and, potentially, to establishing the importance of doctoral-level providers. Ideally, practice guidelines should be based on supporting scientific information and common clinical practice (DeLeon, Frank, & Wedding, 1995). The methodological background common to scientist-practitioner training especially prepares psychologists for an active role in the development of guidelines.

In summary, organized efforts to reform the health care system have dramatically slowed; the factors that first led to the impetus for change—

excessive cost, limited access to service, and poor quality of services—remain national concerns. Exacerbation of these problems in the future will lead to additional efforts to reform the health care system. If psychologists anticipate these changes, there will be many opportunities to enhance the domain of the profession. Moreover, the training used in the scientist-practitioner model provides numerous skills that may be applied to health care systems.

REFERENCES

Behavioral Research Under Attack: APA Picks Up the Gauntlet. (1995). *On Behalf of Science, 8,* 1–2.

Colwill, J. M. (1992). Where have all the primary care applicants gone? *New England Journal of Medicine, 326,* 387–392.

Cummings, N. A., Pallak, M. S., Dorken, H., & Henke, C. J. (1993, September-October). Medicaid, managed mental healthcare and medical cost offset. *Behavioral Healthcare Tomorrow,* 15–20.

DeLeon, P. H., Frank, R. G., & Wedding, D. (1995). Health psychology and public policy: The political press. *Health Psychology, 14,* 493–499.

DeLeon, P. H., Kjervik, D. K., Kraut, A. G., & VandenBos, G. R. (1985). Psychology and nursing: A natural alliance. *American Psychologist, 40,* 1153–1164.

Dunivin, D. L. (1994). Health profession education. *American Psychologist, 49,* 868–878.

Frank, R. G., & Ross, M. R. (1995). The role of health psychology in the changing health care system. *Health Psychology, 14,* 519–525.

Frank, R. G., Sullivan, M. J., & DeLeon, P. H. (1994). Health care reform in the States. *American Psychologist, 49,* 868–878.

Frank, R. G., & VandenBos, G. R. (1994). Health care reform: The 1993–1994 evolution. *American Psychologist, 94,* 851–854.

Inglehart, J. (1995). Republicans and the new politics of healthcare. *New England Journal of Medicine, 332,* 972–975.

Johnstone, B., Frank, R. G., Belar, C., Berk, S., Bieliauskas, L. A., Bigler, E. D., Caplan, B., Elliott, T. R., Glueckauf, R. L., Kaplan, R. M., Kreatzer, J. S., Mateer, C. A., Patterson, D., Puente, A. E., Richards, J. S., Rosenthal, M., Sherer, M., Shewchuk, R., Keigal, L. J., & Sweet, J. J. (1995). Psychology is health care: Future directions. *Professional Psychology: Research and Practice, 26,* 341–365.

Kaplan, R. (1994). The Ziggy theorem: Toward an outcomes-focused health psychology. *Health Psychology, 13,* 451–460.

Prospective Payment Assessment Commission. (1994, June). Report to the U.S. Congress: Medicare and the American health care system.

Medicaid: Spending pressures drive states toward program reinvention. (1995). (No. GAO/HEHS-95-122).

Medical care costs continue to rise faster than overall consumer prices. (1995, May 29). *Medicine and Health*, p. 4.

National Institute of Health. (1994, December). *National Institute of Health Taskforce on Nursing Research: Report to the director.* Department of Health and Human Services, Washington, DC: Author.

Shapiro, G., & Wiggins, J. (1994). A Psy.D. degree for every practitioner: Truth in labeling. *American Psychologist, 49*, 207–210.

Sullivan, M. J. (1995). Medicaid's quiet revolution: Merging the public and private sector. *Professional Psychology: Research and Practice, 26*, 229–234.

Epilogue

Robert J. Resnick

Frank and Johnstone, Kaplan, Hofschire and Foote, and Dunivin have provided provocative and consciousness-raising insights. Although they do not write about Armageddon, they do make a compelling call for action with an end to complacency. These papers warn that psychology must be positioned to show that our services are effective and affordable, as well as cost-effective. It is clear that psychologists will not only compete with each other but will compete with other health providers to provide psychological services. This includes not only "mental health providers" but also primary care physicians, because there is evidence that presently 60% of all visits to primary care physicians' offices are psychologically based (R. Rozensky, personal communication, January 22, 1995). As Hofschire suggests, an implication of this system of treatment is that primary care physicians can control the use and access of psychological services in the future to an even greater degree than they do now. Frank and Johnstone have suggested that 70% of all psychologists are involved in health care services. They also note that the number of psychological practitioners are proliferating at such an alarming rate that sufficient jobs in the marketplace may be lacking for this new group of psychologists.

Unfortunately, psychology is only beginning to recognize the implications of health care reform. The economic reality is that this country cannot continue to spend an ever-increasing percentage of its GNP on the delivery of health services. This is particularly true because there are no data to suggest that these increased expenditures have affected such critical indicators of adequate health care as longevity and infant mortality. Indeed, as health care is presently delivered, an average of 80% of a person's lifetime health costs are consumed in the last 6 months of life.

Psychologists on the local, state, and national level must be prepared to show policy makers and legislators the importance, necessity, and benefit of psychological services and care. We must be able to show not only that what we do is effective and affordable, but also that it is in the best interest of the community, state, and nation to increase access to psychological services. If we do not make the case for our presence on the health care radar scope, who will? Who can make our case better than us? We cannot afford to sit back and allow others, who often have little or no background in psychology, to make policy regarding psychological services. In the absence of psychology's input, uninformed decisions made by otherwise well-meaning legislators and their staff risk damaging the profession and those served by psychology.

Professional psychologists also must reexamine the training programs that are extant today. Graduate programs can no longer train students with little or no concern for their future employment. Indeed, any "call-to-action" must include a discussion of training in underserved areas and not training for the convenience of the training program. We must evaluate what the next generation of psychologists needs to know and how these psychologists can show those competencies. This can be done by developing a core curriculum that every student in every program is required to master. This core curriculum should be balanced with the unique contributions of individual programs and faculty to wrap around these core experiences. Training programs must also place increased emphasis on outcome research to show policy makers the effectiveness of psychological care. Although evidence has been accumulating for more than two decades of medical cost-savings when psychological services are readily available and accessed, these data have not been sufficient to persuade policy makers. A compelling case can be made, however, particularly if well-controlled studies are conducted corroborating the trends in the current literature.

As health care continues to evolve, psychologists must position themselves to offer diverse services in different settings. Although we must not lose our identity as the preeminent providers of psychotherapy and psychological assessment, we must also position ourselves to be providers of multiple services in diverse settings. The more arrows in quiver, the more valuable the archer! For example, psychological principles, strategies, and interventions can be productively used in primary health care settings with generalist physicians. Psychologists offer important services in tertiary settings, such as acute care hospitals, general and surgical hospitals, and psychiatric hospitals. Training should cover the application of psychological services in the areas of consultation and liaison, second opinion (i.e., diagnostic/therapeutic expertise to validate a previously made diagnosis or treatment plan), and employee assistance plan triage.

If psychological practice is to survive, we must also be trained in health care economics, incorporating the "business" of practice. The business side of practice is not an anathema. Indeed, psychologists providing services have expenses, such as office space, telephone, and secretarial support. What is left over are the "profits," which the psychologist keeps as income. If the practitioner's expenses exceed the income, that practitioner, like any other small business, will eventually go out of business. Indeed, we need to understand the evolving health care market from the individual practitioner level to the corporate practice level. Demands from the business side for multidisciplinary practices include bidding on business through HMOs, managed care companies, or capitated programs. We cannot compete successfully if we deny the growing importance of such health care entities or if we do not understand the underlying economics. Accepting the current realities does not imply that individual therapy or long-term therapy is no longer viable. But such services are likely to be prepaid by fewer and fewer health care entities. Psychology is ill advised to produce more and more graduates who seek a share of the dwindling marketplace. Psychology, like medicine with all of its subspecialties, must go through a reexamination of its training and service models. It is not that mental health or psychology has been singled out, but if we do not take some control over our training future, then we will be unable to sit at the table when the important decisions are made about the future of these health care systems.

Finally, what all four sections of the book are suggesting is the necessity for controlling psychology's destiny through training. If we do not become part of the ongoing discussion of the evolution of health care and we are absent in the federal discussion around the size of professional work forces, then we run the significant risk of being seen as an "optional" profession. Should psychology ever be relegated to that position, then we can anticipate receiving no federal funding for training. It is axiomatic that whichever professionals receive federal dollars for training are also the professions that federal dollars reimburse for services. The corollary, then, is that whom the federal government reimbursed is guaranteed a place in health care reform. To paraphrase Charles Dickens, let us now be the hero of our profession, and not its victim.

Index